COLOSSIANS

A Reformed Study of
the Glory and Majesty of Christ

John Dayton

ISBN: 979-8-218-76512-5

Cover design by John Dayton

Table of Contents

PREFACE

Across the landscape of Christianity, doctrinal differences arise from interpretive differences and various presuppositions. While bearing the name Christianity, there is a broad range of theologies containing diverse and conflicting tenets. Suppose you trace the evolution of the church since the 1517 Reformation. In that case, you'll find increasing diversity among the churches, a broadening scope of what is claimed as the Christian religion, and an ever-increasing appeasement and accommodation to society and pagan culture in some quarters. Anyone can write a commentary, but good commentaries draw people to Scripture and the truth that aligns with the saving grace of the gospel.

People explain what biblical theology is according to the presuppositions they bring with them, which they use to interpret Scripture and formulate their theology. In the Reformed tradition, there are only two presuppositions: (1) God is, and (2) the Bible, in its original text, is the inspired word of God and is the only inerrant, infallible, and authoritative rule for faith and life. When these two presuppositions are rigorously used to interpret Scripture within its broadest context, the purest Biblical theology that is systematically deduced is known as Reformed theology. That being true, there is yet some breadth to what qualifies as Reformed theology. Regardless of what your church teaches or whatever commentary you read, you are personally responsible for searching out the truth from Scripture. I hope this Reformed exposition of Paul's letter to the Colossian church can assist you in that effort.

The commentary delves deeply into theology by addressing and dissecting challenging concepts, making every effort to present sound conclusions, consistent with the Biblical text, the immediate and broader context, and the standards of the Reformed faith, in ways that are easy to read but perhaps not so easy to grasp. I recommend that you read the Biblical text of each section of the commentary first. The conclusions drawn in the commentary were based on reasons derived from Scripture, with numerous associated verses referenced for depth, clarity, and confirmation. In many cases, proper theological insight is gained by multiple verses considered together. So, wherever a statement or conclusion made in the commentary raises a doubt or is questioned, please attempt to understand what in Scripture it was based on and what reasoning led to the statement or conclusion.

<https://www.scriptureexposition.com> contains links to book trailers of other Reformed commentaries I have written, as well as information on where they can be purchased.

COLOSSIANS INTRODUCTION

Colossae

Colossae was a small city about 125 miles east of Ephesus. When Paul wrote to the church at Colossae, it was located in the Roman province of Phrygia, in the region of Asia Minor. Today, it is part of Turkey. Laodicea and Hierapolis were neighboring cities only 10 to 20 miles from Colossae, and home churches existed in each (Col. 4:13, 15). Because of the proximity of these cities, people from each knew those from the other. Paul had written a letter to the church at Laodicea and requested that the churches read each other's letters (Col. 4:16).

An earthquake that occurred in 60 AD did considerable damage throughout the region of Phrygia, from which the city of Colossae never recovered. It's traditionally held that Paul's first Roman imprisonment, during which he wrote the letter to the Colossians, began in 60 AD. Since there is no mention of the earthquake in the letter, he likely wrote the letter either before it occurred or hearing reports of it. Likewise, we do not know the condition of the city when the letter was delivered; that is, whether the earthquake had already occurred by the time it was delivered.

In Revelation Chapters 2 and 3, John is told to write letters to seven churches. One is to Laodicea, where Christ rebukes them for what amounts to pride and lukewarmness toward spiritual things. At the same time, though the church at Colossae may no longer have existed, we see from Paul's letter that the saints there had been in dire need of instruction. While Laodicea rebuilt and recovered from the earthquake, Colossae did not. Nevertheless, what has survived is the letter Paul wrote to them, which has become their spiritual legacy to us and to all who have become believers and were saved through its reading.

the letter to the Colossians is not a draft

Some commentators construe the letter to the Colossians as an initial draft of Paul's Ephesian letter. Examining these letters side by side reveals that the topics addressed in both are presented in greater depth and detail in the Ephesian letter. The brevity of statements and the much shorter exhortations to family members in the Colossian letter support such a conclusion.

However, I disagree that the letter to the Colossians is an initial draft or a first edition of the Ephesian letter for the following reasons. Paul's familiarity with these two churches is entirely different. Before anyone claims that it should not make any difference since Paul is writing under the influence of the Holy Spirit, allow me to point out that it is a well-received and accepted belief that the Holy Spirit employs the background, disposition, personality, and skills of the writer, all of which are ordained for this purpose. Therefore, Paul's familiarity with these churches is worth considering. He had not visited Colossae and only knew of the church through Epaphras and perhaps a few others.

In contrast, Paul had spent three years personally teaching and ministering to the Ephesian church. The Ephesian letter was written to believers who were well-versed in the fundamental principles of the faith and who were expected to receive more in-depth and substantial instruction in sound doctrine. Thus, the in-depth presentations in his letter to the Ephesians of the Covenant of grace found in Chapter 1, the former life in Chapter 2, the mystery of the Gentiles revealed in Chapter 3, the unity of the body in Chapter 4, godliness in life and relationships in Chapter 5, and the armor of God in Chapter 6. What is absent from the Ephesian letter are corrections against false practices, beliefs, and teachings. In contrast, the Colossian letter was written to believers with a rudimentary or secondhand knowledge of the Gospel, which they had allowed to become contaminated by various external influences. Paul writes to the Colossians in a manner that is most helpful to them. First, he presents the glorious Christ to them and fills their minds and hearts with his majesty, wonder, and beauty. With no uncertainty, he establishes what Christ has accomplished and secured for them. But Paul also, in a kind, gentle, and loving way, calls them out for having polluted their faith with things that are not of Christ. Paul's task is not merely to scold the Colossians, but to discipline them. Towards that end, many of the doctrinal discourses in Ephesians are presented to the Colossians in a narrower form that is consistent with their ability to grow spiritually. Yet, Colossians contains some of the most beautiful, encouraging, uplifting passages that convey the glory and majesty of Christ, making it a valuable study for all believers.

letters from prison

According to tradition, Colossians was written during Paul's first Roman imprisonment (AD 60-62), along with Ephesians, Philemon, and most likely Philippians as well. Tychicus likely delivered the Colossian and Philemon letters with the assistance of Onesimus, who was a runaway slave returning to Philemon.

CHAPTER 1
THE PREEMINENCE OF CHRIST

CHAPTER 1 INTRODUCTION

The central purpose of Chapter 1, as it is with Chapter 2, is the security of the Gentiles' faith. Several themes are developed in support. From verses 3 through 12, Paul presents the trustworthiness of the source and grounds of their faith. He denotes the gospel as that which was proclaimed to all creatures, faithfully taught to them by Epaphras, and which they heard of the grace of God and understood. It was the hidden mystery of God revealed to the saints. We see in these verses that the Gospel of Grace is proclaimed, not offered. It is the hidden truth of God until it is revealed. It is received with understanding and not acquired by request. Paul causes them to reflect on what they have been called to, their hope of heaven, and an inheritance among the saints.

In verses 13 and 14, Paul presents what the Father and Son have done for the elect to be saved. He explains how the transformation of an elect sinner into a glorified saint is accomplished through deliverance, translation, reconciliation, forgiveness, and propitiation, in which the gospel of Christ and the kingdom are brought to focus. We see this is all of grace according to the Father's will and the work and person of Jesus Christ.

Central to Chapter 1, in verses 15-20, Paul introduces us to the divine person, Jesus Christ, and his relationship to the Father, creation, and the church. The preeminence of Christ is put before us, in which the deity of Christ is established as the creator of all things, the one who holds all things together, who possesses all things, and in whom the fullness of deity dwells bodily. He is the head of the church, our Redeemer through whom the sins of the saints are forgiven. His presence in history with a physical body is made clear, as are his bodily death and resurrection for our sins, by which his preeminence and almighty power to create, sustain, and reconcile all things are revealed. Christ the Redeemer and the one who reconciles all things to himself adds to the encouragement and hope of this Chapter.

The saints are truly blessed by the words of Chapter 1, for there is encouragement, assurance of deliverance from the bondage of sin, and security in the hope of entering the eternal kingdom of our Lord to be presented holy, blameless, and beyond reproach.

COLOSSIANS 1:1-2
GREETING

Epistles open with a greeting that identifies the writer, his authority, the people being addressed, and usually a short benediction. These greetings are not mere niceties but convey important information and promise increases in grace and peace in the names of the Father and Jesus Christ. Most greetings are alike in these matters but vary in some details to accommodate the letter's purpose. In the case of the Colossian letter, Paul introduces Timothy as a brother.

Colossians 1:1
greeting

Paul begins by identifying himself as the author of this letter. Along with him is Timothy. These two are greeting the saints at Colossae. To avoid any misunderstanding about who Paul is, he adds an identifying clause that he frequently uses, which serves a significant purpose. First, he is the apostle Paul. Apostles bear this title as persons of some authority and purpose. They should be taken seriously. Second, although there are various types of apostles, Paul specifically identifies himself as an apostle of Jesus Christ. His authority and power are to be understood as derived from Jesus Christ.

Third, many accusers have falsely charged Paul with being a false and self-proclaimed apostle. In the face of these accusers, Paul countercharges that he is established by the will of God to be an apostle of Jesus Christ. This charge is laid against those who oppose Paul's apostleship, that it is God whom they oppose.

Timothy

In the original text, Paul introduces Timothy as "*the brother*," which the ESV renders as "*our brother*." Paul typically refers to people as "*the brother*," but translators change it to "*our brother*" or "*a brother,*" as done here and also in Colossians 4:9 about Onesimus. The use of the definite article was to establish that Timothy is a man of faith and worthy of respect, as are any of the saints in Christ. It was an important introduction and confirmation of Timothy, who will have an essential role in the church as a leader. The Timothy who is mentioned here is the same Timothy to whom Paul wrote two letters, First and Second Timothy, concerning the oversight of the church.

This brief outline of Timothy will not do this faithful servant justice, as there is much more to this man's service and faith than is reported here. Paul first met Timothy during the early part of his second missionary journey as he and Silas, also known as Silvanus, visited Lystra. We're informed in Acts 16:2 that Timothy was a disciple whose mother, Eunice, was a believing Jew, as was his grandmother, Lois (2 Tim. 1:5). His father was a Greek. For the sake of the Jews in that area, who surmised that Timothy was not circumcised, Paul had him circumcised. Certainly, it was done with Timothy's consent; however, this is not mentioned (Acts 16:3). At Paul's request, Timothy began traveling with Paul and continued to do so throughout Paul's second and third journeys. He was with Paul in Rome during Paul's first imprisonment, led the church at Ephesus (1 Tim. 1:3), taught the gospel in Thessalonica (1 Thess. 3:1-2) and Corinth (1 Cor. 4:17), was at some time arrested himself for his faith, and was asked by Paul to come to him during his second Roman imprisonment (2 Tim. 4:9).

Colossians 1:2
to the faithful saints at Colossae

It is a common charity to acknowledge fellow church members as our brothers and sisters in the Lord, as saints, and as fellow believers without knowing them personally. Paul adds that they are faithful believers in Christ.

A true brother is a faithful believer, which is always charitably considered true of anyone who is a church member. However, such charity is unwarranted and is not implied by the verse when it is known that a church member is guilty of sexual immorality or greed or is an idolater, reviler, drunkard, or swindler. According to Paul, such persons should be *purged* from the church (1 Cor. 5:11-13). The term purged would mean excommunicated today and is an apostolic imperative.

We must be careful to understand what Paul's position is and what it is not. Paul holds this position; the one living as those listed in 1 Cor. 5:11 is not a brother with whom one can associate. The concept here is that they are unremorseful, unrepentant, and do not seek God's grace for deliverance from these sins. So they are, for example, sexually immoral rather than a brother struggling with the sin of sexual immorality. Paul regards such persons as evil and exhorts the church to put them out of fellowship and excommunicate them. It is not Paul's position that brothers struggling to overcome these sins should be ostracized. Generally, Paul speaks charitably unless there is a cause to talk otherwise. When such a cause exists, Paul does not hesitate to exercise judgment against evil (e.g., 1 Cor. 5:1-2). We must also be careful, for Paul is not telling us to judge the eternal state of a person's soul, but rather his fitness for Christian fellowship and access to the benefits of the church.

grace and peace

In verse 2, Paul is not praying for grace and peace as if the Colossians have not yet received them; instead that they continue to receive grace and peace from God. Paul has confidence that the Colossians will be further blessed with peace and grace from God and is alerting them to the understanding that all grace is from God, though they may receive it through various means, including letters written by the apostles. Praying in such manner is Paul's stewardship of God's grace on behalf of the church at Colossae as it was at Ephesus (Eph. 3:2). Now, as we take up the reading and study of Paul's letter to the Colossians, we too will be recipients of God's grace and peace as the Spirit applies its spiritual insights and instructions to our hearts.

Grace is unmerited favor with an intended purpose effectuated by Almighty God. Thereby, all grace is from God (1 Pet. 5:10) and is irresistible (2 Cor. 9:8). We see in Romans 8:32 that the Father *"graciously gives us all things"* (ESV) and in 1 Peter 1:3, we find that the Father's power *"has granted us all things"* (ESV). When these verses are combined, we see that the Father's power works graciously without being merited, so that the saints receive all things necessary for life and godliness (2 Cor. 12:9).

Paul has already acknowledged that those at Colossae have received God's regenerating grace by calling them saints and faithful brothers in Christ. Without the special grace that saves, faith is not possible (Eph. 2:8). This special grace includes the gift of justification through Jesus Christ (Rom. 3:24). The grace Paul is writing about follows the special grace of regeneration, faith, justification, and peace with God (Rom. 5:1). The gifts of the Holy Spirit are according to this grace. By this grace, the Father grants all things to us so that we may be complete in his sight (2 Pet. 1:3).

There are various relationships in which we can find peace. These are peace with oneself, fellow believers, non-believers, and God. God's special grace results in peace with the Father through Jesus Christ. Peace with the Father is the setting aside of his wrath against us (John 3:36), or more properly stated, the redirection of his wrath toward Jesus Christ as our propitiator (Rom. 5:9; I Thess. 1:10, 5:9; Rom 3:25; Heb. 2:17; 1 John 2:2, 4:10). This is a legal matter. The guilt of our sin having been imputed to Jesus Christ, placed Jesus under the law of death by which the wrath of God was poured out upon him. Jesus' forensic righteousness under the law was imputed to us, making us legally righteous before the Father and bringing peace between us. All saints are participants in this peace with God, but the degree to which we are aware of it and its effect on our lives is what Paul is bidding to increase. This peace is through Jesus Christ, as our Redeemer and Propitiator, and it keeps or guards our hearts and minds. These aspects of peace are what Paul refers to and surpass all understanding (Phil. 4:7). Although we may not fully understand this peace, if we keep in mind and cherish in our hearts what Jesus Christ did to make peace for us with the Father we will be more apt to live according to his precepts, to the praise and honor of his holy name, with all thankfulness.

COLOSSIANS 1:3-8
PRAYER OF THANKSGIVING

Verses 3 through 8 are not in the form of a prayer. Paul describes what he prays for and provides reasons for his prayers on behalf of the Colossians. These are profoundly commendable and encouraging words that describe the Colossians in the following ways:

- They are joined to Christ Jesus through their faith.
  Meaning: They have been given to Christ by the Father (John 6:37) that they may believe and be saved (John 6:40).
- They are among all the saints through their love.
  Meaning: They have been joined together into a holy temple (Eph. 2:21, 4:16)
- They are established in heaven by their hope.
  Meaning: They are established in the faith (Col. 2:7) and in the truth (2 Pet. 1:12).
- They have received every spiritual blessing in the heavenly places (Eph. 1:3). By the power of the Holy Spirit, they abound in hope (Rom. 15:13)
  Meaning: They are holy and blameless before God (Eph 1:4) and lack nothing for life and godliness (2 Pet. 1:3)
- They are recipients of the gospel because it has come to them; they have heard it and are bearing fruit in it.
  Meaning: The veil has been removed so that they may turn to the Lord (2 Cor. 3:16). The gospel was proclaimed (Col. 1:23) in truth, and those who believed were sealed with the Holy Spirit (Eph. 1:13).
- They are under God's grace by hearing and understanding.

Meaning: Because they believe and have faith, they are under grace; thus, sin will not rule over them (Rom. 6:14).

- They are connected to the Spirit through love.
  Meaning: God gave them a spirit of love (2 Tim. 1:7), a fruit of the Spirit (Gal. 5:22).

Furthermore, knowing that Paul continuously prays for the Colossians and gives thanks to the Father for them is encouraging. Here, Paul gives an example to all shepherds and reminds them of their duty to pray for those in their care. The Colossians exemplify Christian faith, love, hope, and bearing fruit throughout these verses. Above all, Paul reminds us to be thankful to God, the Father of our Lord Jesus Christ, for all kindness, goodness, and grace are gifts from God.

According to Paul, the pivotal issue on which the Colossians' faith and love are established is explained in verse 5. It is the hope laid up for them in heaven. Hope here is used as a *metonymy*, a word for something related. Paul certainly means the hope for the things laid up for them in heaven, the promise of their inheritance with all the saints, and eternal life. From this hope, the Colossians love their fellow saints and have faith in Christ. Paul immediately dispels any speculation that this hope is a pipe dream or an imagined fantasy by explaining that the origin of this hope lies in the truth of the Gospel that they had heard and received. Neither is this hope, love, and faith peculiar to the Colossians, but Paul testifies that the same gospel is producing these same fruits around the world. Finally, Paul brings us to the very foundation of Christian hope, love, and faith, which is the grace of God revealed in truth and with understanding. The work of the Holy Spirit is not expressly mentioned but can be discerned by necessary inference. Paul addresses yet another necessity. Because many voices claim to hold the truth, primarily Jews, he establishes that the one true gospel of Jesus Christ is what the Colossians learned from Epaphras, a faithful minister of Christ.

Colossians 1:3

God, the Father of our Lord Jesus Christ

According to biblehub.com, the Greek text reads as *the God [and] Father of the Lord of us Jesus Christ.* Paul referred to the God and Father of Jesus Christ frequently (Rom. 15:6; 2 Cor. 1:3 and 11:31; Eph. 1:3). Peter used the expression in 1 Peter 1:3, and John used a form of it in Revelation 1:6. The King James Bible renders the phrase correctly, maintaining the whole relation that God the Father has with Jesus Christ. The Greek does not mean that God is only the Father of Jesus Christ, but also that he is the God of Jesus Christ. The relationship within the Godhead between the First and Second Persons is that of Father and Son, as it applies to the divine nature. However, in terms of the human nature, it is God and creature. However, our Lord Jesus Christ is not two persons joined together. He is one divine person with two natures, one divine and the other human. So, we conclude that God is the God and Father of the divine person who is our Lord Jesus Christ.

The apostles Paul and Peter use the expression *"God and Father"* when addressing their relationship with the saints (Gal. 1:4; Eph. 4:6; Phil. 4:20; 1 Thess. 1:3, 3:11, 3:13). He is our God, as he is to all creatures. But only to the saints is he their Father by his love, care, and adoption. Jesus said this directly after his resurrection when he told Mary, *"go to my brothers and say to them, I am ascending to my Father and your Father, to my God and your God"* (John 20:17 ESV). Our relationship to God is one of the treasures in the Word of God that is too wonderful to fully comprehend. There is an analogy between Jesus Christ's relationship with God and our relationship with God, since the exact words describe both. Indeed, the Lord's federal headship of the elect bears upon this.

Colossians 1:4
a good report

Even though Paul has not been able to visit the saints at Colossae, he keeps them in his prayers and receives reports on their spiritual condition. The verse reports the great joy that permeated the church at that time. That joy was evident in their love for all their brothers and their faith in Christ, which motivated Epaphras to share it with Paul (Col. 1:8).

Colossians 1:5
the word of truth

Here, Paul gives a reason for the Colossians' faith and love, the gospel. The verse contains significant embedded theology, which will be explored. We know that the gospel is proclaimed all over the world, and does not produce faith and love in all people. The difference here is that the gospel was proclaimed to people who had an inheritance kept in heaven for them (Col. 1:12, 3:24; 1 Pet. 1:4; Eph. 1:11). This implies that they were among the chosen elect. You see, there isn't something laid up in heaven for everyone, just for the elect. These Colossian believers had the "*eyes of their hearts*" enlightened so that they may know this hope to which they have been called (Eph. 1:18). Furthermore, this hope kept in heaven is a reference to entering the kingdom of Christ and is an integral part of the gospel. The verse states that it was this hope they heard of when they heard the truth of the gospel. The verse also states that the source of their faith and love lies outside themselves and in the power of God through the gospel, for their faith and love developed only after they heard the truth of the gospel. In particular, hearing the gospel as truth and not as folly is only possible among people who are not perishing (1 Cor. 1:18, 2:14, 3:19).

Colossians 1:6
bearing fruit in the whole world

What has come to the Colossians is the gospel's truth and, thus, the hope laid up for them in heaven. It is confirmed by their faith and love for the saints. Paul then assures the Colossians that this is the same truth that is bearing fruit and increasing worldwide. In hearing this truth, the Colossians understood the grace of God. This is what's so amazing about the gospel: it's according to the grace of God; it's the gospel of the grace of God and not the gratuitous gospel of free will so readily believed and preached today. The gospel bearing fruit in the whole world is the fulfillment of prophecies found in many verses, such as in Isaiah, which Matthew referenced in his gospel, that in Jesus' name, the Gentiles will hope (Matt. 12:21).

Paul states this so clearly in Romans 16:25-27 that it is commonly used as a benediction to conclude church services. He is writing about the gospel coming to the nations, as in Colossians 1:6, "*in the whole world it [the gospel] is bearing fruit and increasing*" (ESV). In Romans, Paul writes that there is a mystery now being revealed to all nations [Gentiles], what had been kept secret for ages, even though the prophets wrote about it long ago. By God's decree, it is now revealed through the preaching of Jesus Christ, the gospel, and is bearing the fruit of saving faith.

During the Olivet Discourse recorded in Matt 24, Mark 13, and Luke 21, Jesus said,

> "*this gospel of the kingdom will be proclaimed throughout the whole world as a testimony to all nations*" (Matt. 24:14).

Once more, we take notice that the only true gospel that has saving grace is proclaimed, preached, or taught, but is never presented as an offer.

The Colossians are commended for hearing and understanding "*the grace of God in truth.*" Paul is commending the Colossians for correctly understanding that the grace being proclaimed to them was according to God's free and sovereign will. As relatively new believers, what they understood was without error. We know there is no grace except that which is from God (1 Pet. 5:10) according to the good pleasure of his will (Eph. 1:5), and whatever is granted according to merit is not of grace (Rom. 11:6). If they had any mixed notions of what God's grace is, Paul could not have written that they understand grace in truth.

Colossians 1:7-8
a faithful minister

Paul further confirms that what the Colossians learned from Epaphras was the true gospel bearing fruit in the whole world. Paul commended Epaphras in several ways. Among the people serving with Paul, Epaphras is beloved and a fellow servant. In addition, Epaphras is a faithful minister of Christ, which strongly implies that Epaphras has been called to a ministry by Christ and faithfully serves, particularly in upholding the truth as it applies to Christ. As to the nature or character of Epaphras' service, it is on behalf of others. We find in Colossians 4:12-13 that Epaphras reported to Paul the faith and love that the Colossian believers expressed. Paul wrote further about Epaphras later in this letter, which will be explored when we reach that point. This apostolic endorsement of Epaphras' ministry must have encouraged Epaphras and aided the efficacy of his service.

COLOSSIANS 1:9-12
PRAYER OF SUPPLICATION

Paul is concluding the exposition of his prayers for the Colossians. First, Paul continually prayed for the Colossians' ongoing spiritual growth and strengthening, providing great assurance. Secondly, Paul was continually thankful to the Father in his prayers, for he says the Father has qualified (past tense) them as saints, so there can be no greater assurance than to hope for something you have already received. In examining how Paul prays and what he includes, we find that he petitions the Lord on behalf of the saints for their most needful things: wisdom, understanding in the knowledge of God, patient endurance with joy, and continued strengthening in the faith. Additionally, we find Paul's gratitude to God for what the saints have already received and continue to receive by grace.

We may lend our thoughts to the prospect that Paul is praying in and according to the will of God, and so deduce that his petitions are an expression of the very will of God and the express work of the Holy Spirit in the lives of the Colossians, and by extension, in ourselves as well. In a manner, Paul's petitions express the substance of what the Colossians will receive from the Father. Furthermore, the contents of Paul's prayer exemplify what we should be praying for ourselves and others.

Colossians 1:9
from this day

Paul has prayed for the Colossians since he first heard of their faith. We may take his words to mean that he included the Colossians whenever he prayed. The first petition is that the Colossians be filled with the knowledge of the Father's will in all spiritual wisdom and understanding. On the one hand, the knowledge of God's will may be revealed extensively, with great clarity and precision. If, however, that knowledge passes us by externally, it avails us nothing. All the things of God that are plainly before the eyes of the natural man pass him by to no avail because they appear foolish to him (1 Cor. 2:14). The spiritual man may understand and gain wisdom because the Holy Spirit interprets spiritual things to spiritually minded people (1 Cor. 2:13-14).

Paul asks that the knowledge of the Father's will be effectually received to produce spiritual wisdom and understanding in the Colossians. Spiritual wisdom, as taught by the Spirit who interprets spiritual things, begins with the fear of the Lord (Ps. 1:7, 111:10; Prov. 9:10) and is distinct from human wisdom (1 Cor. 2:13). *"The wisdom from above is first pure, then peaceable, gentle, open to reason, full of mercy and good fruits, impartial and sincere"* (James 3:17 ESV). In stark contrast, earthly and demonic wisdom produces jealousy, selfish ambition, disorder, and vile practices (James 3:15).

All persons can be sorted into two groups. The first group consists of all natural persons; the Bible has much to say about them. It is never written that they seek God (Rom. 3:11), understand spiritual things (1 Cor. 2:14), please God (Heb. 11:6), or come to Christ on their own (John 6:44). It does say they are slaves to sin (Rom. 6:17), are the corruption that is in the world (2 Pet. 1:4), under the dominion of darkness (Col 1:13). The other group consists of people drawn from the first group by the power of God as he determined pretemporally (before time) according to his free and sovereign choice. These chosen people will become the saints as each is born again and will become the adopted sons of God through Jesus Christ (Eph. 1:5) and have eternal life (John 3:16). Those not chosen, who remain natural persons, perish.

Of all things to understand, one thing stands out as being of paramount importance, and that can only be received from Jesus Christ by revelation and grace. That understanding is to know that the Son of God has come in the person of Jesus Christ, who is truth and the true God and is eternal life and that we are in him (John 14:6; 1 John 5:20). How sorrowful it is to live without knowing Christ in this life and to die separated from him for eternity.

Colossians 1:10
walk worthy of the Lord

It is just as important and necessary that understanding accompanies spiritual knowledge. It is clear that when one understands God's will, one's manner of living changes. Paul petitions that this change in the Colossians is towards becoming worthy of the Lord. In this context, becoming worthy of the Lord does not mean becoming worthy of being saved as if some condition, merit, or standard exists that a man must meet as a prerequisite to salvation. Paul is drawing the minds of those saved to conduct themselves at all times in a manner that honors Christ. That is the understanding part of spiritual wisdom. As it is a shameful thing for a son to dishonor his parents, how much more is it for one who is the recipient of God's grace to reply by living as if that grace were of no effect or value? We may go further and determine from Paul that there is a natural causation that those who are spiritually minded will seek to honor the Lord evermore as they learn the will of God more deeply. The process is pleasing to the Lord and produces successful results when good works are done. As believers increase in their knowledge of God, they become more willing and fruitful in doing good works that please and honor the Lord, which were prepared for the saints to do (Eph. 2:10). How can we fulfill the works God has prepared for us? Because God works in us in such a way that we are willing to do the works foreordained (Phil. 2:13).

Colossians 1:11
being strengthened

We are continually strengthened as our knowledge of God and spiritual wisdom expand our understanding. This strengthening encompasses all aspects of our faith, but the endurance of faith highlights the special qualities of patience and joy. These are needful things in a world where the Christian faith and Christians are under assault. Paul does not leave this here, but adds two things to this strengthening. First, strengthening is with all power. It does not mean that all the power that exists anywhere is being applied. It does mean that all kinds of power work to strengthen believers, from which we may be assured that no remaining power may nullify or prevent Christians from spiritual strengthening. Second, strengthening is according to his glorious might. It is God who wields this power; it is God who strengthens us, and as there is nothing mightier than the Almighty, we may be doubly assured that we are being strengthened.

Colossians 1:12
being thankful; made you qualified

With the petitions being concluded, Paul expresses his thankfulness to the Father as part of his prayers. His thankfulness is because the Father has "*qualified*" the Colossians to share in the saints' inheritance in light. The word "*qualified*" is potentially misleading. It is too soft and might lead one to suspect that being qualified does not guarantee sharing the inheritance with the saints. The Greek word being translated as "*qualified*" is ἱκανώσαντι (hikanōsanti), which, according to biblehub.com, means "to make sufficient or able." Paul expresses that the Father will make the saints able or sufficient to receive their share in the inheritance. Saints are qualified when they become saints, but they are not ready or prepared to receive the inheritance being kept for them in heaven (1 Pet. 1:4). Being qualified means that they can and will be made ready through sanctification, a process with a beginning and an ending.

During his sermon on the mount (Matt. 5:48), Jesus said that the saints must be complete (perfect), even as God is complete (perfect). The Greek word there is τέλειοι (teleioi), which, according to biblehub.com, means *to have reached its end, complete, perfect*. Jesus was referring to the end of the process of sanctification, not when the saints become saints, since they were saints when they first believed. The saints will be complete when they are prepared to receive their inheritance. Just as there is nothing that can be added to God to make him more complete as God, there will be nothing more that can or needs to be added to the saints to make them more complete as saints, for God has given them all things necessary for life and godliness by his almighty power (2 Peter 1:3). Paul, by referring to being qualified, is referring to the very beginning of what starts the process of becoming complete.

Although we are not yet complete or have received all things in this very moment, we are qualified with all assurance that we will lack nothing as saints when we meet Christ in the air, as it is God's will for the saints. When Paul addressed the elders in Ephesus, he said,

> "*And now I commend you to God and to the word of his grace, which is able to build you up and to give you the inheritance among all those who are sanctified*" (Acts 20:32 ESV).

Thus, we see that Paul, Peter, and Jesus present the same theology when their contributions are considered together and in context.

our inheritance

What can we know of this inheritance? In a sense we have already obtained it because we have been predestined in Christ to receive it (Eph. 1:11). The promised Holy Spirit has been given to us as a guarantee of our inheritance (Eph. 1:14). The inheritance itself has been promised and has the following attributes: it is eternal, glorious, imperishable, undefiled, unfading, and it will be shared among the saints (Heb. 9:15; Eph. 1:18; 1 Pet. 1:4; Col 1:12).

Recall the parable of the Prodigal Son. The younger son desired his inheritance before he was ready for it. After receiving it, he squandered it and was left destitute. Our Father in Heaven will not let that happen to the saints in Christ. Our inheritance is kept in heaven until we are made ready by grace and his divine power to receive it.

saints in light

What light φωτί (phōti) is Paul referring to? In Greek, the literal translation is "*saints in the light*" (biblehub.com). Paul is referring to a specific, special, and definite light. This seemingly simple phrase may first appear as a gracious commendation, but it conveys a profound reality with significant meaning.

Jesus is the light of the world

In the New Testament, we first encounter the concept of light in the gospels. Matthew indicates that people were living in a darkness that he characterized as a region and shadow of death until they saw a great light dawn (Matt. 4:16). Luke renders the same concept differently as the mercy of God that makes sunshine to rise on those sitting in the darkness and shadow of death (Luke 1:78-79). Old Simeon in the Temple, when he saw the baby Jesus, said, referring to him, that a light was prepared as a revelation to the Gentiles and a glory to Israel (Luke 2:31-32). We begin to see in these references to light that the light is a reference to Jesus. John clearly states this. John also contrasts this light with darkness (John 1:5), but the darkness that John refers to does not comprehend the light by which we infer that this darkness is a reference to people, whereas, in Matthew and Luke, it is a condition of impending judgment and death. Later, Jesus declares, "*I am the light of the world*" (John 8:12, 9:5 ESV). The light mentioned in the gospels is Jesus Christ. And, of course, this must be true since God is light, and there is no darkness in him (1 John 1:5).

the light of transformation

There is something transformative about Jesus being the light of the world. If you recognize Jesus as the light of the world and walk accordingly, you will not spiritually stumble, just as someone walking in the daylight does not physically stumble. However, if the light of Jesus does not abide in you, you will spiritually stumble just as one physically stumbles when walking in the dark of night (John 11:9-10). People who believe that Jesus is the light of the world become sons of light (John 12:36) and do not remain in darkness (John 12:46). By corollary, the sons of light are no longer under the shadow of death. More so, the sons of light have the light of life (John 1.5). When Jesus commissioned Paul, he was told that he was being sent so that people would turn from darkness to light, from the power of Satan to God, for the forgiveness of sin, and to be sanctified by faith. On the one hand, there is sin, darkness, the power of Satan, and the shadow of death. On the other hand, there is light, forgiveness of sin, faith, sanctification, sonship, and life (Acts 26:18; Matt. 4:16; John 1:5). The identity of the light is further delineated as the light of the gospel of the glory of Christ which we may infer overcomes the power of the god of this world which blinds the minds of unbelievers to this light (2 Cor. 4:4). This light is also the knowledge of God in the face of Jesus Christ (2 Cor. 4:6).

the unapproachable light of God

God dwells in unapproachable light that no one has seen or can see (1 Tim. 6:16). God said to Moses no man can see me and live (Exod. 33:20). Mortal man of perishable flesh and blood cannot even get close for such a one cannot enter the kingdom of God (1 Cor. 15:50). This is not just the Father, but all three persons of the Trinity. To become the incarnate man, Jesus Christ of flesh and blood, the Son had to subdue his essential glory. That does not mean or imply to any degree that he became less God or less divine. We see in his high priestly prayer that Jesus prayed for the glory that he had from all eternity to be returned, indicating that at that time, he was not expressing his glory in its full manifestation (John 17:5). During Christ's incarnation, there was a witnessed transfiguration of Jesus. Witnesses described his face as shining like the sun, and his clothes became like white light, radiant, and his glory was of the only Son of the Father (Matt. 17:2; Mark 9:3; John 1:14). This transfiguration was necessary for Jesus to come into the very presence of the Father. It will be the same or greater manifestation of Jesus Christ that we see on the last day, when the living saints on earth are caught up in the air to be with him and see him as he is, to be changed to be like him.

how we approach the unapproachable

Flesh and blood cannot inherit the kingdom of God (1 Cor. 15:50), yet we have a promised inheritance of an eternal kingdom. At the time we meet Jesus in the air, our blessed hope (Titus. 2:13), we will be changed to be like Jesus; we will then have an imperishable spiritual body (1 Cor. 15:42, 44) that bears the image of Jesus Christ, the man of heaven (1 Cor. 15:4). What the Father had previously qualified the saint for will then be complete. They can then receive the inheritance that has been kept for them all along (1 Pet. 1:4). One aspect of this inheritance is becoming *partakers of the divine nature* (2 Pet. 1:4) and receiving the *glory of the children of God* (Rom. 8:21 ESV). This is the purpose and fulfillment of our holy calling *into his marvelous light* (1 Pet. 2:9 ESV).

conclusion

Verse 1:12 looks forward to our eternal state, having us contemplate the grace by which the Father has qualified us now, the riches of our inheritance, and our participation in the communion as saints in his glorious and marvelous light when we are complete, in our eternal state. The verse contains a now-and-then aspect of our calling. Now we know in part and see dimly as in a mirror, but when we see Christ face to face, the partial will pass away, the perfect will come, and we shall know fully (1 Cor. 13:9-12). Even now, our life is hidden with Christ in God (Col. 3:3). Even now, we are no longer of the darkness but have been transferred to the eternal kingdom of our Lord and Savior, Jesus Christ, the Son of God (Col. 1:13; 2 Pet. 1:11). Even now we are children of light (Eph. 5:8) and what we will be has not yet appeared (1 John 3:2). In the truest sense we who believe are saints in the light now, though dimly, but in our eternal state will be saint in the light in the most complete manner. It is the light of the glory of God in the face of Jesus Christ (2 Cor. 4:6) and draws our minds to the closeness the Father has with the saints, now and forever.

COLOSSIANS 1:13-14
THE GOSPEL

the importance of the truth

The remainder of Chapter 1 is an outline of Paul's Christology. Paul's bullet points are the deity of Christ, his universal preeminence, our redemption and forgiveness of sin, and the Father's overarching sovereign will. As we proceed through this and the following sections, we will systematically explore these points to uncover the details they reveal. In Chapter 2, Paul will bring up many of the details we need to mention here and reference.

Before delving into these verses, let's look ahead to Colossians 2:4, where Paul warns us not to be deceived by anyone making a seemingly plausible argument. The antidote to being deceived is knowing the truth. The mind that is not filled with the truth is more easily persuaded by deceptive arguments that appeal to misunderstandings and misconceptions. In his letter to the Colossians, Paul may be addressing circumstances he knows are occurring in Colossae, such as false teachers misleading believers on various issues. It seems that is the likely case, at least to some degree. We must take Colossians 2:4 at face value: the verse presents a warning that protects the saints from being led astray when properly heeded. With this in mind, recall that in Colossians 1:9, Paul said that he prayed that the Colossians might be filled with the knowledge of God's will with spiritual wisdom and understanding. That, together with heeding the warning in verse 2:4, effectively prevents the saints from being led astray.

Paul has been petitioning the Father for the Colossians for the very things needed to heed the warning of Colossians 2:4. Paul, beginning in verse 1:13, is God's instrument in answering this prayer for the purpose expressed in Colossians 2:4. What Paul accomplishes subtly, and must be drawn out in the Colossians epistle, he pronounces clearly in Titus 1:3.There Paul makes several claims about himself: (1) he is a servant of God, (2) an apostle of Jesus Christ, and (3) a preacher entrusted with his word. Paul then explains the purpose why he is a servant, apostle, and preacher: (1) for the sake of the elect's faith, (2) for their knowledge of the truth, godliness, and eternal life. The culmination of this is that the truth is made known by preaching God's word by those called by God (2 Pet. 1:20-21). So, we may add that the mind filled with the truth, spiritual wisdom, and understanding may not be deluded by false teachers who make plausible arguments.

The truth in preaching the gospel taught by the apostles is substantiated in other places. Jesus said abiding in his words sets one free (John 8:31-32). In his high priestly prayer, Jesus pointed out that the preaching of the apostles (Jesus' words) will lead others to believe in him (John 17:20). Likewise, when the good news is preached, people will hear and believe and call on the name of the Lord to be saved (Rom. 10:14-15). Peter devoted an entire chapter in his second epistle to warn against false teachers and bids us to study the truth laid down by the apostles and the prophets who spoke from God so as not to be led astray (2 Pet. 1:19-21).

Knowing that those appointed by Christ, the holy prophets and the apostles, who spoke the truth from God, and with hearts desiring to know and understand the truth from the very words of God, we will be prepared to receive the truth set before us by Paul in these next two important verses.

the covenants of redemption and grace

Upon the first reading of verses 1:13 and 14, a person should perceive the Father's and Son's grace as it applies to the salvation of the elect. These verses declare that the Father and Son extricate sinners from the darkness that separates them from God, redeem them, forgive their sins, and transfer them to the kingdom of the Lord. Examine these two verses for evidence of human merit, will, or cooperation, and you will find none. Neither is any such thing implied. Verses 1:13 and 14 are all of grace, grace alone, for there is nothing of human merit associated with what the Father and Son have done as expressed in these verses. Together, they express the ***covenant of grace*** that runs through human history from Genesis to Revelation. God saves sinners by grace alone, through faith alone, by Christ alone, according to Scripture, all to the glory of God alone.

The grace proclaimed in verses 1:13 and 14 is not limited to New Testament saints, as it expresses what the Father and Son have covenanted to do for all saints throughout history. We must include the Holy Spirit in this covenant, as will be explained. The three Persons of the Godhead, in eternity past, covenanted together. Eternity past is an expression that indicates this occurred before creation, before time, or pretemporally. Although we cannot know how this covenant was determined, as it lies in the secret things of God, there are revelations of it in Scripture. Theologians have referred to this as the ***covenant of redemption***, in which the Father established a definite plan of redemption that would unfold following creation and the fall. The Son agreed to take on the duties of the Redeemer put forth in the Father's plan, and the Holy Spirit covenanted to apply all the merits of the Redeemer to the elect chosen by the Father. The Father, Son, and Holy Spirit have faithfully kept this covenant of redemption, and we see its administration in human history as the covenant of grace.

A covenant is an agreement between two or more parties that contains conditions and promises. We can find the elements of a covenant between the Father and Son in many verses. Among them that shed light on the covenant of redemption is Ephesians 1:3-14.

1. The agreement between the Father and Son
    a. What the Father agreed to:

i. Before creation, the Father chose who would be redeemed (Eph. 1:4).
ii. The Father decreed the incarnation of Jesus Christ (Psalm 2:7-8; Eph. 1:5).
iii. Our redemption through Jesus Christ was planned according to the Father's will (Eph. 1:7-10).
iv. God's secret and hidden wisdom in the gospel was decreed before the ages (1 Cor. 2:7).
v. Jesus Christ was known and loved by the Father before the foundation of the world (1 Pet. 1:20; John 17:24).

b. What the Son agreed to:
   i. The Son came into this world to do the Father's will (Heb. 10:5-7).
   ii. Jesus accomplished the works given to him by the Father (John 5:36, 12:49, 17:8).
   iii. The Son agreed to lay down his life as the Messiah according to the charge given to him by the Father (John 10:17-18).
   iv. Jesus was crucified according to God's definite plan and foreknowledge (Acts 2:23).
   v. Jesus Christ, *"... the Lamb having been slain from the founding of the world"* (Rev. 13:8 – Greek interlinear).
   vi. Jesus would be the mediator of a new covenant (Heb. 9:15, 12:24).

2. The commands of the covenant:
   a. The elect would be chosen by the Father and predestined according to his will and purpose (Eph. 1:4-5)
   b. The Father sent the Son into the world in the flesh (Heb. 10:5).
   c. Jesus was to be born under the law and redeem the elect for adoption (Gal. 4:4-5).
   d. Jesus was not to lose any of those the Father had given him (John 6:39).

   e. The elect would be made holy and blameless before the Father (Eph. 1:4).
   f. Jesus was commanded what to say and speak under the authority of the Father (John 12:49).
   g. Jesus was to bear our iniquities, be crushed, put to grief, and suffer the anguish of his soul (Isa. 53:10-11).
   h. All things are to be united in Jesus (Eph. 1:10).

3. The promises of the covenant:
   a. The Father assigned Jesus a kingdom (Luke 22:29).
   b. The Father gives all authority in heaven and on earth to Jesus (Matt. 28:18)
   c. Jesus was glorified (John 12:23, 13:31)
   d. Jesus was exalted and given a name above every name (Phil. 2:9)

   e. Jesus was given the authority to judge the world (2 Tim. 4:1; Rev. 20:4)
   f. The church as a bride (Rev. 19:7, 21:9)

Colossians 1:13
one work but in many parts

Several parts of verse 13 must be dealt with separately, even though each part occurs in conjunction with the others when the entirety of the verse is considered.

the Father, the originating cause

In verse 3, Paul begins to explain what he has been praying for on behalf of the Colossians and to whom he is praying. It is God, the Father of our Lord Jesus Christ. The Father is the antecedent of "He" in verse 13. Verse 13 states that the Father did what the verse goes on to say was done to us. It begins or originates with God, the Father. Explaining that the Father is the originating cause of salvation is not unique to this section of Scripture or to Paul. According to Paul's letter to Ephesus, the Father chose us before the world began and predestined us to adoption through Jesus Christ (Eph. 1:3-5). Being chosen by the Father is also expressed in 1 Thessalonians 1:4,

James 2:5, and Romans 11:5. Peter states that the Father, by his divine power, called us to his own glory and gave us all things for life and godliness (2 Pet. 1:3-4).

In the complex of salvation, all that occurs to turn a godless sinner into a saint is initiated by the Father and occurs according to his purpose and will (Eph. 1:5) in conjunction with the Father's definite plan (Acts 2:23). Jesus expressed the Father's sovereign causation in several ways. Jesus said the chosen are given and drawn to him by the Father (John 17:24, 6:44). Thus, Jesus can say that his sheep know his voice and come to him (John 10:27), but those who are not among his sheep, those not given to him or chosen by the Father, will not believe and will not come to him (John 10:26; 6:44). Jesus welcomes all who the Father has given him and bids them to come (Matt. 11:28), for it is only them who can come to Jesus. Jesus describes them as knowing they labor under the burden [of sin] that they bear. Therefore, it is said that the Father alone is the ***originating cause*** of salvation. No causation by human will, works, or inclination exists that precedes the Father's or on which the Father's is predicated.

dominion of darkness

According to biblehub.com, the Greek word that the ESV translates as "*domain*" is ἐξουσίας (exousias), which is correctly translated as "*dominion*", "*power*", or "*authority*." Many English Bibles render it as power. The Amplified Bible has dominion.

Darkness in Scripture is an all-encompassing state of existence that possesses the power to hold people in bondage (2 Pet. 2:4; Jude 1:6). Thus, the unbeliever is of the darkness and is the darkness (1 Pet. 2:9; Eph 5:8). Darkness is also a place of judgment (Matt. 8:12) but in all its power, it is unable to overcome the light of Christ (John 1:5).

The word darkness, as used, is a metonymy, a single attribute of the misery in which unbelievers live that encompasses the whole of their fallen state. People who are "in darkness" have the following extensive list of attributes:

Their relation to God:

- They are the children of wrath by nature (Eph. 2:3), sons of disobedience, and under God's wrath (Eph. 5:6).
- They do not seek God (Rom. 3:11) and are ungodly sinners (1 Tim. 1:9; 1 Pet. 4:18).
- They are under the debt of death (Rom. 5:12; 6:23).
- They are unrighteous (Rom. 3:10) and establish their own (false) righteousness (Rom. 10:3).

Their minds:

- They cannot see the light of the gospel because their minds have been blinded (2 Cor. 4:4).
- Their hearts and minds are veiled to the gospel (2 Cor. 3:16).
- They are futile in their thinking, and their hearts are dark (Rom. 1:21).
- They set their minds on the things of the flesh (Rom. 8:5).

They are in and of the darkness:

- Their own nature enslaves them to things that are not gods (Gal. 4:8).
- They are under the dominion of sin (Rom. 6:14), slaves of sin (Rom. 6:17).
- They are the corruption that is in the world (2 Pet. 1:4).

You may regard these characteristics as the attributes of everyone who has not been delivered from the darkness, unbelievers in Christ. Unbelievers should not be considered merely suffering from some external influence, like a sickness or a lack of information. As it is said, the sinner is not a sinner because he sins; he sins because he is a sinner. The unbeliever is trapped in darkness, being of the darkness, and thus unable to free himself from his own nature, nor incline himself to be free. Darkness holds the unbeliever with an unshakable grip that will not release him until divine power is applied when the Father delivers him from its bondage.

the Son

The Son being written of is the incarnate, risen, and glorified Son, Jesus Christ, who is preeminent over all things (Col. 1:18). When people hear the name Jesus Christ, they tend to think of Jesus during his earthly ministry as recorded in the Gospels, apart from the various future prophecies Scripture contains. Perhaps the suffering servant of Isaiah 53 comes to mind most readily. However, in verse 13, I think it is more fitting to consider Jesus Christ glorified in heaven and reigning over his kingdom. The apostles wrote of Jesus Christ being seated at the right hand of God (Eph. 1:20; Col. 3:1; Heb. 8:1, 12:2). Just before his ascension, he told the disciples, *"All authority in heaven and on earth has been given to me"* (Matt. 28:18 ESV). The Father raised Jesus and

> *"seated him at his right hand in the heavenly places, far above all rule and authority and power and dominion, and above every name that is named, not only in this age but also in the one to come. And he put all things under his feet and gave him as head over all things to the church, which is his body, the fullness of him who fills all in all"* (Eph 1:20-23 ESV).

Jesus said that the Father has given all judgment to him (John 5:22). When the Son of Man comes in his glory, he will be seated on his glorious throne (Matt. 25:31). Later in this Chapter, Paul will extol the preeminence of Christ and it is the preeminent Son whose kingdom the saints have been transferred to.

delivered from the darkness

The darkness described above is where all believers were when they were called to Christ. Unless people are called to Christ, they will remain in darkness. But verse 13 specifies a two-step work of the Father: a deliverance and a transferal. The first is the deliverance from the bondage of darkness; the second is the transfer to the kingdom of his beloved Son. It is a single work, not two. Paul graciously included all the Colossians among the "us" he referred to as being delivered from the domain of darkness. We can get a better understanding of who this deliverance applies to. Does it apply to all people in all circumstances, those who autonomously choose to be delivered, or to particular people sovereignly chosen by God?

Jesus said that people who do not believe in him remain in darkness and thus perish (John 3:16, 12:46). The implication is that there are people who are not saved and never enter the kingdom of Jesus Christ. Jesus amplified this by saying,

> *"If anyone does not abide in me he is thrown away like a branch and withers; and the branches are gathered, thrown into the fire, and burned"* (John 15:6 ESV),

That's an apt description of perishing. Some people do perish, and it is because they haven't been delivered from their corruption, which is the darkness that binds them. To such people, the cross of Christ remains folly, as do the things of the Spirit (1 Cor. 1:18, 2:14). Those who have been delivered go on to believe in Jesus Christ. Their deliverance is by the Father's will since faith and belief are not possible when a person is under the power of darkness.

Not all people will be delivered from the domain of darkness. Some will perish. So, this disposes of the first possibility of who can be delivered. Those still in darkness, whether elect or not, are held within its dominion and cannot effectuate or initiate their escape. They lack both the ability to escape and the desire to escape. A person who is dead in trespasses and sin also does not seek God (Rom. 3:11), cannot please God (Heb. 11:6), has a veil over their eyes and minds (2 Cor. 4:3), and their minds are futile (Rom. 1:21) and unable to discern spiritual things (1 Cor. 2:14) which is precisely how the power of darkness that enslaves them is manifested. Peter expresses the inability of an individual to extricate himself from their corruption by stating that God's divine power is necessary to accomplish this (2 Pet. 1:3-4).

In the effort to know who can be delivered from darkness, Scripture informs us that not all people will be delivered, and no one can deliver themselves, not even incline themselves to seek deliverance. Only those whom the Father has chosen, a particular people, will be delivered.

For a person to be delivered from darkness, the darkness must lose its dominion over them. The power of sin over them must be defeated. But until the debt of death is paid, which they legally owe for their sin (Rom. 6:23), sin maintains its hold on them. We will explore this further in detail when we examine verse 14 and discuss the work of Jesus Christ. For now, the Father delivered his people from the power of darkness through Jesus Christ, as we find in verse 14.

the kingdom

The Father is transferring his chosen people to an eternal kingdom that cannot be shaken (Heb. 12:28), whose king is King of kings and whose lord is Lord of lords (Rev. 17:14). There is a wide variety of beliefs about how a person can enter this kingdom of heaven and who is allowed in. There are even misunderstandings about the historical meaning of Christ's kingdom. As we undertake this study, many erroneous beliefs will be exposed for what they are. When the mention of Christ's kingdom arises in Scripture or discussion, we should pause to contemplate the precious and marvelous wonder of all the saints of God taking possession of it and dwelling there forever, especially considering its central role in our faith.

In Chapter 2 of the book of Daniel, Daniel interpreted King Nebuchadnezzar's dream of a great image. In summary, the parts of the image represented several earthly kingdoms. In the dream's interpretation, the God of heaven established an eternal kingdom with one king, forever ending the earthly kingdoms with their destruction. The common understanding of Daniel's interpretation of Nebuchadnezzar's dream is that there are four kingdoms, the fourth of which is Roman. Rome is the final kingdom when the Messiah is revealed and inaugurates the eternal kingdom of God. See John Calvin's commentary on Daniel for a thorough exposition of Daniel's interpretation.

In Chapter 7 of the book of Daniel, Daniel had an extensive vision of four beasts coming out of the sea. An angel explains to Daniel that they represent four kingdoms of the earth. Still, the saints of the Most High shall receive and possess a kingdom that shall last forever and ever (Dan. 7:14). The fourth beast had a horn that made war against the saints of God and prevailed over them until the Ancient of Days came and judgment was given to the saints who then possessed the kingdom (Dan. 7:21-22). In verse 7:27, the saints of the Most High receive the greatest kingdom under heaven, whose king has everlasting dominion over all. The Ancient of Days is the

Messiah, Jesus Christ. Calvin comments that this "depicts for us a visible image of Christ's kingdom." See John Calvin's commentary on Daniel.

The prophet Nathan, having been instructed by God (2 Sam. 7:4), prophesied to King David that one of his descendants would be king of an eternal kingdom, a kingdom that would be made sure forever (2 Sam. 7:16). There is no other kingdom that Colossians 1:13 refers to than the one prophesied in Daniel and promised to David, it is the kingdom of the beloved Son.

These prophecies predict an eternal kingdom and one king who is king forever. The good news is that the King and kingdom have come. The New Testament refers to this kingdom as the eternal kingdom, the kingdom of God, the kingdom of heaven, the kingdom of Christ, the kingdom of our Lord, and the kingdom of his beloved Son. According to the eschatology of Amillennialism, the kingdom of verse 13 is the millennial kingdom, where "millennial" is understood to be figurative. The kingdom itself is eternal.
New Testament statements about Christ's kingdom:

- John the Baptist proclaimed that the *"kingdom of heaven is at hand"* (Matt. 3:2). The time is fulfilled, and the kingdom of God is at hand (Mark 1:15).
- The kingdom is for the poor in spirit (Matt. 5:3), whoever is persecuted for righteousness' sake (Matt. 5:10).
- The coming of the kingdom should be prayed for (Matt. 6:10; Luke 11:2).
- When the twelve apostles were given authority and sent out, their instruction was to proclaim that the kingdom of heaven was at hand (Matt. 10:7; Luke 9:2).
- Jesus spoke in parables to keep the secrets of the kingdom from those who were not granted to know them (Matt. 13:11; Mark 4:11; Luke 8:10)
- The righteous will shine like the sun in the kingdom of their Father (Matt. 13:43).
- Mary was told that her son, whose name would be Jesus, would be the Son of the Most High, who would be given the throne of David (the promised kingdom), and of his kingdom, there would be no end (Luke 1:31-33).

- The kingdom of God comes in ways that cannot be observed (Luke 17:20).
- The Father assigned the kingdom to Jesus (Luke 22:29).
- You must be born again to see the kingdom of God (John 3:3).
- Jesus said his kingdom was not of this world (John 18:36).
- The kingdom of God is about righteousness, peace, joy, and the Holy Spirit (Rom. 14:17).
- The kingdom of God consists in power (1 Cor. 4:20).
- The kingdom cannot be shaken (Heb. 12:28).
- The kingdom is promised to those who love God (Jas. 2:5).
- The kingdom of our Lord and Savior, Jesus Christ, is eternal (2 Pet. 1:11).
- After destroying every rule, authority, and power, the end will come, and Jesus will deliver the Kingdom to God the Father (1 Cor. 15:24; Rev. 12:10).

This kingdom is eternal, not limited to one thousand years; it has been at hand since Jesus began his earthly ministry. It is not an earthly kingdom to which the Father has transferred the saints. We are no longer in darkness because we are children of the kingdom ruled by Jesus Christ, in which we participate now by faith while waiting eagerly for the consummation of our hope when we are made fit to take possession of it.

the gospel

Prophecies of the Old Testament foretold of an eternal kingdom. It is to be ruled by Jesus Christ, who will be given dominion over all things, and where the saints will be forever. But what does this have to do with salvation? The Bible teaches us that people are saved by grace alone, by Christ alone, through faith alone. These principles are the essential components of the covenants God made with people at various times in history. Each of these covenants is an expression of the overarching covenant of grace that spans all of human history. No one is ever saved apart from grace, without the merits of Jesus Christ personally applied, or without faith in Christ. God's mercy and his divine power are the enabling force of his grace that calls the dead to life in Christ (John 5:21; Rom. 4:17). The person and work of Christ are the legal and just bases for our redemption, justification, and sanctification. Our faith trusts in God alone and glorifies his name as we live godly lives.

The Israelites longed for the coming Messiah and his promised kingdom for centuries. Then, at the right time, in the fullness of time, Jesus was born, God incarnate, and the good news of the coming Messiah went forth. He had arrived. But, and this is important, not only had the King arrived, but also his promised and foretold eternal kingdom. This is the gospel of the kingdom, the promised kingdom of God's beloved Son. It is at hand to welcome the saints to take possession of by faith. It is this kingdom that dead sinners are transferred to as saints after being delivered from the bondage of sin and born again.

Since John [the Baptist], the good news of the kingdom has been preached (Luke 16:16). Jesus taught in the synagogues throughout Galilee, proclaiming the gospel of the kingdom (Matt. 4:23, 9:35; Luke 8:1). It was his purpose to preach the good news of the kingdom. During the Olivet Discourse, Jesus stated that the gospel of the kingdom would be proclaimed throughout the world as a testimony to the nations (Matt. 24:14). Peter, in turn, preached the good news of the kingdom of God and the name of Jesus Christ in Samaria. People believed and were baptized (Acts 8:12). These verses form a critical foundation for understanding that the whole of the gospel is the good news that our Lord Jesus Christ has come and taken possession of this eternal kingdom to rule forever with his saints in glory.

The Biblical story of human experience does not lead us to an ending. It guides us to contemplate a perpetual state of glory as the eternal ages roll forever onward, revealing *"the immeasurable riches of his [the Father's] grace in kindness toward us in Christ Jesus"* (Eph. 2:7 ESV). One of these great events, involving the kingdom, will occur when the great day of judgment concludes with Jesus Christ presenting the eternal kingdom to the Father (1 Cor. 15:24) in which all the glorified saints dwell in righteousness (2 Pet. 3:13). We will be revealed as sons of the living God (Hosea 1:10; Rom. 9:26) and creation will be liberated from its bondage to corruption (Rom. 8:21, 23).

Colossians 1:14

Working our way through this verse will be challenging. There are many details to discuss, and we endeavor to examine them logically, guided by Scripture. In this effort, we will explore what it means to be a redeemer, how Christ became our redeemer, the nature and circumstances of Christ's offering, and how our redemption was eternally secured, leading to life and the forgiveness of our sins.

Christ, the meritorious cause, a redeemer

Redemption was integral to Hebrew law and culture, and Paul's reference suggests that the Colossians may have had a similar understanding of the concept. Nevertheless, Paul explains that in our case, the outcome of redemption by the Son is the forgiveness of sins.

What is a redeemer?

Verse 14 informs us that we have been redeemed by Jesus Christ, the Son. We should understand that this redemption was legally sound according to Levitical law (Lev. 25). A redeemer, at his own expense, restores property to a relative who had previously lost or sold it and then shares in the interest of that property. A redeemer may also redeem a person, such as a slave or someone who has lost all means of support or has fallen into debt. In the story of Ruth, Naomi's husband had sold some land before the family moved to Moab. Years later, when she and Ruth returned to Bethlehem, they were alone and destitute. Boaz, a good man and a relative of Naomi's husband, wanted to redeem the land that had been previously sold, which would also redeem Naomi and Ruth. However, another man had the first right to be the redeemer. Unless he relinquished that right, Boaz could not be the redeemer. Rules had to be followed, but it eventually worked out, and Boaz redeemed the land and married Ruth.

Who are the "we" that Paul is writing about?

Precisely, who has been redeemed? A phrase appearing in many places in Scripture is "*his people.*" When the angel appeared to Joseph in a dream, he told Joseph that Mary would bear a son who would save "*his people*" from their sins (Matt. 1:21). In Luke's gospel, we are told about Zachariah, the father of John the Baptist, being filled with the Holy Spirit, who prophesied that the Lord God has visited and redeemed "*his people*" (Luke 1:68). "*His people*" were foreknown by God (Rom. 11:2) which includes Gentiles (Rom. 15:10), not just Jews. When the New Heavens and new Earth appear in a vision, an angel proclaims that God will dwell with "*his people*". He will be with them (Rev. 21:3). Those who were chosen "*for his own possession*" (1 Pet. 2:9) were called out of darkness into his marvelous light (1 Pet. 2:10; Col. 1:13). By these references to "*his people*," we may conclude "*we*" in verse 14 are "*his people*" - the elect. They are chosen, redeemed, saved from their sins, and are God's possession to be with him. They are the elect who alone were redeemed by Christ. Whatever Christ did or accomplished on the cross and following was for and only for the elect. All that has been done and is being done for the elect is by grace alone, through Jesus Christ alone, to effectually redeem "*his people*" and does not extend beyond them for any purpose.

What was the debt owed that the elect were redeemed from?

Sin is not to be understood as an external influence that renders a person morally ill in the eyes of God. It is unlike a disease that one can recover from. All people are descended from Adam and have inherited his corrupt and spiritually dead nature (Gen. 5:3, 6:5; Jer. 17:9; Titus 1:15). Because all men are born "*in Adam*" they have all spiritually died (1 Cor. 15:22), that is they are dead in trespasses and sin even before they sin and trespass (Eph. 2:1; Ps 51:5). All people are at first spiritually dead, meaning separated from God. They are thus subject to physical death and eventually eternal death in hell, which comprises the debt they owe. Therefore, according to the law, a debt is owed for sin, even for trespasses, which is eternal death or perishing. A good explanation of spiritual deadness is found in Ephesians 2:12. Although it is addressed to Gentile believers, it applies to all believers as a description of their spiritual deadness before coming to Christ in faith. All the phrases in this verse mean essentially the same thing: being "*without God*" is key. During our former lives (1) we were separated from Christ, (2) we were outsiders, (3) had no access to the covenant promises, (3) had no hope in the world, and (4) were without God.

Following a sacrifice for sin, the remnant left over from the sacrifice belonged to the priest (Lev. 5:13). Under certain conditions, in addition to the offering for the sin and restitution of losses incurred by sin, the guilty person was to pay the priest an additional fifth of the value of the restitution (Lev. 5:15-16). To ensure that we understand we owe a debt for our sins, Paul pointed out that we are not only dead in sin but also in trespasses (Eph. 2:1). Trespasses refer to inadvertent errors and accidental infractions of the law. If a person is dead because of accidental infractions, they are most surely dead for intentional ones. Because of sin and corrupt nature (Eph. 2:3), all people were unrighteous before God (Rom. 3:10) and owed a debt of death under the law (Rom. 5:12, 6:16, 23). But this death is no less than eternal death, perishing, condemnation (Matt. 25:41; Luke 13:3; John 3:16, 5:29; Rom. 5:16,18; 2 Thess. 1:9, 2:10; Heb. 6:2; 10:27). The elect, "*his people*," owed this debt of death for sin just as much as did the rest of the human race. They could have paid that debt themselves and perished. Instead, the Father had planned for them to be redeemed by Jesus Christ (Rom. 3:23-25).

It is necessary to restate what has just been presented regarding the covenant of works. The covenant of works was inaugurated in the Garden of Eden with Adam. It promised the benediction of eternal life with God if Adam continued in perfect obedience and the malediction of eternal death upon the advent of sin. We all know, even non-believers, that Adam did not fulfill the terms for eternal life by his disobedience and sin. Immediately, Adam died spiritually, being cut from the blissful relationship he previously had with God. His body became subject to decline and physical death, and he incurred a debt of eternal death.

Additionally, Adam's nature became enslaved to sin and thus corrupt. Because Adam was a representative person or federal head of the entire human race, we are obligated to the covenant of works, as he was. However, we receive the guilt of his sin through imputation and his corrupt nature by being descended from him. Therefore, as we come into the world before we do good or evil, we are spiritually dead, enslaved to sin, and indebted to the same malediction stipulated in the covenant of works, which is eternal death.

We now come to how Jesus remedied this for his people. Although he is descended from Adam, it is not in the ordinary way because the Holy Spirit conceived him in the womb of Mary. Coming into the world as a man, Jesus was under the covenant of works, but he was not under Adam's federal headship. He did not receive Adam's guilt, corrupt nature, or the debt of eternal death. Jesus was then free to fulfill the covenant of works as a man, which he did through a life of perfect obedience under the law. By fulfilling the covenant of works, as the federal head of his people, it was imputed to them as if they completed it themselves. The offering of his blood atoned for our sins and canceled the debt of eternal death we owed, and his fulfillment of the covenant of works led to our justification. When we say Jesus was qualified to offer his own blood as the spotless lamb of God, it is only because he first fulfilled the covenant of works through his perfect obedience to the law.

What was required of a redeemer to pay the debt owed by the elect?

To redeem the elect from this debt, a high priest (Lev. 16; Heb. 5:1) would have to make a blood sacrifice (Heb. 9:22) of a kinsman redeemer (Lev. 25) who was blameless under the law like a lamb without blemish (Lev. 4; 1 Pet. 1:19). To furthermore justify his people, the redeemer would have to fulfill the covenant of works. A special kinsman redeemer and a special high priest are needed. The sacrifice must first be prepared by having the guilt of all the sins of the elect imputed to him so that he is genuinely guilty under the law (Isa. 53:6; Rom. 3:25; 2 Cor. 5:21; Col. 2:14; 1 Pet. 2:24). The blood sacrifice must then be reckoned as full payment of this debt for divine justice to cancel the record of sin or eternal death would prevail over the offering and those for whom the offering was made.

How did the Son become qualified to be the redeemer of his people?

To be a kinsman, the Son had to be made in the flesh just as we are in the flesh (Heb. 2:17). This was accomplished when Mary conceived Jesus by the Holy Spirit. Why was Mary chosen for this? Her genealogy can be traced back to Abraham through David (Luke 3:34). God had told Abraham that all nations would be blessed in him (Gen. 12:3), which meant that the Messiah would be his descendant. Fourteen generations later, God instructed the prophet Nathan to inform King David that one of his descendants would possess an eternal kingdom (2 Sam. 7:12-13, 16). Christ's kingdom does not exclude Gentiles because Rahab and Ruth, both Gentiles, are in Mary's lineage (Matt. 1:5; Ruth 4:17). The child born to Mary was the Son of God and would be called holy (Luke 1:26, 31, 35). By his conception, the Son was made in the flesh (John 1:14; 1 Tim. 3:16; 1 Pet. 4:1; 1 John 4:2), he was under the law (Gal. 4:4), and under the covenant of works. Jesus' conception was the incarnation of Jesus Christ by which the Son became our kinsman. As he grew into adulthood, he was tempted in every way as we are without sin (Heb. 4:15). Thus, according to the law, Jesus was a lamb without blemish (1 Pet. 1:19).

Jesus was our High Priest

As to a high priest who could perform this particular sacrifice, none among the Levites were qualified. Every high priest is from the tribe of Levite (Num. 3:12), men burdened with their own sins. Before they can sacrifice for the sins of others, they are required to sacrifice for their own sins (Heb. 5:3). The complex nature of the once-for-all sacrifice for sin, necessary to redeem God's people, precluded all Levitical priests who would need such a sacrifice for themselves first. Being unclean themselves, they could not conduct a once-for-all and perfect sacrifice. Now, Jesus would not need to sacrifice for his own sins first because he has no sin, but he's of the tribe of Judah (Heb. 7:14) and cannot serve as a Levitical priest. It seems like an insurmountable legal problem, but then there's Melchizedek.

We are introduced to Melchizedek in Genesis 14. Abraham, Abram at the time, rescued his nephew Lot from four kings who had taken him and the people of Sodom captive. Abraham had all the rescued people and all their possessions with him, which were the spoils of war. Out of nowhere, Melchizedek comes to Abraham with bread and wine and a blessing from God. He's introduced as a priest of God Most High and king of Salem, the original name of Jerusalem. Abraham's response was to pay a tithe of the spoils to Melchizedek (Gen. 14:18-20). We learn more about Melchizedek from Psalm 110. There is an order of priests that follow after Melchizedek, who are priests forever (Ps. 110:4). Their relevance to Jesus is explained in Hebrews Chapter 7. The name Melchizedek first means "king of righteousness" and then "king of Salem" (meaning "peace").

Melchizedek is said to resemble the Son of God because of an unusual conclusion based on the silence of Scripture about him.

> "*He is without father or mother or genealogy, having neither beginning of days nor end of life, but resembling the Son of God he continues a priest forever*" (Heb. 7:3 ESV).

Hebrews 7:17 and Psalm 110:4 state, "*You are a priest forever after the order of Melchizedek*" (ESV). The priest referred to is Jesus. He can be a priest forever by the power of an indestructible life (Heb. 7:16), and Jesus' priesthood is of the order of Melchizedek by God's unchangeable oath (Heb. 5:6, 10, 7:12, 20-21; Ps. 110:4). Jesus is the perfect high priest in his righteousness and holiness and is thus able to offer a perfect sacrifice. The Levitical priesthood established by commandment was set aside because of its weakness in making anything perfect (Heb. 7:18-19). This weakness stems from the covenant of works, which was never repealed. The Levitical priesthood cannot remove its pending malediction or satisfy its conditions for benediction.

Jesus performs the duties of our High Priest.

The picture is almost complete. We have a kinsman without blemish under the law, who has fulfilled the covenant of works, can offer his own blood for our sins, and is a qualified high priest to perform the sacrifice. Our redeemer and high priest is Jesus Christ (Heb. 6:20). As the spotless lamb to be offered for sin, the sins of the elect were laid upon him (Isa. 53:6; Rom. 3:25; 2 Cor. 5:21; Col. 2:14; 1 Pet. 2:24). As high priest, Jesus offered up himself to God for the sins of his people (Heb. 7:27, 9:14). But he only becomes our redeemer when God accepts his sacrificial offering.

Christ's role as high priest was prophesied by Isaiah in the phrase,

> "*because he poured out his soul to death and was numbered with the transgressors; yet he bore the sin of many, and makes intercession for the transgressors*" (Isa. 53:12 ESV).

Jesus Christ poured out his soul and made intercession – the very duties of a high priest. As to this intersession, we are told that Christ, our high priest, entered into heaven using his own blood, into the presence of God, to offer himself for us once for all time, thus marking the start of a new age and securing an eternal redemption having put away our sin (Heb. 9:11-12, 24-26).

What were the nature and circumstances of Jesus' offering that made it acceptable?

We have not addressed how eternal death has been avoided. So far, we have discussed only Jesus' physical death and not the experience of his soul. The Apostles Creed states, "he descended to hell." This phrase was later added to the original text of the Creed and has been a subject of dispute ever since. It is not found in the Nicene Creed, and it is never stated anywhere in the original language of the Bible that Jesus descended or visited hell, the place of the eternal torment of the damned, also known as the fiery pit, the second death, and eternal death. In defense of the current Creed's statement, 1 Peter 3:19 is often interpreted to mean that after Jesus died, he descended into hell to preach the gospel to the souls imprisoned there.

> *"in which he went [in the Spirit] and proclaimed to the spirits in prison"* (1 Pet. 3:19 ESV)

I believe the correct interpretation of 1 Peter 3:19 is as follows and does not warrant the phrase's inclusion in the creed.

> Noah, by faith and through the Holy Spirit, witnessed the gospel to his generation, thus further condemning them (Heb. 11:7). This means that, as Paul says, Jesus proclaimed or preached it through the Holy Spirit to that generation via Noah. That generation was destroyed, and their souls are now in prison. That prison is the lower part of Hades, where the souls of the lost are sent following death and kept until the day of judgment. The Old Testament refers to Hades as Sheol.

> (An explanation of 1 Peter 3:19 and why "he descended into Hell" should not be in the Apostles' Creed.)

I don't dispute the intent of the Creed to address our redemption most fully, but I suggest it employs the wrong terminology. For many years, the Creed has led people to believe Jesus literally descended into Hell following his death to rescue some from its torments. This account cannot be found explicitly in Scripture and thus cannot be properly deduced. Scripture. Jesus told us where he would be following his death when he responded to the thief on the cross, "*Truly, I say to you, today you will be with me in paradise*" (Luke 23:43 ESV). Paradise, also known as Abraham's bosom and Abraham's side (Luke 16:22), is the upper part of Hades where the souls of the righteous are during their intermediate state. Jesus' soul went to Paradise, not to the fiery pit of hell or the lower part of Hades, and it is there that the thief who had been crucified next to him joined him. However, before Jesus arrives in Paradise, he still has high priestly work to conduct. So far, this explains that Jesus did not literally descend to hell.

We must examine the circumstances of Jesus' death as they apply to his soul. According to Old Testament law, every person who has committed a crime punishable by death is to be hung on a tree, an action indicating he had been cursed by God (Deut. 21:22-23; Gal. 3:13). Numbers 25:1-5 records that Moses, following instructions from God, hung the Israelite men who had committed idolatry upon being seduced by Moabite women. Besides the curse demonstrated by the hangings, a plague accompanied the idolatry from which twenty-four thousand died. Death by hanging from a tree was, and is, to be taken seriously as a representation of being cursed by God. Such a curse applies to Jesus' death since he was hung on a tree, that tree being the cross (Acts 5:30, 10:39, 13:29; 1 Pet. 2:24). When the guilt of our sin was laid upon Jesus (Isa 53:6; 2 Cor. 5:21), he became a cursed man and his death by crucifixion was a manifestation of that curse. His death was the curse of the law (Gal. 3:10, 13). Jesus not only suffered on the cross but also previously from the physical abuse he received at the hands of the Jewish leaders and the Romans.

Notwithstanding the authorities who abused Jesus, it was the will of God to crush Jesus, to put him to grief, as Jesus made an offering for our guilt (Isa. 53:10). This offering came from his soul, in some manner, and in that offering and being crushed Jesus suffered the anguish of his soul (v. 11) having been poured out to death (v. 12). Embodied in Isaiah's language is more than the shedding of blood and physical death. It appears most certain that there was a torment of the soul most profound as to be judicially reckoned propitiatory. Isaiah employs what may be considered a metonymy in the phrase, "*upon him was the chastisement that brought us peace, and with his wounds, we are healed*" (Isa. 53:5 ESV). The chastisement and wounds that Isaiah mentioned encompass his physical death; they certainly point to it and lead to it, but they refer to much more, all that Jesus experienced following his arrest. Thus, it can be rightly stated that by his chastisement and wounds, we have been healed of our iniquity and have peace with God (v. 5). By the time Jesus died, he had already been cursed, bruised, crushed, descended into the anguish of his soul, and forsaken by God (Ps. 22; Matt. 27:46; Mark 15:34). In particular, just before Jesus died, he said, "*It is finished* (John 19:30)." What was finished was his full payment for sin. This ransom was required to redeem his people. The cup of his suffering was only then filled to the brim to meet the demands of divine and holy justice. So, when Jesus' suffering was consummated by his physical death, the justice of God was satisfied, and Jesus' offering of his own blood for our sins was accepted.

When the impenitent thief who was crucified next to Jesus died, his soul descended into the lower region of Hades, a place of torment (Luke 16:19-31). There, he would wait for the day of final judgment to be cast into the lake of fire (Rev. 20:15). This thief died as a man forsaken by God.

Jesus, laden with the guilt of our sins and cursed, was also crucified and died. As with the thief, there is more than mere physical death involved. Before he died physically, Jesus cried out, "*My God, my God, why have you forsaken me* (Matt. 27:46; Mark 15:34)?" Jesus bears the guilt of the sins of others whereas the thief bears his own but they are both guilty and reckoned as having the same debt of death to pay (Luke 22:37). If God is to follow and apply the law with impartiality, they must both be dead spiritually before they can die physically. Keep in mind that Jesus Christ is a divine person. He is both fully man and fully God. As a man, he possesses a physical body and a human soul, characterized by a sinless human nature. When the guilt of sin is laid upon Jesus, it is laid upon his human soul. The divine person, Jesus Christ, becomes forensically guilty of sin without corruption in any part of his person. Becoming legally guilty of sin, he is now subject to the wages of sin, which is death. For a human person, this means spiritual death to be followed by physical death and eventually eternal death. Spiritual death is a separation from God, and since Jesus is both forensically guilty of sin, cursed, and forsaken, there is some separation taking place that is or is likened to spiritual death. Just as the divine person Jesus Christ physically died in his physical body, he experienced this separation or forsakenness in his human soul. Although Jesus told us of his forsakenness when he was about to die, I suggest the imputation of our guilt, becoming a curse for us, and being forsaken occurred just before the beginning of his torment.

When Jesus died physically, his soul entered the intermediate state in which body and soul were separated (John 19:30). He was still the divine person Jesus Christ, guilty of our sins, and with his physical body dead on the cross. Dead on the cross was where being our high priest and the spotless lamb of God, offering his own blood for our sins, made all the difference. Instead of following the impenitent thief into the lower region of Hades, Jesus Christ entered the holy place in heaven, into the presence of God by his blood (Heb. 9:12) to offer it on our behalf as a sacrifice of himself for sin. Divine justice weighed the offering, the totality of Christ's suffering, his wounds, the travail of his soul being poured out to God, his shed blood, his essential and forensic righteousness under the law, and reckoned it sufficiently propitiatory for sin and equitable for the debt of eternal death. Christ's payment for the debt of sin was accepted as a full and complete redemption; thus, he was no longer guilty and under the curse of the law. As our federal head Jesus Christ was declared righteous, and so were the elect, as his human soul was raised to spiritual life, so were the elect raised to spiritual life with him (Col. 2:13). If Jesus Christ, being our federal head, had not died spiritually in his human soul and been raised to spiritual life, it would not have been possible for the saints, being already spiritually dead, to have risen apart from him.

Looking ahead to Colossians 3:1, it says, "*you have been raised with Chris*" (ESV). This entire phrase is one word in the original Greek text, συνηγέρθητε (synēgerthēte), that means *"to raise together", "to awaken together:* (biblehub.com). So, we may ask, "How do we rise from spiritual death to spiritual life together with Christ if he does not rise with us from start to finish?" Spiritual death is not eternal death and does not involve descending into Hell. It is an abandonment or spiritual separation from God.

We have previously established that Jesus was legally qualified to be a redeemer of his people. Was the redemption that he was qualified to make legally conducted? The Old Testament priests followed the Levitical law of Temple service, sacrifice, and sin offerings. Although Jesus was a high priest of a different order, he still had to fulfill this law (Matt. 5:17; Luke 24:44). When a high priest makes an offering for sin, he lays his hands on the animal to be sacrificed, which represents the transfer of sin to the animal. That action by the priest and sacrifice is a type of Christ's sacrifice or a foreshadowing of it. In Christ's case, the elect's guilt was imputed to Jesus (Isa. 53:6; 2 Cor. 5:21), and he became forensically guilty of sin but not a sinner himself. As it is written, he was made to bc sin for us, the elect (2 Cor. 5:21). Isaiah contributes to this by having written, "*the LORD has laid on him the iniquity of us all*" (Isa. 53:6). The fact that Jesus did not make an offering for himself defeats all notions that he became a sinner, corrupt, or so constituted. The guilt laid upon Jesus was sufficient to make Jesus legally obligated to pay the penalty of a cursed death, but that sin and its guilt were external.

In the case of the Levitical high priest, he would take the blood of a bull sacrificed for his own sins and sprinkle it on the mercy seat. Then, he would take the blood of a goat sacrificed for the sins of the people and sprinkle it on the mercy seat. This sacrifice was done in the Holy Place inside the veil once a year, every year, on the Day of Atonement (Lev. 16). Jesus, our high priest (Heb. 2:17, 3:1), did not make an offering of blood for himself because he had no sin (Heb. 7:26-27), but for the sins of his people he offered his own blood once for all (Acts 20:28; Heb. 9:12, 7:27) under the conditions previously mentioned. In his flesh, Christ took the elect's sins to the cross so that they might die to sin (1 Pet. 2:24). Upon his death, Jesus did not enter the temple in Jerusalem as would a Levitical high priest; he entered into heaven and the presence of God on our behalf (Heb. 9:24) to present his offering of blood. Thus, having done all, Jesus, our high priest, fulfilled the moral and Levitical laws and satisfied the demands of divine justice by how he lived, suffered, and sacrificed himself.

The day of Christ's crucifixion is not called the day of atonement in the New Testament. Still, the Old Testament implies that it fulfills every preceding day of atonement. Christ's consummate Day of Atonement ends for all time, all sacrifice for sin (Heb. 10:12, 26). An exchange was made when Jesus presented his blood to the Father. That blood was the blood of the Word of God, who had become flesh and lived under the law without sin. It was the blood of the Lord of Glory, the light of the world, who suffered the anguish of his soul, who poured out his soul unto death for the sake of his people. It was the blood of the righteous sacrifice of the perfect lamb of God without spot or blemish. His life, suffering, and blood fulfilled the demands of divine justice, and so his offer, having been received, was reckoned for redemption and the reconciliation of his people. When divine justice could demand no more, his bloody sacrifice was reckoned payment for sin and propitiatory. He redeemed his people by paying their debt of death and took possession of them as was his right as their redeemer. The guilt that was laid upon Jesus was the record of our debt. It was nailed to the cross and has been canceled for all time (Ps. 103:12; Col. 2:13-14; Heb. 8:12, 10:17). Sin, having been judicially dealt with, no longer has a claim for eternal death upon the elect (John 3:16-18; Rom. 8:1, 33). Paul stated this so clearly,

> "*And you, who were dead in your trespasses and the uncircumcision of your flesh, God made alive together with him, having forgiven us all our trespasses, by canceling the record of debt that stood against us with its legal demands. This he set aside, nailing it to the cross*" (Col. 2:13-14 ESV).

Thus, we note that everything that had been taken from Jesus was restored to him, and he passed into Paradise as he had foretold the thief.

the lamb of God

As noted previously, on the Day of Atonement, the Levitical high priest sacrificed a goat for the sins of the people (Lev. 16:15; Heb. 9:12). These sacrifices for sin were conducted once every year by the high priest. Each represented, by type, the once-for-all sacrifice of Jesus Christ by the offering of his own blood. But Jesus is never referred to as a goat, but as a lamb. Why? In John 1:29 and 36, Jesus is called "*the lamb of God.*" He is referred to like a lamb led to slaughter and without blemish or spot (Acts 8:32; 1 Pet. 1:10). In the Exodus account of Passover, the people were to sacrifice a lamb without blemish and put its blood on the doorpost and lintel of their doorways (Exod. 12:1-7). On that night, God was going to execute judgment on Egypt by killing the firstborn of men and animals across Egypt. The blood of the lambs on the doorposts was to be a sign to pass over, and the destroyer would not enter the house to strike down the firstborn within (Exod. 12:23). The entire event is known as Passover. A lamb slain for this is known as a Passover or paschal lamb (Mark 14:12). Jesus Christ is not just a lamb without blemish; he is our Passover lamb, πάσχα (pascha) (1 Cor. 5:7, biblehub.com). It is no coincidence that Christ instituted the Lord's Supper and was crucified during Passover week (Mark 14:22-25, 15:42). Just as the sacrament of baptism replaced circumcision as the sign of the covenant, the Lord's Supper stands in the place of the Passover meal.

There is something about Christ's shed blood we need to examine. Believers who have been sanctified and justified have also been washed (1 Cor. 6:11). Justification was by Christ's shed blood (Rom. 5:9), so there is a connection between Christ's blood and being washed. Revelation 7:14-17 presents a vision of the saints in heaven, specifying that they have washed their robes white in the blood of the Lamb (v. 14). There is also mention of the saints being sprinkled with the blood of Christ (1 Pet. 1:2; Heb. 12:24). Finally, as Jesus was washing the disciples" feet, Peter protested and Jesus answered saying, *"If I do not wash you, you have no share with me"* (John 13:8). The situation was an example of service to one another and humility. Still, Jesus' response to Peter contained theological significance. The blood of the sacrifice was always used to clean and consecrate objects and people (Exod. 29:21; Lev. 16:19). In like manner, believers even now have confidence to enter the holy places and full assurance of faith with hearts sprinkled clean by the blood of Jesus (Heb. 10:19, 22). All of these verses imply that it is by the shed and sacrificial blood of Jesus Christ that believers are made and kept holy, in addition to being redeemed and freed from the power of sin.

a transfer of federal headship

The concept of federal headship is very important in all of this. Briefly, a federal head is a representative person whose actions, merits, and demerits are legally counted or reckoned to all persons under his federal headship. The entire human race begins life under the curse of Adam because all people enter life under his federal headship. Adam's fall from grace was our fall from grace. Like King David, we were in a state of sin and corruption when conceived (Ps. 51:5). Adam is everyone's federal head as they come into the world (Rom. 5:12). We received the condemnation of Adam's original sin and his corrupt nature (Rom. 5:18-19). We are thus born sinners, as is our nature, and enemies of God (Eph. 2:3). It is a state we can do nothing to extricate ourselves from (John 6:44, 65). It is called corruption and darkness and possesses the power to enslave us (John 8:34; Rom. 6:6, 17, 20; Gal 4:3, 9; Titus 3:3). Many people remain under Adam's federal headship throughout their lives. They will never come to a saving faith in Jesus Christ and will perish (John 3:16).

in review

God the Father has a definite plan that includes a group of people that can be identified in several ways. They are called his people, the chosen, and the elect. After a person is born again, we may refer to them as the faithful, believers, redeemed, and saints. For this review, these people will be called the elect in deference to God's sovereignty. The elect begin under the dominion of sin because they are all initially in the same fallen state of sin and corruption as Adam, due to his sin and their descent from him. Sin and corruption are a state of pending judgment and wrath from which no ordinary means of deliverance exists. Verse 13 refers to this as the domain of darkness, but the power of the darkness enslaves them. According to the Father's mercy and grace, the elect are delivered from this darkness and brought to the kingdom of his beloved Son.

The person and work of Jesus Christ alone accomplish this deliverance and transfer. Deliverance from darkness is the gospel of the kingdom of God in the person and work of Jesus Christ, our Lord. The Father terminated Adam's federal headship over the elect and gave them to Jesus Christ for Jesus to be their new federal head (John 10:27-30). The work of Jesus is this: he redeemed those under his headship so that their sins are forgiven, and he took possession of them as is a redeemer's right. He first had to live a perfect and sinless life under the law to complete the covenant of works and be our redeemer. According to the law, the elect owed a debt of death for all their sins. To pay their debt, Jesus would have to die a legal and just death for sin. The guilt of all the sins of the redeemed was imputed to Jesus, making Jesus personally guilty of sin and subject to the law of sin, but not a sinner himself. When Jesus was put to death as the elect's federal head, all the elect's sins were forgiven; they died to sin, were released from its power over them, fulfilled the law, and were delivered from the darkness. Their debt was paid, and they were redeemed. When the elect rose with Christ, they were, or had been, transferred to his kingdom. The sequence of events from Jesus' incarnation to his ascension is as follows.

Jesus is incarnate by the Holy Spirit in the Virgin Mary.

1. Jesus lives perfectly under the law and fulfills the covenant of works.
2. Jesus has the guilt of the elect laid upon him, imputed, and becomes cursed.
3. Jesus is arrested and abused.
4. Jesus offers himself as a high priest and redeemer.
5. Jesus is crucified and dies. His body is laid to rest in a tomb.
6. Jesus presents his offering, his blood, in the holy places in heaven.
7. Jesus secures eternal redemption and life.
8. Jesus goes to Paradise.
9. Jesus is bodily resurrected from the grave in his physical body.
10. Jesus ascends, is glorified, and takes his place at the right hand of the Father.

our abiding redemption

From verse 14, believers have redemption "*in*" Jesus Christ, a most important "*in*", which is by far more significant than "*by*" Jesus Christ. No true believer should ever claim to be redeemed by Jesus Christ once and for all and then be apart from Jesus Christ. While believers have been redeemed, their redemption remains with and abides in Jesus Christ. Peter alluded to this when he wrote to believers scattered across Asia Minor, reminding them of the necessity of the ongoing sprinkling of the blood of Jesus Christ (1 Pet. 1:2). The author of Hebrews makes a similar remark about the sprinkled blood (Heb.12:24) as does John (1 John 1:7). These references about the sprinkled blood have more to do with believers' sanctification than justification in so much as it is necessary to subdue the lingering effects of sin and release believers from it as they mature in the likeness of Christ.

plausible arguments

Though others have said more, this systematic exposition of verses 13 and 14 was in-depth. Several beliefs and practices within Christian circles do not conform to verses 13 and 14, yet they are widely accepted due to various plausible arguments supporting them. Four familiar ones are briefly stated below, with a brief explanation of their errors.

1. *The forgiveness of sin can be accomplished by other means than the blood and grace of Jesus Christ.*

   The only lawful means by which a person can escape the due penalty of sin, which is eternal death, is to be redeemed by Jesus Christ. Forgiveness of sin cannot be accomplished by an earthly priest, a repeated prayer, or penance in purgatory (John 14:6). There is no other savior or means of salvation other than Jesus Christ (Acts 4:12). Jesus is called the Savior of the world (John 4:42; 1 John 4:14), not because he saves the entire world, but because he is the only one in the world who saves.

2. *You will enter the kingdom of heaven if you are a church member.*

Many church members will enter the kingdom of heaven when they die, but entering does not depend on church membership. Entrance into the kingdom depends on whether or not the Father delivers you from darkness and forgives your sins through Jesus Christ. This is the only gospel that saves. If a person is never delivered from the darkness, their fallen state of sin and corruption, they remain subjects of judgment and wrath, regardless of what church they are a member of.

3. *Jesus Christ's work, particularly on the cross, had a universal benefit that applies to everyone.*

   The people who are the beneficiaries of what verses 13 and 14 describe are particular people. They are the ones delivered from darkness, who are redeemed by Christ, whose sins are forgiven, and who are transferred to the kingdom of Christ. Salvation is an all-or-nothing set of circumstances foreordained according to the Father's definite plan. It involved these same persons being delivered from Adam's federal headship and transferred to Jesus Christ's federal headship. What Christ does, in its entirety, is for all who are given to him as their federal head and is counted to them as if they had done it themselves. Those whom the Father has not given to Jesus eventually receive judgment and wrath.

4. *A person can initiate their own salvation.*

   Who delivers whom from the darkness? Who is the Redeemer? It is the Father who delivers. It is the Lord Jesus Christ who redeems. Before a person is delivered, they are under the domination of their own sin and corruption, enemies of God, unable to please him, and unable to come to Christ. Divine power is necessary to escape that corruption (2 Peter 1:3-4). Until that power is applied to a person, that person remains an enemy of God (Rom. 5:10). Consider the extraordinary details of our redemption and the preeminence of Christ, his glory, majesty, power, and authority described in the remaining verses of this chapter which are all applied to the salvation of his chosen people and then realize how demeaning of Christ it is to think salvation is left to the will of the creature.

COLOSSIANS 1:15-17
THE PREEMINENCE OF CHRIST, PART 1

As we consider the preeminence of Christ, we are forced to reshape our understanding of the law and the prophets. As we consider Christ's preeminence, it refers to his being superior and first in order. These were the things that the holy angels longed to look into to gain whatever glimpse they might of the Lord (1 Pet. 1:12). The laws about priestly service, the moral law, and being a redeemer were not items in a list of qualifications that Christ was obligated to check off by conforming himself to them. Collectively, they are a reflection of who Christ is. Many things in the Old Testament are types of which Jesus Christ is the antitype. David is a type of Christ the King. Boaz is a type of Christ the Redeemer. Melchizedek is a type of Christ concerning the eternal nature of his priesthood. The Levitical priesthood was a type of Christ's concerning his priestly service. It is always the type that is constructed and conformed to the antitype.

Colossians 1:15
Christ, the image of God

Verses 13 and 14 refer to the incarnate Son, Jesus Christ, who died in the flesh on the cross for our sins. This same Jesus Christ is the antecedent of "He" in verse 15 as he is in verses 16 and 17.

1. *Jesus Christ is God:*

   The Son, the second Person of the Trinity, was not always Jesus Christ. The Son became Jesus Christ during the incarnation when the Son became man in the flesh by the Holy Spirit (Luke 1:31; John 1:14; Heb. 2:14, 5:7). Paul often refers to Jesus as a man (Rom. 5:15, 17; 1 Cor. 15:21, 48, 49; 1 Tim 2:5). Being a man in the flesh, Jesus Christ died in the flesh (Col. 1:22; Heb. 2:14, 5:7; 1 Pet. 3:18). In the process of becoming a man in the flesh, the Son did not cease to be God.

John refers to the Son as the Word, and the Word was God (John 1:1), and the Word became flesh (John 1:14). In the Greek text (biblehub.com) of John 1:18, it is written of Jesus Christ μονογενὴς Θεὸς (monogenēs Theos) that translates as *[the] only begotten God.* Jesus plainly said that he was God when he said that he preexisted Abraham (John 8:58). Jesus also said that he and the Father are one (John 10:30). When responding to Jesus, Thomas said, *"My Lord and my God"* (John 20:28)! The writer of Hebrews opens by referring to Jesus Christ as the Son of God who is the radiance (effulgence) of the glory of God and the exact imprint of his nature (substance) (Heb. 1:1-3). Not only was Jesus Christ God before and after the incarnation, but he did not become God or a god by adoption or merit. The word "*imprint*" can be translated as "*copy*," but "*copy*" shouldn't be used, as it fails to properly represent how Jesus Christ possesses the same nature as God. God has chosen to enlighten us to his glory as we behold it "*in the face of Jesus Christ*" (2 Cor. 4:6 ESV). We recognize three Persons in the Trinity, but one divine nature that is not copied or duplicated among them. Neither is it shared. They each fully possess it. Jesus expressed this as *"I and the Father are one"* (John 10:30) and *"you, Father, are in me, and I in you"* (John 17:21). This mutual indwelling is referred to as ***perichoresis***.

In Jesus Christ, the fullness of God dwells bodily (Col. 2:9), being physically descended from the Israelites, yet is God overall. Thus, we are compelled to this conclusion that Jesus Christ is fully man and fully God, comprising two natures: one human, with a human will, and the other divine, with a divine will. As to his personhood, Jesus Christ is one divine person, not a human person. According to the Westminster Confession of Faith, Chapter 8, Section 2:

> "So that two whole, perfect, and distinct natures, the Godhead and the manhood, were inseparably joined together in one person, without conversion, composition, or confusion. Which person is very God and very man, yet one Christ,

> the only mediator between God and man." (WCF -8.2)

This union is called a ***hypostatic union***, which involves two perfectly complete natures in one person.

2. *The image of the unseeable God:*
   God is Spirit (John 4:24) and dwells in unapproachable light (1 Tim. 6:16). No one has seen God (1 John 4:12), nor could they live (Exod. 33:20). It states in a familiar doxology that the only God is King eternal, immortal, and invisible (1 Tim. 1:17). This applies to all three Persons of the Godhead, the Father, the Son, and the Holy Spirit equally and without exception because each is fully God.

So far, we have established that Jesus Christ is fully man and fully God and that God is invisible in each of the three Persons of the Godhead. We now contend with the issue of Jesus being an image of the invisible God. There are two aspects of this. First, we turn to Romans 1:19-20. We must see how creation reveals God's invisible attributes. God has revealed to people what can be plainly known about him. God is not passive in this knowledge. Although his attributes are invisible, they are clearly perceived through the things he has created. Creation would be dull and muted if God had not chosen to reveal his attributes through creation. In a far more profound way, God is revealed in a personal and saving way through the person and work of Jesus Christ (Matt. 11:27; Luke 10:22). By seeing Jesus, one sees the Father (John 14:9). During Jesus' high priestly prayer, he mentioned knowing about the Father several times. He prayed that the disciples would know the Father (John 17:3), that he glorified the Father on earth (John 17:4), that he manifested the Father's name to the people whom the Father had given him, that he gave them the words of the Father (John 1:8, 14), and that he has made the Father's name known to them (John 17:26). By seeing and receiving the work, words, and person of Jesus Christ as the incarnate Son of God, one comes to know the Father in a saving way for eternal life (John 17:3). John 14:9 expresses how Jesus Christ is the image of God in this first way. If you have seen Jesus (with the eyes of faith), you have seen the Father. But many of the Jews did not see because it must be revealed by God (Matt. 11:25).

We discovered the Father through our journey with Jesus, observing his work and receiving his words. However, there is a more profound way in which Jesus Christ is the image of the invisible God. The mutual indwelling of the Trinity is unabated by the incarnation. Jesus in the flesh is fully God, and Jesus in the flesh is how God is revealed to man (Heb. 1:2; Luke 10:22; John 14:9; 2 Cor. 4:6). Jesus is not a type of God or a foreshadowing of God to come. Suppose you see Jesus and see nothing more than a man of flesh and blood. In that case, it is because the god of this world has blinded you (2 Cor. 4:4). But if you see Jesus as King of kings and Lord of lords, it is because, by the grace of God, your eyes have been opened to his glory as God the Son (John 1:14). By knowing Jesus as he claims to be, you would also know the Father, and as believers, you do know and have seen the Father, an allusion to Jesus (John 14:7 ESV)

But now, the incarnate Son, Jesus Christ, is visible. During his earthly ministry, he was visible to all, and now he is visible only to the saints in heaven. To truly know God, we must know him in the person of Jesus Christ (John 14:6). If we are to worship the one true and living God, it can only be through his only-begotten Son, our Lord Jesus Christ. The unregenerate mind sees only the flesh, whereas the regenerate mind perceives the divine person. We began in darkness, but the Father transferred us into the kingdom of his Son, our Redeemer, having paid the penalty of death for our sins and freed us from that debt. The Son, who is our redeemer, is God.

the firstborn over all creation

We are dealing with the phrase "*the firstborn of all creation*" as it is rendered in the ESV and NASB. The NIV and the NKJV have "*the firstborn over all creation*." The literal translation of the Greek text is, "*firstborn all creation*." However, the interlinear has it as, "*[the] firstborn over all creation*" (biblehub.com). The definite article is implied and whether "*of*" or "*over*" precedes "*all*" falls to the interpreter's preference.

A firstborn always possesses a special status, even preeminence. It is that particular character, preeminence, possessed by a firstborn that Paul is using to draw out for us the preeminence of Christ in multiple ways.

Mark opens his account of the gospel with, "*The beginning of the gospel of Jesus Christ, the Son of God*" (ESV). In many other places Jesus Christ is called the Son of God (e.g., 2 Cor. 1:19; Heb. 4:14). More specifically, he is called the "*only begotten Son of God*" (John 1:13, 3:16, 18; 1 John 4:9), which is translated from μονογενής (monogenés) (biblehub.com). Thus, it is correct to say that the Son of God is the firstborn of God since he is the only Son of God. This is substantiated by verses that refer to how precious he is to the Father (1 Pet. 2:4, 6), how precious his blood is (1 Pet. 1:19), and that he is beloved by the Father (Luke 3:22, Matt. 3:17, 12:18, 17:5; Mark 1:11, 9:7; Eph. 1:6; 2 Pet. 2:17).

The Son is the firstborn of God, but is also described as the firstborn of the dead in Colossians 1:18. In that verse, as we will get to, the Son receives this identity as the firstborn because he is the first to be born from the dead, to rise from death to life, and further ascend to glory. The Son also is described as the firstborn among many brothers (Rom. 8:29). This parallels being the firstborn from the dead, as many brothers, saints, will succeed him from death to glory. In these references, the Son received his identity as the firstborn through his work and Person as the Redeemer.

The divine Person, as firstborn, is "*of the dead,*" and is "*of many brothers,*" but he is not "*of* creation". As we move past verse 15, it becomes clear that the phrase in verse 15 should be "*the firstborn over all creation.*" We also have to accept that Paul is attributing all things to the divine Person, the Son, whether incarnate or not.

If we take the preceding text into account, that the only begotten Son of God is the one in whom we have redemption and is the image of the invisible God, we see that Paul is referring to the incarnate Jesus Christ. As the Son, he is, by divine nature, the firstborn of God. As we move into verse 16 and proceed further, we see that it is presented as the reason why Jesus Christ is the firstborn concerning creation. This same divine Person is the Creator for whom all things were created and by whom all things subsist. As the beloved Son, the only Son, and thus the firstborn, he has rule, authority, and preeminence over all creation. Jesus Christ is over all creation as is the right of a firstborn, the firstborn of God, for the reasons stated in verses 16 and 17. The firstborn is more precious to the Father than all created things and is preeminent in everything (v. 18).

Colossians 1:16
Christ the Creator

As we delve into these verses, we encounter some difficulty in determining to whom they refer. The incarnate Son is Jesus Christ, our redeemer, but the Son of God created all that there is long before his incarnation. The difficulty is resolved when we understand these verses refer to the one divine Person who is now and forever Jesus Christ. In other words, the pre-incarnate Son and the incarnate Son are the same divine Person, and we may attribute creation and redemption to him.

Verse 16 explains how Christ is the firstborn over all creation, as indicated by the word *for* or *because*. The explanation is a matter of preeminence due to his Sonship and right as firstborn. *"By him"* indicates that the Son performed the entire work of creation. Christ's creative work involved all things; nothing was made that was not made by Christ (John 1:3). John, in the opening of his gospel, seamlessly shifts from presenting the divinity of Christ to his presence among us in the flesh while maintaining throughout Christ's creative power. Like Paul, John is writing about the one divine person we now know as Jesus Christ. Things invisible include things that are not seen. Although including rulers appears in many translations, it is likely incorrect. From the original language, it seems to refer to things that have priority or came first, even from the beginning, among which are the forces of nature and principles of logic and reason.

From the original language, it should be *"in the heavens and on earth"* (biblehub.com). Many Bibles render it this way. The plural *"heavens"* is more extensive than just heaven. *"Through him"* indicates he was acting as a surrogate, carrying out the will of the Father. "*For him*" indicates he is the intended recipient or possessor of all that was created. However, our English translations miss a much more important concept. All things are not only for Christ; they are purposed to point to and draw attention to him and glorify him. Since the world's creation, the things that have been created reveal his eternal power and divine nature (Rom. 1:20). The heavens declare the glory of God (Ps. 19:1), and we can take this to mean that it is in the person of Jesus Christ.

Colossians 1:17
***Christ, by whom all things hold togethe*r**

Paul continues to explain how Jesus Christ is the firstborn over all creation. Paul writes in verse 17 that the Son is "*before all things*." First, *before* means to precede. Paul expresses an issue of Christ's divine being on a larger scale than Jesus, telling the Jews, "*Before Abraham was, I am*" (John 8:58) because Paul refers to the entire work of creation. Secondly, this signifies that the Son, and thus Jesus Christ, transcends what he has created. To transcend means to be above and beyond in a superior way. Christ is not of the creation; he transcends it. So that we may avoid contemplating being left alone to fend for ourselves in this universe, Paul adds that "*in him [Christ] all things hold together*." "*in him*" are very important words as they mean that what holds the universe together inherently comes from within Jesus Christ, so only Jesus Christ can sustain creation; it cannot be sustained on its own or without him. Thereby, Paul elevates our minds to the realization that Christ is both transcendent and immanent and can govern all things. Being immanent means to be present and indwelling. We often substitute the word omnipresent. We may recall verse 15, in which Paul writes that God is invisible, which aligns with his transcendence. He also writes that Christ is the image of God and the firstborn over all creation, which accords with his immanence. These three verses, 15-17, portray, in the widest sense, the majestic glory of God in the person of Jesus Christ in his creative and providential work, who is the God with whom we must deal.

Paul and Peter go on to write that the very power which formed and sustains the universe is also applied to the elect in personal ways, as all things work together for good for those who love God and are called according to his purpose (Rom. 8:28), granting by his divine power all things necessary for life and godliness (2 Pet. 1:3).

COLOSSIANS 1:18-20
THE PREEMINENCE OF CHRIST, PART 2

We should consider verses 18-20 together to grasp the theme that Paul is developing regarding reconciliation and the preeminence of Christ. Paul's logical argument is that since Christ has preeminence over creation and governs it (v. 15), he then has preeminence over the church and governs it. While this is true, there is another layer to it. Christ took upon himself a body of flesh and a sinless human nature. He then assumed our debt of sin by taking upon himself the guilt of our sin to make full restitution by his own blood and death on the cross. Thus, after making propitiation for our sins, he rose from among the dead to redeem and justify the church. Christ's preeminence, glory, Lordship, power, and headship are displayed in all things. Because all saints rise to new life in Christ following his resurrection, he is the firstborn among many brothers (Rom. 8:29), which aligns with his preeminence.

Colossians 1:18

Christ, the head of the church

Paul draws our attention to the church and Christ's preeminence over the church. The church is led or governed by Christ as its head. On one level, Paul uses the metaphor of the physical head and body to represent the organic relationship between Christ and the Church, to indicate that there is more to his headship than simply being in charge. Yet, on another level, there is an even deeper meaning to Christ being the head of the church if we recognize his headship as a special type called federal headship, which was previously explained in detail.

the body of Christ

Paul refers to the church as a body. He uses the phrase "*body of Christ*" to refer to the church in several places (1 Cor. 12:27; Eph. 4:12,5:23; Col. 1:24). In other places, the use of the word body refers to a physical body, even Christ's physical body. But in the verses listed, "*body of Christ*" refers to the entire group of elect individuals who have been or will be redeemed by Christ. When redeemed, you belong to Christ (Rom. 1:6, 8:9; Titus 2:14; 1 Cor. 6:20, 7:23, 15:23;

Gal. 5:24; and more). The concept of "body" being a group or a mass is not uncommon. We use the phrase "*body of water*" to refer to a large lake or ocean. Paul refers to our collective mass of sin as our "*body of sin*," not to be misunderstood as our body that sins (Rom. 6:6).

We should recognize that there is a church within the church, just as "*not all who are descended from Israel belong to Israel*" (Rom. 9:6 ESV). Christ is the head of the church, both as it exists here on earth and in heaven. The membership of the church on earth includes both believers and non-believers, people who have been or will be born again, and people who will never be born again. Therefore, participating in the church on earth does not necessarily mean Christ redeemed you or that he is your federal head. Yet Christ's headship over his church is extensive. When the apostles say Christ redeemed the church, or any such statement to the same effect, they refer to the perfected church consisting of only those among the elect and none other. When the apostles describe the church, they are describing the perfected or invisible church, allowing that description to graciously fall upon the visible church on earth.

Christ, the beginning

The word *beginning* is applied to Christ; Christ himself is the beginning. We see this reference to him in other important places as *the Alpha and the Omega, the first and the last, the beginning and the end* (Rev. 21:6, 22:13). But here in verse 18, it has a specific reference to Christ being the beginning of the reconciliation of all things (Col. 1:20), beginning first with the church by being the firstborn from the dead.

firstborn from the dead - death first

Christ is presented in verses 15 and 18 as the firstborn in different ways. In verse 15, the Son is presented as "*the firstborn over all creation*." This was explained as the Son being eternally begotten of the Father and the creator of all things. In verse 18, he is presented as "*the firstborn from the dead*," which has a different significance. The incarnate Son was resurrected from the dead and ascended as the Redeemer and head of the Church.

Several important points concern the Son as *"the firstborn from the dead."* Christ had to first be dead to be *"from the dead."* The how and why of Christ's crucifixion have already been explained. Death and sin are tied together, as we see in Romans 6:23, "*...the wages of sin is death..."* If Christ did not die after the guilt of the elect's sin was imputed to him, there would have been a breach of justice. Scripture repeatedly tells us that Jesus died. He was handed over to lawless men and killed (Acts 2:23). When he physically died, *"he gave up his spirit"* (John 19:30). There are six verses with the phrase *"Christ died"* and two verses containing *"Jesus died."* Many more verses clearly state that Jesus Christ died. The crucified one was the Lord of Glory (1 Cor. 2:8), and he died (2 Cor. 5:15). There is no doubt as we explore Christ's death in Scripture, we find it was a sacrificial death (Eph. 5:2), under Law (Rom. 6:23, 8:2), according to Scripture (1 Cor. 15:3), and in the Father's definite plan (Acts 2:23).

In Acts 2:24, the Greek word translated in various English Bibles as "*pangs*," "*pains*," "*agony*," or "*throes*" that Jesus suffered in death is ὠδῖνας (ōdinas), which refers to the intensity of pain a woman experiences during childbirth.

> 5604 *ōdín* – properly, the pain of childbirth (travail); (figuratively) the pain *necessary* to *open up* (introduce) something new, i.e., to bring in *more*. [5604 (*ōdín*) suggests *intense suffering* (similar to birth pain) – hence, "to suffer greatly, great pain" (*L & N*, 1, 24.87) like "a birth-pang, travail-pain; figuratively, extreme suffering" (*A-S*).] [http://www.biblehub.com]
>
> *"God raised him up, loosing the pangs of death, because it was not possible for him to be held by it."* (Acts. 2:24 ESV)

The intensity of Jesus' agony cannot be adequately described in human language. It is a testament to the level of pain women experience in childbirth that it is the only human experience by which Jesus' agony can be remotely represented. While Jesus was dead, he experienced an agony likened to, but much greater than, the agony a woman experiences during childbirth. As the verse indicates, this occurred until he was risen. When God confronts Adam, Eve, and the serpent for their sin to curse them, he pronounces to the serpent what is known as the "***protoevangelium,***" an indication that an offspring of the woman will crush his head, but he will be bruised in the process (Gen. 3:15). This is a veiled pronouncement that Jesus Christ will destroy the power of Satan, but not without suffering. Then, God turns to Eve and informs her that she will bring forth children in pain (Gen. 3:16). I suggest that every woman who has experienced the pain of childbirth thoughtfully reflect that it was through such pain, but to a much greater extent, that Jesus Christ was brought forth and through the pain he suffered in death for you, not unlike yours, he is your Redeemer and Savior. Likewise, men ought to realize how precious women are and the precious hope we all have through pain and promise (Gen. 3:15).

firstborn from the dead - risen from the dead

We have yet to deal with Christ being the firstborn in the aftermath of his death. John stated plainly that in love, Jesus freed us from our sins by his blood (his death) and is the firstborn of the dead (Rev. 1:5).

There is honor in being a firstborn. Being a firstborn is a special and unique status. The striking down of the firstborn in Egypt was among the plagues. It was an execution of judgment against the Egyptian gods (Exod. 12:12). That which was most precious to Egypt was taken from them in judgment and to demonstrate the impotence of their tutelary gods. In striking down the firstborn of Egypt and sparing the firstborn of Israel, the firstborn children of Israel were consecrated to God (Num. 3:13). To be consecrated is to be set aside or prepared for a holy purpose. That purpose was to be in the priestly service, but God substituted the Levites for them (Num. 3:12). The Levites were a redemption of the firstborn in a one-to-one ratio. Each additional firstborn over the number of Levites had to be redeemed for the cost of five shekels paid to Aaron (Num. 3:46-51).

There is no doubt that there is significance in the firstborn. But the Father did not spare his own Son, the firstborn over all creation, to do what previously demonstrated the impotence of false gods and idols. However, the story does not end there because the firstborn over all creation is the firstborn of the dead. "*He has risen from the dead,*" proclaimed the angel at the tomb (Matt. 28:7). Having the power of an indestructible life (Heb. 7:16), death couldn't hold him (Acts 2:24). By this power, God raised him up (Acts 2:24).

The firstborn of Egypt died in judgment and remained forever in the grave. The gods they worshiped were powerless and could neither spare, redeem, nor restore them. But the firstborn over all creation, the Son of God, the offspring of David, "*has risen from the dead*" (2 Tim. 2:8). The Son was raised with power by God (Col. 2:12). Paul is writing about the God of power who demonstrates his power in creation, through the resurrection of his Son from the dead, by the redemption of his people, and by the restoration of all things through his Son. If we examine Acts 2:23 closely, we see that God applies His power according to a definite plan, his plan, his will. Why was it not possible for death to keep hold of Christ? Because God's power is immutable.

Jesus raised many people from death, yet none of them are considered as firstborn from the dead. Something significant must distinguish Jesus from them as the firstborn from the dead. Each person whom Jesus raised later died, whereas after Jesus rose from the grave (Matt. 28:6-7; Mark 16:6; Luke 24:6; 2 Tim. 2:8), he bodily ascended to heaven (Mark 16:19; Acts 1:2, 11, 22; 1 Tim. 3:16; John 20:17, 27; Eph. 4:8-10). Thus, Jesus, after being dead and in the tomb, rose to life and ascended into heaven, never to die again.

Peter said in his great sermon in Acts chapter 2 that it was not possible for death to keep its hold on Jesus. The root of Peter's statement is that God swore an oath that the Christ would be a priest forever after the order of Melchizedek (Ps. 110:4; Heb. 5:6). Thus, Jesus Christ is not hindered by death, death cannot overcome or make void God's oath, and he continues with an indestructible life as a priest permanently, forever, making intercession for his people (Heb. 7:23-25). God fulfilled his oath by his almighty power that raised Jesus Christ from the tomb (Rom. 1:4; 2 Cor. 13:4; Col. 2:12).

Enoch and Elijah are two notable figures whose situations require examination. The saints who have died are said to be in the *intermediate state*, the condition of the soul apart from the body. In the *glorified state*, the body and soul are reunited after the physical body has been changed into a spiritual body (1 Cor 15:44). The glorified state occurs after Jesus Christ comes in glory, reunites the departed souls with their spiritual bodies, and raptures the saints on earth as they are drawn up into the clouds to be with him (1 Thess. 4:17). The anomalies are Enoch and Elijah because both were raptured (Gen 5:21-24; Heb 11:5; 2 Kings 2:11). Since neither of them had physically died, neither could be said to be from the dead let alone firstborn from the dead. It remains that *Jesus Christ is the firstborn from the dead.*

firstborn among many brothers

Since there is a firstborn, it follows that others will, in succession, also be raised. There are two aspects to being raised, which depend on Jesus Christ being our federal head. The first aspect of being raised is from spiritual death to spiritual life. This is being born again (John 3:3), also referred to as regeneration (Titus 3:5). Let's rewind and begin with Jesus' death. We died with Christ (Rom 6:8; Col 2:20, 3:3) in a particular way. For us, this was not a physical death nor a spiritual death. We were already spiritually dead in trespasses and sin (Eph. 2:1). It was a death to the law (Rom. 7:4, 6; Gal 2:19) and death to sin (Rom 6:2). By this death we can say that we truly died to all things that held us captive to corruption and darkness (Col. 1:13; 1 Thess. 5:5; 1 Pet. 2:9; 2 Pet. 1:4) and the record of debt that stood against us (Col. 2:14). Being raised to spiritual life is not being raised from the death that we died in Christ (Rom. 7:4), but from our spiritual death. We first had to die to spiritual death before we could be raised from it. Just as it is said that we had to be buried with Christ in death to the power of sin so that we might have newness of life (Rom. 6:4). Everyone who has been born again has died to spiritual death since sin has lost its power over them. They can never again die spiritually, and thus the life they have in Christ is eternal (John 3:36, 5:24).

Let's examine what it means for us to have risen to "*newness of life*" with the Lord from death, as recorded in Romans 6:4. In this passage, Paul is speaking of the Father.

> "*We were buried therefore with him by baptism into death, in order that, just as Christ was raised from the dead by the glory of the Father,*

> *we too might walk in newness of life."* (Rom. 6:4 ESV)

The verse highlights various aspects of rising from the dead. In our case, "*we too might walk in newness of life*" is only possible if we have risen from spiritual death, separation, or estrangement from God to spiritual life reconciled to God. The phrase means that we have risen from spiritual death to spiritual life. We did not rise from physical death to physical life as did Jesus, but the verse makes a strong connection between Christ's rising from the dead and our rising to spiritual life, that there is something shared in common, if only in part. If our rising is to be "*as*" his rising, then his rising must in part be "*as*" ours, from spiritual death to spiritual life, as previously discussed. In this, too, Jesus Christ has preeminence (Col. 1:18). Christ's rising from the dead and our rising to spiritual life are bound together in his federal headship and the glory of the Father. Eventually, we will physically die, and at the resurrection when Christ comes, we will rise and be taken up to meet Jesus in the air (1 John 3:2; 1 Thess. 4:17).

A verse that captures the end of our spiritual death and the beginning of our spiritual life is 2 Corinthians 5:17: "*the old has passed away, and the new has come"(* ESV); we are new creations in Christ. The elect, when born again, are raised with Christ (Col. 3:1). Being raised with Christ to new life means we are enabled to walk according to the Spirit (Rom. 8:4), have faith (Col. 2:12), and have eternal life (John 3:36, 5:24; 6:47, 54). Even now, we have eternal life since we are dead to spiritual death and can no longer die spiritually, which would be to become estranged from God again (1 Cor. 1:8; Phil. 1:6, 4:7; 1 Pet. 1:5). These are the aspects of what it means to be raised with Christ while we remain dead to the law and dead to sin (1 Cor. 15:56).

Consider the phrase "*in everything he (Jesus Christ) might have preeminence."* In Christ's priesthood, he was a perfect high priest. Being without sin, he did not need to sacrifice for himself or sacrifice repeatedly for the sins of others, as do earthly priests. He offered his own blood once, making a more perfect offering that was based on a promise sworn by an unchangeable oath, not on a commandment that through weakness made nothing perfect (Heb.

7:19). It is said that he is a priest forever after the order of Melchizedek (Heb. 5:6, 6:20, 7:17). In this priestly order, Christ is preeminent as can be seen in the following: In Ephesians 1:4-5 we are told of God's plan that through Jesus Christ his chosen people would be holy and blameless and adopted as sons. We have seen how that plan unfolded over time and how Jesus accomplished the Father's will, but what Jesus accomplished as our high priest was predestined before creation. In this manner, Jesus Christ has always been our perfect high priest. Although Melchizedek's name means king of righteousness and king of peace, Jesus Christ, in his person, is the King of Righteousness and the King of Peace from all eternity.

Colossians 1:19
Christ, the fullness of God, the divine essence

The point Paul desires us to grasp is that all that Jesus Christ is and has done — his person and work — is true because the fullness of God is in him. Paul is somewhat redundant because he has already explained that Jesus is the image of the invisible God; however, this further clarifies why he is that image.

When John baptized Jesus, the Father spoke from heaven, *"This is my beloved Son, with whom I am well pleased"* (Matt. 3:17). When Jesus was transfigured, the Father spoke from a cloud, *"This is my beloved Son, with whom I am well pleased; listen to him"* (Matt. 17:5; Mark 9:7; 2 Pet. 1:17). Following Jesus' triumphal entry into Jerusalem and predicting his death, while in prayer a voice came from heaven saying about the Father's name, "*I have glorified it, and will glorify it again*" (John 12:28). Jesus foretold of his authority that would come about soon after his trial that he will be seated at the right hand of the Power of God (Matt. 26:64; Mark 14:62; Luke 22:69).

The literal translation of Col. 1:19 reads: *because in Him was pleased all the fullness to dwell* (biblehub.com). The English Bibles make the verse more readable and clear that the fullness refers to the fullness of deity (God), as it explicitly does in Col.2:9.

"*In him*" refers to the head of the church, the beginning, the firstborn from the dead, who has preeminence over all things. To avoid getting lost in the complexities of these concepts, Paul quickly reminds us that Jesus Christ, who died and was raised, is our Lord and Redeemer, and has the fullness of God dwelling within him. It does not mean that Jesus wasn't a real man with a physical body, or that the man Jesus became God, or that Jesus the man became possessed by God. It does mean that Jesus is both man and God in one divine person. All the fullness of God, the essence of the divine nature in its entirety, indwells Jesus Christ. The Greek word, which is translated as *"dwell,"* has a meaning that is more closely aligned with *"inhabit"* and *"fixed"* (biblehub.com 2730[e]). This is by far different than Jesus having temporarily dwelt among us. The dwelling of the fullness of deity in Jesus is permanent and not subject to change over time. The Holy Spirit joined the two natures, one human and one divine, at conception (Matt. 1:20).

Jesus acknowledged his deity many times. He plainly spoke when he said, *"...before Abraham was, I am"* (John 8:58). Speaking about his relation with the Father, Jesus said, "*I and the Father are one"* (John 10:30). In his high priestly prayer, Jesus prayed, "*... just as you, Father, are in me, and I in you...*" (John 17:21). John described Jesus as the Son of God who became flesh, who was in the beginning and was with God and was God (John 1:1, 14).

This fullness would be all that God is in holiness, righteousness, power, knowledge, mercy, grace, and so forth, dwelling in Jesus Christ, the head of the church. As such, he may supply all things necessary for the care, growth, and perseverance of the church so that we may find our fullness in him alone (Eph. 1:23; Rom. 8:28; 1 Pet. 1:5).

Paul has written more explicitly about the fullness of Christ in Ephesians 1:15-23 and what it means for the church, particularly in verses 18-23, which closely parallel Colossians.

> *...having the eyes of your hearts enlightened, that you may know what is the hope to which he has called you, what are the riches of his glorious inheritance in the saints, and what is the immeasurable greatness of his power toward us who believe, according to the working of his great might that he worked in Christ when he raised him from the dead and seated him at his right hand in the heavenly places, far above all rule and authority and power and dominion,*

> *and above every name that is named, not only in this age but also in the one to come. And he put all things under his feet and gave him as head over all things to the church, which is his body, the fullness of him who fills all in all.* (Eph. 1:18-23 ESV)

Paul extols Christ's majesty, glory, and supremacy, leading to the church. He [Jesus Christ] is the fullness of him [deity] who fills all in all. We must consider that no authority or power exists that is not under Christ's rule and governance; all things are under his feet. Christ is above all things and rules all things and to his people, the church, which is his body; he fills all needs so that the saints may be complete and fit for glory (Matt. 5:48; Eph. 4:10). What a wonderful and blessed assurance it is that Jesus Christ fulfills every need for life and godliness (2 Pet. 1:3). We may conclude that it is a rejection of the work, merit, and person of Jesus Christ if one looks elsewhere for such fulfillment.

Colossians 1:20
reconciliation

When Adam fell, he caused all humankind to fall with him into sin and misery. Additionally, the entire creation became corrupted (Gen. 3:17-18). We see from this that both people and creation need to be restored. As head of the Church, Jesus Christ is the beginning of this restoration.

The Father chose and predestined the elect before the creation of the world. The sole condition of our predestination was that it would be through the person of Jesus Christ (Eph. 1:4-5). We can then determine that Christ became the head of the church before the creation of the world. As head of the church, he assumed the duties and responsibilities of the Christ, which included propitiation and redemption, acts which required his blood sacrifice. As the Son assumed the duty of Christ, he became the beginning of all restoration, first of the Church by his death, and then the restoration of all things. The restoration of all things can only follow the restoration of the church. Only then will it be set free from its bondage to corruption. This occurs after the children of God are revealed in glory, which is what the whole creation has been waiting and groaning for (Rom. 8:9-22).

reconciliation of all things

The reconciliation accomplished by the Son is according to the Father's eternal plan. There are no other means than through the Son, specifically the incarnate Son, Jesus Christ, by which we may be reconciled to God (John 14:6). Now, the reconciliation Paul writes of is more extensive. It is the reconciliation of the elect and all creation. From verses 15 through 23, Paul draws our minds to the preeminence of Christ over all things, as stated in verse 18. Paul's overall view of Christ's preeminence is that of Christ as the firstborn, a position in itself of preeminence. Paul begins with the preeminence of Christ in its most general and extensive sense, his preeminence over creation. Whether Paul is writing about the pre-incarnate Son or the incarnate Son, Jesus Christ, does not matter because in either case, there is only one divine person, the Son, who is now Jesus Christ. This divine person is the firstborn over all creation, indicating that he is before creation, being the eternally begotten Son of the Father through whom all things were created.

As the firstborn over all creation, he has rule and lordship over all things; as stated in verse 17, "*in him all things hold together.*" Paul then narrows the perspective of Christ's preeminence to being head of the church. In verse 18, we have the sentence, "*He is the beginning, the firstborn from the dead, that in everything he might be preeminent.*" Let's take this apart. Remove the middle clause, and it reads: He is the beginning that in all things he might be preeminent. This statement indicates that Christ's preeminence is established because he is the beginning. Paul has causation in mind, and the very beginning of this causation lies in the middle clause we temporarily removed; he is "*the firstborn of the dead.*" Being the firstborn of the dead makes Christ the beginning of something. What is it that Christ is the beginning of or the causation of? Paul's approach in presenting Christ's preeminence is from his wider preeminence over creation to his narrower preeminence over the Church. He is the beginning of something that starts with being the firstborn from the dead, which has far-reaching consequences for creation. That is revealed in verse 20, the reconciliation of all things. Verse 20 concludes and restates all that proceeded from verse 15. Paul's statement of reconciliation follows the same construct, from the wider to the narrower. The broader reconciliation encompasses all things. The narrower is the reconciliation of the church.

As we explore reconciliation, we find that it occurs in stages. The first is the reconciliation of the elect to the Father, as stated in verse 20, "*making peace by the blood of his cross.*" Through the redemptive work of Christ, the Spirit regenerates the soul (Titus 3:5) and justifies the person in his name (1 Cor. 6:11). At this point, only the souls of the elect have been reconciled. Their physical bodies remain unchanged and have yet to be addressed. The total human person consists of a soul and a body (Matt. 10:28). This is where all reconciliation begins and why Christ is the beginning of reconciliation.

The second stage of reconciliation occurs with the redemption of our bodies, which precedes our full adoption as sons (Rom 8:23). When we die, our souls are separated from our bodies, and we enter what is referred to as the *intermediate state*. The reconciliation of our bodies involves several changes when the Lord comes. The bodies of the saints who have died will be raised first, followed by the living saints, and together they will meet the Lord in the air (1 Thess. 4:16-17). Body and soul now joined will be sanctified completely, meaning that our physical bodies of flesh and blood will be raised as spiritual and imperishable bodies (1 Thess. 5:23; 1 Cor. 15:44). Thus, when we see him as he is (1 John 3:2), our bodies will be transformed to be like his glorious body, our sanctification will be complete, we will bear the image of God like Jesus (Phil. 3:20-21, 2 Cor. 3:18; Matt. 5:48; 2 Pet. 1:4), and we will appear with Christ in glory (Col. 3:4).

The ultimate state of the saints in the united church is with sanctified souls and spiritual bodies. This is the state of glory which the saints will inherit. Then, the third stage of reconciliation can occur, the reconciliation of creation, when the glorified saints are presented as the sons of God. Romans 8:19-23 lays out the progression that reconciliation follows. Just like creation that has been subjected to corruption, we groan within ourselves, having been spiritually raised with Christ. Spiritually rising with Christ is the reconciliation of our fallen nature. It is the beginning of reconciliation. We groan as we wait for the reconciliation, the redemption, of our bodies when the Lord of glory appears to gather his church. Then, when the united church is presented to the Father for adoption as sons, the waiting creation will be set free.

In summary, when Christ is raised as the firstfruits from the dead, he becomes the beginning of the reconciliation of all things, a process that goes through three phases. All things have their time and place. First, the souls of the saints are reconciled to God by Christ's blood. Then, when Christ comes again, the bodies of the saints are transformed into spiritual bodies, making them acceptable to enter the kingdom and thus reconciled. The saints' souls and spiritual bodies are united, and the saints are thereafter in their glorified state, presented as the sons of God. Once this occurs, the remainder of creation has the futility of the curse lifted. *Christ will then have reconciled all things*.

propitiation

The main focus of verse 20 is the reconciliation of the elect, which involves "*making peace by the blood of his cross*" and introduces a new concept, ***propitiation***, which is the act of making peace by setting aside God's wrath. Before our redemption, we were just like the rest of mankind, living in a manner that builds up the wrath of God against us (Rom. 2:5; Eph. 2:3) that would eventually lead us to destruction (Rom. 9:22). To be reconciled, the wrath of God must be dealt with.

Paul has already indicated that Christ is our redeemer, having paid the debt of our sin, which is eternal death. Now, Paul writes about making peace, which raises the question of peace between whom and in what manner peace is being made. Examine the first part of verse 20, *"and through him [the Son] to reconcile to himself [the Father] all things,*" where the antecedents have been added. Reconciliation of the elect, as well as all things, is with the Father through Jesus Christ. We have seen in verse 14 that in Christ, we have redemption, the forgiveness of sin. As we have stated, redemption from the debt of sin requires the payment of death. This debt is sometimes referred to as a ransom (1 Tim. 2:6; Rev. 5:9). The debt is owed to God, and the ransom is paid to God. As a result, sin is forgiven, and the elect are reconciled to God. However, this reconciliation includes peace, which we may conclude is peace with the Father. Thus, reconciliation is not complete until we have peace with the Father.

The justice of God was satisfied; in this case, when the blood of Jesus Christ paid the debt of death that we owed to God. As stated previously, the guilt of the elect's sin was imputed to Christ, making him legally guilty, for which God's holy justice necessitated his death. By that, the elect have been redeemed and their sins forgiven, but they have not yet been reconciled or at peace with the Father. Peace with the Father, and thus reconciliation, occurs when Jesus Christ's forensic righteousness is imputed to the elect (Rom. 5:1). This introduces another concept, *justification.* Christ's forensic righteousness is the righteousness he acquired while living under the law without sin and perfected by his death under the law. It is in distinction to the essential righteousness of his divine nature.

All that Jesus Christ accomplished is applied to individuals in time. The elect are baptized into Christ's death and raised to new life, becoming born again into spiritual life. This occurs at a particular time for each of his chosen people. By grace, they come to faith and are justified (Rom. 5:1). Justified means that the forensic righteousness of Jesus, their federal head, is imputed to them. Their legal standing before the Father is righteousness, specifically the forensic righteousness of Jesus Christ, which becomes their forensic righteousness. It is an external or alien righteousness that is imputed to the saints. An alien righteousness sets aside God's wrath toward us, and the faithful are at peace with the Father. God and his people are reconciled so that peace now exists between God and his people rather than wrath (Rom. 3:25, 5:9; 1 Thess. 1:10, 5:9; Heb. 2:17; 1 John 4:10). They have been propitiated, and their souls have been reconciled to the Father.

Paul mentions blood in verse 20, alluding to the ceremonial blood sacrifices for sin conducted by the priests of Israel. Christ's crucifixion was bloody. From his bloody sacrifice, the elect have received redemption, the forgiveness of sin, propitiation, reconciliation, eternal life, faith, and justification. By his blood, Jesus Christ, our high priest forever after the order of Melchizedek, is the propitiation for our sins (1 John 2:2, 4:10) and is truly the King of Peace.

COLOSSIANS 1:21-23
THE PREEMINENCE OF CHRIST, PART 3

Verses 21 through 23 form a conditional sentence around "*if indeed you continue in the faith...*"(ESV). It is not uncommon for Paul to write generally about Christ and the church and then switch to writing about what Christ has done for individuals within the church. The people Paul addresses as "And you" are collectively those among the elect who meet the condition in verse 23. The word *you* in this verse is plural, addressing everyone, so that we must all bear its meaning personally.

Overall, in these verses, Paul continues to express the preeminence of Christ and his reconciliation of all things. Since verse 21 begins with "*And*," it connects Christ's reconciliation of all things (v. 20) with his death and the church's reconciliation. Paul takes a moment to remind you who you are so that you can understand your need to be reconciled. Paul's presentation of Christ's reconciliation began with the reconciliation of all things, then the church, then individuals, but the actual working out of reconciliation commences with individuals, then the church, when it is perfected, and then creation, which culminates as all things in order are being reconciled to the Father through Christ.

Colossians 1:21

The elect's former condition, the need for reconciliation

Paul's use of "*once*" is not about one specific moment. It means that your former life has now come to an end. Throughout your former life, you were alienated from God (Eph. 4:17-18), which is to say that you were far from God or spiritually dead. You were hostile in mind (Rom. 8:7; 1 Cor. 3:19), which means you were hostile to the things of the Spirit (Eph. 2:3). And you did evil things (1 John 5:19). Paul wrote the very same thing to the Ephesians, that they were dead in the trespasses and sin in which they once walked (Eph 2:1-2). Notice that the conduct being written about was ongoing.

Verse 21 was written to cause you to reflect on your former corruption and to prove your inability to incline yourself towards God, much less establish your reconciliation. It is proof of your former blindness to your absolute need for Jesus Christ to accomplish what you were incapable of and unwilling to accomplish yourself. Verse 21 establishes that the saints did not come to Christ or were reconciled to God by their personal choice. The saints should realize that such a choice is impossible when alienated from God (Eph. 2:12), hostile in mind (Rom. 8:7), and walking in evil (Col. 3:5; 3 John 1:11). Ever since Adam sinned by arrogating independence and personal sovereignty, thereby plunging mankind into sin and misery, people have been vainly working to make themselves acceptable to God or God acceptable to them rather than recognizing Christ's sovereignty and their inherent inabilities. Paul establishes this. Once we realize these things, all praise and thankfulness should spring from us as we extol his glory, majesty, loving-kindness, and grace. However, if we persist in the claim of personal autonomy of choice, are we not engaging in the same sin as Adam?

Colossians 1:22
mission accomplished

There came a moment in your life that changed you forever. You may not have known it at the time, but you do now. Before that moment, even up to that moment, you were hostile in mind and doing evil things, alienated from God. That is what verse 21 says of you. Up to that moment, you were dead and walking in trespasses and sins, following the spirit of the sons of disobedience, and like the rest of mankind, you were a child of wrath (Eph. 2:1-3). But that moment that had been decreed from eternity past came, and you were then, as you are now, reconciled to God in Christ by his blood.

Before God created the heavens and the earth, he chose a people and predestined them. What we know of this is limited. How election was done is somewhat of a mystery. It was done in love (Eph. 1:4-5), according to the counsel of his will (Eph. 1:11), and for his purpose (Rom. 8:28; Eph. 1:5, 9, 3:11; Heb. 6:17). To affirm anything beyond what the Bible reveals of election is speculation and presumption. Why it was done has some clarity. The Father chose the elect to be holy and blameless (Eph 1:4) and predestined the elect to adoption as sons through Jesus Christ (Eph. 1:5). From this, it is proper to say that Jesus Christ, the incarnation of the Son, was foreordained with a mission of works to accomplish (Heb. 3:1). This work was done at the right time, in the fullness of time according to

God's definite plan (Acts 2:23) to unite all things in Jesus Christ (Eph. 1:9-10). We are now living in a time after Jesus Christ has fulfilled all that the Father gave him to accomplish for the reconciliation of his people. (Heb. 8:1, 12:2).

Paul wrote that Christ died in his body of flesh to make it resplendently clear that it was the incarnate Son of God in the person of Jesus Christ and that this was an actual physical death of a real body as opposed to some mystical occurrence or apparition. Paul went on to specify what this reconciliation includes and what Christ has accomplished. You are now presentable to the Father as holy, blameless, and above reproach. Holy means to be called out, set aside, or consecrated (1 Pet. 2:5,9). Blameless means to be without guilt, justified, and at peace with the Father (Rom. 3:24, 5:9; 1 Cor. 6:11; Phil. 1:10, 2:15; Titus 3:7; Jude 24). Above reproach means no charge can be laid against you (Rom. 8:1, 33). Thus, Jesus Christ fulfilled all the Father had given him to do for those he had chosen (Eph. 1:4-5).

The verse mentions the saints being presented to the Father by Jesus Christ. This presentation (Rom. 8:19; 1 Cor. 15:24) occurs after Christ comes on the Last Day with his mighty angels (2 Thess. 1:7) to collect his church by gathering together all the elect among the living and the dead (Matt. 24:31; Mark 13:27; Rom. 14:9). Every saint will be fully sanctified (Matt. 5:48) and be transformed in body to be like the Lord's (Phil. 3:21; 1 John 3:2). Jesus told us that he will have accomplished the will of the Father when he makes this presentation (John 6:39-40) and at such time the creation will be released from its curse and all things will have been reconciled to the Father through Jesus Christ. The Scripture says for such reasons as stated here that the name of Jesus is above every name (Phil. 2:9) in this age and in the age to come (Eph. 1:21) so that at the mention of his name, every knee should bow and *"every tongue confess that Jesus Christ is Lord, to the glory of God the Father"* (Phil. 2:10-11 ESV).

Colossians 1:23
the conditional part of verses 21 through 23

All of verse 22 applies to you if you are among the faithful who have been born again. If you are not among the faithful, then verse 21 continues to describe your condition before God. When people say reconciliation with God is unconditional, they mean that individuals being reconciled do not have to prepare themselves or accomplish something on their own before they can be reconciled. There are no preconditions that an individual must meet or perform to be reconciled to God. The previous verses establish the impossibility of such preconditions.

God reconciles individuals to himself through Jesus Christ, but how do you know whether or not Christ has reconciled you to God? Paul explains how you can be assured of your reconciliation. There is only one thing on Paul's assurance checklist: faith. It is not simply having faith in anything, as some teach today, saying all faiths lead to God. That's a lie. Paul will write more about faith after he prepares us for that.

Paul knows the Colossians have heard the true gospel because he knows it was taught to them by Epaphras (Col. 1:7). They must safeguard the hope they have of the gospel and stably and steadfastly continue in the faith. Paul adds this note of confirmation regarding the gospel that the Colossians had heard: it was the same as that proclaimed throughout the whole world and the same as that of which Paul became a minister. This closing phrase is Paul's authoritative confirmation that the gospel they have heard is the one true gospel, thereby confirming their hope in it.

It is important to discern that the gospel was proclaimed, not offered, which has wrongfully become part of our way of thinking about the gospel. Are the gospel and salvation offered according to Scripture? There are only two verses we need to check. In 1 Corinthians 9:18, according to the NASB, we find the phrase "*offer the gospel*," while the NIV translates it as "*offer it*," referring to the gospel. The ESV and KJV do not use the word *offer* in any verse regarding the gospel or salvation. In 1 Corinthians 9:18, the NASB and NIV have an incorrect translation of θήσω (thēsō). According to biblehub.com, this Greek word (5087[e]) means to place, lay, or set, and its usage is to put, place, set, fix, and establish. In Titus 2:11, the NIV uses the phrase "*offer salvation*." In this case, the NIV has an error in translating σωτήριος (sōtērios). Biblehub.com defines this Greek word (4992[e]) as saving or bringing salvation with the same usage. None of the other Bibles have the same error. Apart from these errant translations, the ESV, KJV, NASB, and NIV do not claim that the gospel or salvation is offered. In that light, it is proper to disregard the notion that the gospel or salvation is ever offered in Scripture. The gospel does not come as an offer to be presented as a choice. The gospel is conveyed through the word preached (Rom. 10:14; 1 Peter 4:6), with the power of God (Rom. 1:16), and in the Holy Spirit (1 Thess. 1:5).

We've heard time and time again that Jesus is knocking at your door and wants to come in and save you. You just have to open the door for him. Do you not see the multiple errors in such a scenario, the weakness of Jesus, your inability to open the door, your inability to hear the knock, and Jesus' preference that you perish in hell rather than open the door himself and actually save you?

The gospel is never offered because God has already predestined all outcomes. He chose the elect in love, according to his own counsel. He predestined them through Jesus Christ to be adopted as sons, being made holy and blameless (Eph. 1:3-4). Thus, by the guarding power of God (1 Pet. 1:5), the elect will, through grace (Eph. 2:8), fulfill the condition of faith set before us in verse 23. They will be made holy and blameless and then presented to the Father just as the Father willed and predestined through Jesus Christ, who fills all in all. Thus, the saints may be steadfast in the hope of the gospel that there is no other name under heaven than Jesus Christ by whom we must be saved (Acts 4:12).

Verses 21 to 23 also serve as a warning. The absence of faith and hope in the gospel of Jesus Christ leaves a person in a state of alienation from God, from which he cannot escape (John 6:44, 65). Furthermore, those wavering in their faith have no cause for assurance. We often say that a person struggling with their faith is a sign that the Holy Spirit is at work within them, but a steadfast faith, not a wavering one, assures us of our salvation.

Paul teaches in 1 Timothy 6:11 that the man of God should flee evil and pursue righteousness, godliness, faith, love, steadfastness, and gentleness. Peter teaches the same in 2 Peter 1:5-8. A man of God already possesses those things which Paul and Peter exhort us to pursue. We may take this pursuit to be a matter of seeking and engaging the means of grace to improve all the spiritual gifts we have received by grace and, in so doing, confirm our calling and election (2 Pet. 1:10). It is by the means described in 2 Peter 1:10 that we can confirm our calling and election, not by thinking we must be among the elect because God loves and saves everyone or one day we chose to follow Christ ourselves.

COLOSSIANS 1:24-29
PAUL'S MINISTRY TO THE CHURCH

Paul's ministry is revealed as a means of revelation, a revealing of the mystery of Christ to those chosen by God. Points to be made here include (1) God chooses those called saints, (2) they have been given to know what has been hidden for centuries, (3) the hidden mystery is Christ in them, the hope of glory. Paul explains that his focus is on presenting all the saints as mature in Christ.

Colossians 1:24
suffering for the sake of the elect

Paul wrote about his suffering and toiling for the sake of the body of Christ, the church. He described this as no ordinary work, for it required the energy of God working powerfully within Paul. There are reasons for this. (1) The unregenerate elect are unable to come to Christ and must be drawn against a depraved will (John 6:44). (2) The opposition of the world to the gospel is forceful and cruel (2 Cor. 4:4). (3) False teachers and heretics infiltrate among new believers to lead them astray and stir up trouble (2 Pet. 2:1). Nonetheless, Paul rejoiced because the work he had been doing had been for the sake of the church.

We know there is no deficiency whatsoever in the sacrifice of Christ. So, what did Paul mean by writing, *"I am filling up what is lacking in Christ's afflictions"* (ESV)? There is no cheap grace. Does the preaching of the Word lead some to Christ? What has the preacher done and sacrificed to prepare himself to preach? Do the poor, when ministered to, find their way to Christ? What have those who minister to the poor given up in time and resources? Do the efforts of evangelists and missionaries ever lead anyone to Christ? Have missionaries lost their lives in foreign countries for the sake of Christ? All the means of grace that involve the efforts and gifts of others require some amount of sacrifice, even the least of which was in addition to that which Christ rendered in his afflictions. However, in every case, they were made possible and effectual for the elect by Christ and by his afflictions.

If there is any explanation as to why Paul can say he rejoices in his suffering, it is best expressed by himself in Philippians 3:8-11, in which he makes the following points. (1) The value of knowing Jesus Christ as his Lord is worth the loss of everything else that he has. (2) The suffering of all losses is worth gaining Christ and being found in him. (3) There is a righteousness that comes from God through faith in Christ, not from the law. (4) Paul desires to know Christ, even to share in his suffering. (5) By any means, attain the resurrection from the dead. While Paul states all this in a personal way, many aspects of it apply to all believers. We all suffer in Christ's suffering (1 Pet. 4:13). Righteousness is through faith in Christ, not by the law (Rom. 1:17, 3:1, 26). Whoever has been united with Christ in his death will have a resurrection like his (Rom. 6:5).

Colossians 1:25
to make the word of God fully known

Paul always made it clear to people the source of his calling and the governing authority by which his ministry was conducted. It served several purposes. (1) To dispel the rumors and accusations that Paul had appointed himself or was appointed by other men. (2) To ensure the word he proclaimed is received as the word of God. (3) To give God the glory for whatever fruit resulted from his ministry. Paul also pointed out that the intended beneficiaries of his stewardship were the Colossians and thus made the word of God fully known to them.

The phrase in the verse "*make the word of God fully known*" (ESV) is rendered differently in each of the various Bibles. I suggest that the phrase, as rendered in the ESV, conveys the intended meaning. This is important for what's coming next about a long-hidden mystery. We will discover that this mystery has two levels. The first thing that Paul will bring forth is the inclusion of the Gentiles in the church.

Colossians 1:26
the word of mystery

Paul had just written that he is a minister of God's word and began to present the fruit of that ministry; the first fruit is having made the word of God fully known. As to this word of God, Paul had something specific in mind, a mystery. A mystery that had been hidden for ages and generations is now revealed to the saints. The very nature of a Biblical mystery is that it cannot be known by ordinary means. It is among the secret things of God (Deut. 29:29). Paul emphasized that this mystery was purposefully kept hidden for so long that ages and generations passed without it being revealed. However, this mystery is now being revealed to the saints everywhere, and we should understand that this revelation is exclusive to the saints, especially to the saints to whom Paul was writing. Revealing this mystery was the very purpose of Paul's ministry: to make the word of God fully known. Now, the word is no longer hidden away in a mystery, but it is being brought forth to be made known, even today.

Colossians 1:27
a two-part mystery revealed

The mystery had been hidden until God chose to reveal it. Until then, it was unknowable. Many places in the Old Testament indicate that the nations will be blessed and worship God (Gen. 22:18; Ps. 22:27, 86:9; Isa. 42:1, 49:6, 55:5, 60:3; Dan. 7:14; Mal. 1:11). Other verses indicate the same but do not directly mention the nations (Isa. 9:2; Hosea 2:23). In these verses, the Gentiles are the nations referred to and at the time of their writing, they were not God's people. So, how was this a mystery? It was a mystery as to when and how it would happen. God is now making it known that this is the time when the Gentiles are coming into the church, the family of God, in great numbers, with great riches of glory. Now, the innermost secret part of this mystery is revealed. The Gentiles have Christ in them and share with the saints all the hope of glory, which is their entrance into the eternal kingdom of Christ.

New believers who have been delivered from the despair, misery, and hopelessness of living without Christ greatly value and cherish the new hope to which they have been delivered by and in

Christ. God is pleased to remind all the saints how precious Christ is to them by announcing the great joy of new Gentile believers.

Colossians 1:28
proclaiming Christ

Christ is proclaimed so that all the saints may be mature believers. Paul may have referred to himself and Timothy by writing "*Him we Proclaim.*" Paul repeated the use of *"we"* later in the verse, indicating that they have a ministry to the saints to present them as mature in Christ. In the intervening phrase that contains "*we,*" Paul explained that they, with all wisdom, warn everyone and teach everyone to accomplish their ministry. Who but the special ministers of the gospel have such grace to proclaim Christ with all wisdom? Indeed, Paul was referring to himself and Timothy, but I would not leave out others, such as Epaphras (Col. 1:7).

To proclaim something is to announce, declare, or extol it openly or publicly. This is how Christ has been taught, proclaimed, and declared with confidence and certainty. Warnings and teachings have been included, which will be discussed further in this epistle. Of special importance, these warnings and teachings have been conducted and put forward with *"all wisdom.*" It necessarily means that all counterarguments against their proclamation of Christ are foolish and lack wisdom. Such are made by people who lack understanding and are the purveyors of delusions (2 Tim. 3:13; 2 Pet. 2:1-2; Jude 1:4). Paul's reference here to wisdom is positive as it is a wisdom from above (1 Cor. 2:7). In other places where Paul referred to wisdom, it is of another sort that is meant to be appealing in and of itself in opposition to Christ (1 Cor. 2:1). James helps us understand that the word *wisdom* by itself may convey different meanings and needs to be understood within the context it is used (James 3:13-17).

Among the purposes for proclaiming Christ is its outcome on the saints and their maturity in Christ. The concept of being mature in Christ deserves some explanation. One of the purposes for leaders, teachers, shepherds, and overseers in the church is to build up the body of Christ to mature manhood (Eph. 4:11-13). Being mature in Christ consists of a way of thinking (1 Cor. 14:20), to press ever onward toward what lies ahead in our calling without being impeded by the past (Phil. 3:13-15), being able to distinguish good from evil

(Heb. 5:14), ever steadfast in the faith and not wavering under every wind of doctrine and human schemes (Eph. 4:14), and finally being "*sober-minded, dignified, self-controlled, sound in faith, in love, and in steadfastness*" (Titus 2:2 ESV).

Paul had already written that his goal was for a man to be mature in Christ. Such a man is *"filled with the knowledge of his [the Father's] will in all spiritual wisdom and understanding"* (Col. 1:9 ESV). He walks in a manner worthy of the Lord, bears fruit in every good work, and increases in the knowledge of God (Col 1:10). He endures with patience and joy, giving thanks to the Father (Col. 1:11-12).

The work Paul had done as a minister of Christ had been done in the power of Christ and for his glory. When Paul wrote, "*...we may present everyone mature in Christ...*" he was giving glory to Christ for including the Gentiles. Salvation came to the Gentiles to make Israel jealous (Rom. 11:11). Paul saw that the Gentiles coming to faith would in some way make the Jews jealous and save some of them (Rom. 11:14). Thus, the coming of Gentiles into the faith must not occur secretly but be presented with glory and revealed to the saints everywhere for the sake of the elect, yet unbelieving, Jews.

The mystery of the Gentiles is an issue that directly impacts the correctness of our understanding of election. The Father freely and sovereignly chose all those who would be adopted as sons through Jesus Christ pretemporally, before time (Eph. 1:4-5). Election includes the Gentiles, and when the Gentiles would be called, following the gospel going forth to the nations. Just as the Father is sovereign over whole nations, when they may be called, he has sovereignty over every individual. The Father's sovereignty in election is precisely what Paul meant in Romans 9, concerning Jacob and Esau, representatives of two nations, by which the free sovereignty of God over election is upheld and human will and works are denied (Rom. 9:11, 16; Gen. 25:23).

Colossians 1:29

Paul's purpose

It was for Christ to be proclaimed and the saints to be mature in Christ that Paul toiled and struggled. Given his history, Paul only acknowledged what people knew of his efforts—that he struggled and toiled—but he directed them to the source and power of his efforts and the power that lay behind their faith, the fruit of his ministry. Paul still directs all who are called to ministry to the one who called and to the source of all fruit that comes from their efforts. It is Christ in them who effectuates their ministries and brings forth fruit. Recall in verse 7 that it was Epaphras who first proclaimed the gospel to the Colossians, and later, Paul wrote this epistle to them. One planted, and another watered, but God gave it growth (1 Cor. 3:7).

CHAPTER 1 SUMMARY

Introduction

Throughout the letter, Paul addresses the Colossians as a pastor. As he usually does, he began by identifying himself and his authority as an apostle of Christ. Epaphras reported to Paul in Rome about the faith of the Colossians, which motivated Paul to write this letter. Paul sets out to commend the Colossians for their faith, love for the saints, and hope in heaven. He then confirms that their faith is in the gospel of truth that has been received throughout the world.

the fundamentals of the Christian religion

Paul issues a lengthy description of what he prays for the Colossians to receive from God. It is used to express several fundamentals of the Christian faith. The Father is the originating cause of salvation, delivers the elect from their bondage to sin, and translates them into the eternal kingdom of his beloved Son. Verse 13 is an all-encompassing statement of the gospel, for it declares that the long-awaited Messiah and the eternal kingdom have come. This eternal kingdom is one in which the saints participate by faith now through Jesus Christ and in substance when they are in glory. Jesus Christ, the Son, is the means of the elect's deliverance from their bondage to sin by redemption, which is the forgiveness of sin. Jesus Christ is the meritorious cause of salvation. This gospel of grace originates in the divine will and is effectuated by divine power. Verses 13 and 14 stand in monolithic opposition to the gratuitous gospel of human free will, which claims that all of verses 13 and 14 occur only after an individual freely chooses to follow Christ, as if the individual were the originating and meritorious cause of their election and salvation. In all, the beauty, glory, and majesty of Jesus Christ are proclaimed, leaving us thankful to praise our gracious Father and our Lord Jesus Christ.

Several important topics were discussed in detail in the commentary, including the covenants of redemption and grace, the domain of darkness, the kingdom, how Christ is Redeemer and High Priest, and federal headship.

the preeminence of Christ

Paul presented a wonderful description of the glorious preeminence of Jesus Christ in verses 15-23. The incarnate Son of God is the divine person Jesus Christ, the visible image of God in whom the fullness of deity dwells bodily. In his being, he is before his creative work. He is the firstborn over all creation, through whom all things on earth and in heaven, visible and invisible, were created, including all principalities and rule, and through whom all things have their being, consist, and hold together. All things were created by him and for him. He is the head of the church and the beginning of the reconciliation of all things by being the firstborn from the dead. By the blood of his cross, the elect are reconciled to the Father by his death, and have redemption, the forgiveness of sin, so that they may be presented holy, blameless, and beyond reproach. Jesus Christ reconciles all things and is preeminent over all things. Both the preeminence of Christ and his reconciliation were discussed in detail in the commentary.

once alienated but now reconciled

Paul brings the weightier matters of faith just presented to a personal level as he explains what the Colossians have experienced in Christ. They were previously alienated from God because of the evil way they lived. But Christ, by his death, has made them holy and beyond reproach before the Father. But they must not stray from the gospel as they first learned it and continue steadfastly in the faith. They are reminded that the gospel they first learned, and of which Paul is a minister, is spreading throughout the world.

ministry and mystery

The mystery of Gentiles coming into the church and their inclusion in the covenant of grace was a significant issue to discuss with the Colossians. Their inclusion was a pivotal event in history. To help the Colossians appreciate the significance of this, Paul explained his own suffering on their behalf, using it to reveal the mystery of Christ to them and to Gentiles everywhere through his ministry. He went on to stipulate that his ministry included teaching to present everyone mature in Christ.

A memorable passage is the beautiful section that extols Christ's preeminence, power, glory, majesty, and deity, found in verses 15-20. Two verses that express God's eternal plan and the covenant of grace, worthy of reflection, are

> *And you, who once were alienated and hostile in mind, doing evil deeds, he [Christ] has now reconciled in his body of flesh by his death, in order to present you holy and blameless and above reproach before him [the Father],* (Col. 1:21-22 ESV)

CHAPTER 2
ALIVE IN CHRIST

CHAPTER 2 INTRODUCTION

The Chapter focuses on the Colossians' faith, which is under assault from false teachers using plausible arguments, deceit, human traditions, and legalisms to lead the saints astray and shipwreck their faith. To counter this, Paul intermingles several arguments throughout the chapter and masterfully uses contrasting realities. But he first discloses the ultimate remedy against all false teachings – full assurance of understanding and the knowledge of the mystery of Christ.

Throughout, Paul outlines what was done for the Colossians to come to faith in Christ and what they would be walking away from if they continued to follow false teachings. They were uncircumcised but are now circumcised in Christ. They were once spiritually dead in trespasses but are now spiritually alive, having been buried and raised with Christ. The entire record of debt against them has been legally canceled, as if it were nailed to the cross.

Christ is contrasted against the elemental spirits. In Christ lie all the hidden treasures of wisdom and knowledge, but in human precepts and teaching, there is only the appearance of wisdom. The whole fullness of deity dwells in Christ, but festivals and sabbaths are mere shadows, and self-made religions of no value. Christ is the triumphant head of all rule and authority, but those who speak against Christ are puffed up without reason.

The glory and grace of Christ presented in this chapter renew and elevate our joy, praise, and thankfulness to God. We are thus encouraged to hold steadfastly to Christ and the wisdom, knowledge, and understanding we have received in him and not search for spiritual fulfillment elsewhere. The Chapter presents Christ as the victor over sin, Satan, and the law.

COLOSSIANS 2:1-5
ENCOURAGEMENT

These first verses of chapter 2 outline what Paul will address. The central message of these verses is a warning about being led astray and an exhortation that the knowledge of Christ they presently possess will keep them from stumbling, so they should be encouraged. Paul affirms that they not only have this knowledge but also understand it. Paul also exhorts the saints to cultivate brotherly affection, for isolated individuals are most vulnerable to being led astray.

Colossians 2:1
suffering for fellow saints

Paul referred to the last section of what he had written in Chapter 1 concerning his suffering and afflictions. Here, he was making it clear that this struggle has been of no meager degree, that they know its magnitude, and that it was for their spiritual benefit, their brothers in Laodicea, and even those whom Paul had not seen. Paul was referring to believers in Laodicea, a city located near Colossae. Many people in these two cities were acquainted with one another. Later in Chapter 4, Paul again mentions the brothers and the church at Laodicea. There seems to be a subtle shift in who he addresses, being directed more towards the saints he had not yet met and who may be hearing his message for the first time.

Paul was not writing about his suffering and struggle to aggrandize himself with the Colossian believers. His purpose was to instill the value of struggling for the faith, theirs, and others. If their souls were worthy of this stranger Paul struggling for them, how precious ought their own souls be to themselves and the souls of their fellow believers? Paul will disclose a reason for this struggle in verse 4. Until then, he is preparing us for further instruction.

Colossians 2:2

The exposition of this verse will begin at its end and work backward.

God's mystery of Christ

A Biblical mystery involves something hidden or kept from human sight and understanding. Divine revelation is necessary to know and understand hidden things; otherwise, they will remain hidden. Human reason and intellect cannot penetrate a mystery to disclose its meaning and purpose. For example, we know that Jesus Christ is coming again, but it is a mystery as to when (Matt. 24:36; Mark 13:32). The prophets disclosed that the covenant of grace would include the Gentiles, but when it would happen remained a mystery until it was revealed (Col. 1:26-27; Gen. 22:18; Pa. 22:27, 86:9; Isa 42:1, 49:6, 55:5, 60:3; Dan 7:14; Mal. 1:11; Rom. 9:30; Gal. 3:8, 14; Eph. 3:6).

Paul refers to "*God's mystery*" and then says the mystery is Christ. The verse discloses that believers possess the knowledge and understanding of this mystery by which it is no longer a mystery to them. But it remains a mystery to nonbelievers. 1 Corinthians 2 explains why Christ remains a mystery to the unregenerate mind. Before plunging into 1 Corinthians, James informs us there are two types of wisdom, that which is from above and that which is unspiritual, even demonic (Jas. 3:15). Paul refers to the latter wisdom as the wisdom of this age, calls it foolish (1 Cor. 1:20), and points out that it belongs to those who are the shapers and influencers [rulers] of this age and who are passing away (1 Cor. 2:6). Paul purposely avoided clever language, that belongs to that latter wisdom, when he preached the gospel. He didn't want to draw people in by earthly wisdom, which has no saving grace. As he pointed out, faith rests on God's power, not men's clever words. (1 Cor. 1:4-5). No one comes to Christ through human wisdom but by the Spirit, who then speaks spiritual things to those born again, to the spiritually minded (1 Cor.

2:13). Only those born again are spiritually minded (1 Cor. 2:12). Paul explains that speaking from the Spirit imparts real wisdom to spiritually minded people. He calls this wisdom the secret and hidden things of God, which would otherwise be a mystery (Deut. 29:29; 1 Cor. 6-7). These are things that God decreed pretemporally (1 Cor. 2:8), which include election in Christ, redemption through the blood of Jesus—the forgiveness of sin, and predestination as sons through Jesus (Eph. 1:3-10). This hidden and secret wisdom is revealed only through the Spirit (1 Cor. 2:10), but the natural person, the non-believer, cannot discern spiritual things because they are folly to him. (1 Cor. 2:14). The gospel is veiled to those whose minds are blinded by the [demonic] wisdom of this world, and it remains veiled to those who are perishing (2 Cor. 4:3-4). We were all slaves to sin (Rom. 6:16-17) and under the dominion of darkness (Col. 1:13) until the Father called us out of it (1 Pet. 2:9) and into the kingdom of his beloved Son (Col. 1:13), thus "*making known to us the mystery of his will*" (Eph. 1:9 ESV).

In Paul's letter to the Ephesian church, in Chapter 3, he brings up the mystery of Christ. He says the Holy Spirit revealed what was hidden for generations to the prophets and holy apostles. That mystery was that the Gentiles are now "*fellow heirs, members of the same body, and partakers of the promise in Christ Jesus through the gospel*" (Eph. 3:6 ESV). However, the context of Ephesians is different than what Paul is dealing with here. In his letter to the Ephesians, Paul emphasizes the union of Jews and Gentiles into one body of believers and members of the same household of God. Here, Paul prepares his readers to persevere in the faith that is under attack. Due to the present context, Paul refers to all things about Jesus Christ that must be revealed for people to grasp and understand their meaning, including the gospel (2 Cor. 4:3). All things Christ and the gospel are the focus of what Paul refers to in verse 2 as a mystery. The inclusion of the Gentiles is not an entirely separate mystery because they are brought into the family of God as Christ is revealed to them.

Paul points out that this is God's mystery, as are all secret things (Deut. 29:29). We may infer that Paul is referring to the Father. We must always have before us the origin and ownership of all we have through the revelation of Jesus Christ that the Father, according to his will and purpose, has made known to us. Since it is God's mystery, it is up to his sovereign will to determine to whom, when, and how he reveals it. Even as the mystery of Christ has been revealed to the saints, it continues to be God's who does not transfer sovereignty over it to individuals to determine, by reason or will, if it is disclosed to them. In other words, individuals do not mediate God's mystery of Christ (1 Tim. 2:5). Any saint may preach the gospel to nonbelievers who may then know its meaning, but understanding that lifts the veil from one's mind (2 Cor. 4:3) and overcomes the perception of folly (2 Cor. 1:18) is according to the will of God (Eph 1:5, 9, 11) and the work of the Holy Spirit.

Paul wrote to the church at Corinth, which is relevant here and worth examining. There is a light that shines in the hearts of men. It is the "*knowledge of the glory of God in the face of Jesus Christ*" (2 Cor. 4:6). Without that light, men remain in darkness and will forever stay there unless God grants the light to shine (2 Cor. 4:6 ESV). There is depth to the mystery of Christ, which, when God shines the light of his glory in our hearts, evicts the darkness that abides there, and we behold his glory in the face of Jesus Christ. Shining the light of his glory is one of several expressions of how Christ is revealed to the elect. Notice that the light God commands shines "*out*" of darkness, not into darkness. This light is an internal light that now shines in the hearts of the saints only upon God's command. It is the internal knowledge of the glory of God in the person of Jesus Christ. Such light and knowledge are unattainable apart from the Father's command.

In another place, Paul associates God's mystery with God's definite plan (Acts 2:23), which we will examine in more detail. Corrections based on the Greek text and annotations have been added for clarification.

> [3] *Blessed be the God and Father of our Lord Jesus Christ, who has blessed us in Christ with every spiritual blessing in the heavenly places,* [4] *even as he [the Father] chose us in him [Jesus] before the foundation of the world, that we should be holy and blameless before him [the Father]. In love* [5] *he predestined us for adoption to himself as*

> *sons through Jesus Christ, according to the ~~purpose~~ (good pleasure) of his will, 6 to the praise of his glorious grace, with which he has blessed us in the Beloved [Christ]. 7 In him [Jesus] we have redemption through his blood, the forgiveness of our trespasses, according to the riches of his [the Father] grace, 8 which he [the Father] lavished upon us, in all wisdom and insight 9 making known to us the mystery of his [the Father] will, according to his purpose, which he set forth in Christ 10 as a plan for the fullness of time, to unite all things in him [Jesus], things in heaven and things on earth.* (Eph. 1:3-10 ESV, clarifications and corrections added)

There is a translation issue in verse 5. The phrase "*according to the purpose of his will*" should be "*according to the good pleasure of his will*" as rendered in the KJV. From the Greek text, εὐδοκίαν (eudokian) means "*good pleasure,*" not "*purpose*" (biblehub.com). The Father and Jesus, whom we are directed to in this Ephesians passage, have been annotated for clarity.

We need to explore several essential theological concepts in this Ephesian passage. The passage is theocentric (God centered) and presents a gospel that is monergistic (of one means) in nature. Paul's letter to the Ephesians is addressed to the saints, whom he addresses here as "*we*" and "*us*." This passage applies to specific individuals, not to all people universally. Something happened "*before the foundation of the world,*" meaning it occurred pretemporally and consequently atemporally. What happened is the Father choosing particular people before time, pretemporally. Choosing before time establishes that the Father did not peer through time, not having been created, to base election on what he would then learn of people's choices. The erroneous concept that election results from God peering through time to learn fashions God as a spectator of human activity and demeans his freedom, sovereignty, and omniscience at the very least.

Paul explains that the Father made this pretemporal choice in love and that those chosen would be holy and blameless in his sight. Those chosen, Paul explains, were predestined through Jesus Christ to be adopted as sons, to be redeemed by Jesus' blood for the forgiveness of sins. These statements disclose essential aspects of the Father's pretemporal plan: (1) following creation, mankind would be in sin, guilty, and unholy; (2) the incarnation of the Son as Jesus Christ (1 Pet. 1:20) and his bloody sacrifice that would redeem certain people, those chosen, was decreed for the forgiveness of their sins, to be made holy and blameless, and to adoption as sons. Furthermore, these statements imply: (1) Adam's fall was foreknown and so ordered as the Father is most free and sovereign to have ordered otherwise; (2) Adam's sin, guilt, and resulting corruption were ordered to be passed on to his descendants by imputation and ordinary generation; (3) all who were not chosen remain in sin and corruption. In other places, we find that God ordered Adam's fall for his own glory (Rom. 9:23, 15:7; 1 Cor. 1:20; Phil. 1:11, 2:10; 1 Pet. 4:13). God's predetermination of the incarnation of Jesus has a profound bearing on Adam's fall. Because God had pretemporally chosen "*his people*" in Jesus, it was necessary to preserve the bloodline derived from Adam that would lead to Jesus as a kinsman redeemer. Since the chosen were to be adopted as sons, they were inexorably united to Jesus Christ before creation. Specifically, election and predestination are according to his purpose and will as a matter of pretemporal grace that unites the saints in Jesus Christ.

In verse 7, Paul provides further details about God's redemptive plan. Those chosen by the Father are to be redeemed. This redemption has two crucial aspects: (1) it is the forgiveness of our trespasses (Col. 1:14), and (2) it will be by the blood of Jesus Christ, his death. Redemption is necessary, or the chosen will not be holy and blameless in his sight and will not be worthy to be adopted as sons. Verse 9 mentions mystery, described as "*the mystery of his will,*" that Paul says he has made known to us. From this, we should understand that God's will for redemption, forgiveness, and adoption is only through Jesus Christ and is revealed only to those chosen and predestined along with Jesus Christ to be so blessed.

Paul then explicitly connects God's mystery with his definite plan in verse 10. Everything described in this Ephesian passage is realized in Jesus Christ "*as a plan for the fullness of time.*" This expression once again shapes our understanding that the entirety of God's plan originates pretemporally and plays out in history as it has been planned. "*Fullness of time*" means the entire expanse between eternity-past and future. It indicates that God's plan is eternal and unchanging. In doing so, all things, in heaven and on earth, will be united in Jesus Christ. God's plan is not only the reconciliation of the elect but also the reconciliation of all creation. Therefore, it is comprehensive. Otherwise, the Apostle could not write,

- "in everything he might be preeminent" (Col. 1:18 ESV),
- "*all things work together for good*" (Rom. 8:28 ESV),
- "*he who began a good work in you will bring it to completion*" (Phil. 1:6 ESV), and
- *"him who works all things according to the counsel of his will*" (Eph. 1:11).

The grace the Father lavishes on the elect, including election, is in "*all wisdom and insight.*" All wisdom precludes any notion that the Father had to learn or discover whom to elect before election. Paul uses this phrase to establish once and for all that you cannot know how this was done (Rom. 11:33), that it lies among the secret things of God (Deut. 29:29). The verse is a statement of the Father's omniscience and transcendence over time, space, and creatures, especially since they didn't exist pretemporal. It is also a statement of the immutability and infallibility of God's eternal plan. Having been established in all wisdom and insight precludes any effectual opposition and reinforces what was stated earlier: that election is "*according to the pleasure of his will*" and is conducted freely and sovereignly. Paul presents and reinforces the truth that the Father did not lack any wisdom or insight that he needed to learn or discover before choosing who to elect and having elected some, freely and sovereignly chose, for his pleasure, to lavish upon them absolutely free and unconditional grace.

Upon reviewing Ephesians 1:3-10, we must conclude the following to base our understanding of election, predestination, the gospel, and the mystery of God. These verses present God's definite and eternal plan, which encompasses the mystery of Christ, known as the gospel. By whatever means it is revealed to the elect, it is revealed in truth and power. Otherwise, whatever gospel we profess that is inconsistent with Scripture and not according to the mystery of Christ is not of grace nor unto salvation.

1. God's definite and eternal plan originates pretemporally, before creation, and in all wisdom and insight according to the good pleasure of his will.

2. The Father purposed and ordered Adam's fall since he planned some people's redemption from its consequences. God did not take a risk by creating Adam, not knowing what he might do. Furthermore, God was free not to create Adam if he so willed. Of Adam's fall, the Westminster Confession of Faith states, "This their sin God was pleased, according to his wise and holy counsel, to permit, having purposed to order it to his own glory" (WCF VI.1).

3. Being absolutely free, God sovereignly chose to redeem some people from the consequences of Adam's sin. Redemption was not an issue about fairness but of God's love, grace, and sovereign freedom. God remained free, holy, just, and righteous to have allowed all to perish if he so willed.

4. God also predestined those he chose to be adopted as sons through Jesus Christ, thus predestinating the incarnation of his Son and his mediation and intercession as high priest.

5. The chosen are redeemed from eternal death, the consequence of Adam's sin, by the blood of Jesus Christ, which we understand to predetermine his incarnation, suffering, and death.

6. God's plan is according to the mystery of his will and purpose, which includes revealing aspects of his plan to the saints. We cannot conclude that this is an exhaustive revelation of God's will, but rather only a partial one. But it is revealed in truth and power (Col. 1:6; 2 John 1:3; Rom. 1:4; 1 Thess. 1:5).

7. God's plan is all of grace by which he *"blessed us in Christ with every spiritual blessing in the heavenly places"* (Eph. 1:3 ESV) and *"lavished upon us, in all wisdom and insight"* (Eph. 1:8 ESV). This grace, nor any part of it, is preconditioned on any actual or foreseen merit. The creature receives salvific grace when he is born again. God's plan is unconditional, including the gospel, apart from the free sovereign will of God for his good pleasure and glory.

8. God's plan makes no special accommodations for those he had not chosen. They are left to perish according to God's holy justice. From the Ephesians passage, we may conclude that those not elected remain destitute of all the blessings and graces lavished on the elect.

9. God's plan unfolds in time, culminating in all things united in Christ. We can refer back to Colossians Chapter 1 to understand what this means, particularly concerning Christ being the firstborn over all creation.

10. By establishing his plan, God did not limit his sovereignty, subordinate his freedom, establish creaturely conditions, or share his glory. The Ephesian passage reveals God's free and sovereign will, righteousness, knowledge, wisdom, power, mercy, and grace.

Christ offered himself, his blood, to the Father as a ransom payment to redeem the elect from the penalty of sin. He did not offer himself, his blood, to mankind. When the Father accepted Christ's sacrificial offer of himself, the elect's sins were expiated, the Father's wrath was propitiated, and the elect were at peace with God. As Paul says, the Father chose us to be holy and blameless, not to give us a choice. Paul leads us to conclude that all those chosen will become holy and blameless (Rom. 8:29-30). Election and predestination are the work that the Father began pretemporally by lovingly, sovereignly, and freely choosing particular people who will, according to Scripture, be raised to glory *"at the day of Jesus Christ"*

(John 6:44; Phil, 1:6). This work proceeds because all things necessary for its completion have been fulfilled (John 19:30), but the work's completion only occurs at the day of Jesus Christ (Phil. 1:6).

It is God who, in all freedom, initiates an individual's redemption when he elects them pretemporally. God brings it to fruition with all efficacy, resulting in adoption as a son with all that it entails. Philippians 1:6 is a statement of pure grace and God's free, sovereign will and power, inherent to his divine nature, plan, mystery, and the gospel, encompassing biblical soteriology. No one could be assured that God would fulfill his promises if he were not always sovereign over all things. Yet, Colossians 2:2 bids us to strive for complete assurance that the knowledge we possess of God's mystery in Christ is altogether trustworthy, as it is derived from God and not from man.

Whoever is in Christ is a member of the household of God and a fellow saint, regardless of how they believe that has occurred. Their faith is equally precious before God (1 Pet. 1:7; 2 Pet. 1:1). Nevertheless, only one gospel saves, and it is according to grace alone (Acts 20:24), apart from human reason, will, and works. Whoever is saved is saved according to it and by no other means. What we've systematically exposited from Scripture on the mystery of God, which is Christ, should challenge anyone who believes that nonbelievers, the unregenerate, can reason or will their way into a saving relationship with God. Human reason, autonomous free will, and works are not pathways to salvation.

The mystery of God encompasses secret and hidden things that belong to God (Deut. 29:29) and lie beyond the reach of the natural mind. There is no access to them until a person is born again, and that only happens according to the good pleasure of God's will (Eph. 1:5), not human will or reason. The absolute sovereignty of God over election appears unjust and unfair to many people, who often rationalize this perception by citing the phrase "*God is love*" from 1 John 4:8 and 16. When doing so, to the exclusion of all else that God is, they embrace a constrained view of God that accommodates him to a man-centered theology.

understanding and knowledge

The knowledge Paul refers to is the depth of the knowledge of Christ. Anyone can pick up a Bible and read with the knowledge of what the words mean. Any number of unbelievers can recite the Christmas account of Christ's birth and the Easter account of his crucifixion and resurrection. However, they lack belief because they have no spiritual understanding (Rom. 3:11). It seems to them as folly (1 Cor. 1:18). Paul adds understanding to this knowledge, which is essential for belief. Of course, Paul refers to the understanding of the knowledge of Christ that belongs to salvation (1 Cor. 2:12) and remains inaccessible to nonbelievers (1 Cor. 2:14) unless the Father reveals it (Eph. 1:17). Thus, we see that there are two types of people. The Father presents Christ as a hidden mystery to nonbelievers, but to the saints, Christ is presented with understanding and knowledge. Jesus Christ is a mystery to the elect until he is revealed as their Savior. However, Jesus Christ is a mystery to the non-elect until he is revealed as their judge. We can again refer to 2 Corinthians 4:6 to see that the understanding and knowledge Paul refers to is the light of God's glory shining in our hearts.

Psalm 82 describes the works of evil people and says,

> "*They have neither knowledge nor understanding, they walk about in darkness; all the foundations of the earth are shaken*" (Psalm 82:5 ESV).

Thus, we see what the lack of knowledge and understanding leads to.

encouraged in their hearts to reach

Paul stated his struggles in verse 1 to encourage the saints he had not met face-to-face, which we can glean as an encouragement to all saints. Paul will come to the necessity for this encouragement in verse 4, but here, he wants their encouragement to be a motivation for reaching a particular goal, as it were, their heart's desire. As saints, they currently possess the knowledge of Christ (Col. 1:9; 1 John 5:20), but there is something more they need to strive for, which is what Paul encourages them to do. We should not think Paul is attempting to engender warm, fuzzy feelings in our hearts. He has far more serious matters in mind for the saints, particularly their endurance and perseverance in the faith that requires determined steadfastness.

all the riches of full assurance

It is good to know and understand something, but holding it as true and trustworthy is the current matter. Paul's desire, effort, and suffering are for the saints to have full assurance that their understanding and knowledge of Christ, which has been revealed to them by the Father, is true and trustworthy. His encouragement is so that they will strive for this assurance and strive for its fullness, in all its completeness, which comes in two parts: (1) the knowledge of Christ that has been revealed to them through the holy Apostles is the true and trustworthy word of God (1 Cor. 1:18; 2 Cor. 2:17; 1 Thess. 2:13; Heb. 13:7; 1 Tim. 1:5; 2 Tim. 2:11), and (2) as recipients of this knowledge with understanding, they may confirm their calling and election among the saints (2 Pet. 1:10).

The riches that Paul refers to are not simply in having an assurance of the heart only, but lie among all that the saints may be assured of. It is a precious thing to know with full assurance that you are in Christ and thus heir to the kingdom (Rom. 8:17; Gal. 3:29, 4:7; Eph 3:6; Titus 3:7; 1 Pet. 3:7; Jas. 2:5) and have an inheritance kept ready in heaven (Eph. 1:11, 14, 18; Col. 1:12, 3:24; Heb. 9:15; 1 Pet. 1:4). In Romans, Paul tells us about the wisdom and knowledge of God as he marvels at the depth of its riches and extols the immutability of God's purpose in election. Even though God imparts wisdom and knowledge to the saints, his ways and judgment remain beyond our understanding (Rom. 11:3).

Full assurance and confirming one's calling and election are biblical tenets of the Christian faith that some churches deny. The notion that a saved person can lose their salvation stands only on plausible arguments and human reason while denying the truths of Scripture. Many people think they are right with God, though their lives show no evidence of it. Unless they are born again, regardless of what they think their relationship is with God, they will discover they have no part in Christ. They haven't lost something they never possessed. But anyone who is among the elect will be saved for all eternity. The phrase "once saved, always saved" is true, regardless of the skepticism some people have toward it. The teaching that a person must face the day of judgment for the Lord to decide only then to allow them into heaven, confine them for a time in purgatory, or damn them to hell is foreign to Scripture and no part of a sound, Christian theology. People who teach that a saved person can forfeit their salvation or that a person can never be assured of being saved find their audiences among those who do not study the Bible to seek out the truths of the Christian religion as taught by the Prophets and Apostles.

knit together in love

Being knit together is an expression of how the saints have been joined. David used the phrase *"knit together"* to describe how God formed him in the womb (Ps. 139:13). This is an apt comparison to how diverse people come together in one faith to be united in peace, love, service, and worship. Paul uses this same expression again in Colossians 2:19. While knitting is a process, Paul draws our thoughts to the result of that process, that we have come together in love by God, who has truly, but metaphorically, knit us together. Thus, being knit together, we are being built into a spiritual house, a holy priesthood, and, in Christ, a dwelling place for the Spirit of God. Being knit together is what we have been called to by a holy calling bringing us together to one hope, one Lord, one baptism, one God who is Father to all (Eph. 2:22, 4:4-6; 1 Pet. 2:5). Thus, believers have a unique brotherhood and fellowship (1 Pet. 2:17, 5:9; 1 John 1:1) that distinguishes us from the world.

Because people have a lingering tendency toward independence and disunity, Paul clarifies that the saints need each other's love and affection, which can only come from God, because full assurance exists only among members of the household of God striving together with one mind. His own efforts for their souls had been set before them as an example to regard each other's spiritual welfare as precious as their own. Paul explained this in his letter to the Philippian church. Striving together for the faith that ensues from receiving the gospel is part of what it is to live in a manner that testifies to the indwelling word of Christ (Phil. 1:27). Notice in the Philippians passage the phrase "s*triving side by side for the faith of the gospel.*" Paul added this phrase to convict us of the importance of our unity in Christ and the necessity to actively seek each other's complete assurance of hope, a means of our perseverance.

The "*in love*" part of this clause expresses two aspects of love. First, our loving Father joined us together as he had chosen and predestined us in Christ (Eph. 1:4-5). God's love that elected and predestined us for adoption is the love with which he "*knit*" us to one another. Jesus Christ's love surpasses understanding (Eph. 3:19), from which nothing may separate us (Rom. 8:38-39). Keeping with the metaphor of knitting, we can say it produces a garment that can not be unraveled. Second, the result of our coming together, being fit together into a spiritual household according to Peter, is brotherly affection and love (2 Pet. 1:7). On the other side of this, John informs us that the failure to love your brother in Christ is a serious offense that betrays a failure to love God (1 John 3:10, 4:20).

all the riches

Encouragement is not an end in itself. There is something of great value to strive for that Paul presents to our mind's eye, which requires encouragement to reach. Paul is addressing us as the body of Christ, the church. His goal, as it should be the church's, is to reach the riches God has put before us. Specifically, Paul wants us to see this goal, strive for it, and be encouraged, as he explains, with the full assurance in our hearts that we will obtain it.

And what are these riches that Paul encourages us to reach for? They lie in two parts that lead to Christ. The first is Christ, who is presented to the world as a mystery (1 Cor. 2:14; 2 Cor. 4:4) but to the saints with understanding and knowledge. This gospel leads to eternal life in Christ, ushering us into the everlasting kingdom of our Lord and Savior Jesus Christ. The second is our full assurance of our participation in Christ, our citizenship in the household of God, and even the confirmation of our calling and election (Rom. 16:25; Eph. 2:19; 2 Pet. 1:10). It is more than assenting to the gospel. The author of Hebrews describes faith as the assurance of what we hope for, an assurance that is a conviction of things we have not seen (Heb. 11:1).

Colossians 2:3
hidden treasures

Paul emphasized the value of knowing Christ in verses 2 and 3 with words like "*all the riches*" and "*all the treasures.*" Paul also directed us to know that knowledge alone is an insufficient goal. Real understanding and wisdom can only come by revelation from Christ, but we can seek the full assurance of its veracity, for God only reveals it for his glory.

Along with the desired assurance are certain riches associated with the knowledge and understanding of Christ. Even now, all the treasures of knowledge and wisdom remain hidden in Christ, a mystery to the world. However, the saints have been granted access to Christ and all these treasures with complete assurance. Paul desired the Colossians to possess them all and draws us to assurance and conviction in things unseen and hoped for. Paul has written that Jesus Christ is the wisdom of God in other places (1 Cor. 1:24, 30; Col. 3:16; Eph. 4:14).

Nonbelievers are left with a mystery that belongs to God and which they cannot mediate. The treasures of wisdom and knowledge remain hidden and cannot be uncovered or discerned unless one is born again.

Colossians 2:4
plausible arguments

In verses 1 through 3, Paul has outlined what the Colossians possess if they remain in the faith and do not allow themselves to become deluded or frustrated by attractions to other things that appeal to their minds. In verse 4, Paul contrasts (1) the assurance of Christ they have in their hearts with the delusions of the mind and (2) the treasures of the knowledge of Christ with plausible arguments about false treasures. Precious possessions are at stake, and a deluded mind does not embrace them with the proper esteem.

True riches are found in Jesus Christ, in his glory (Rom. 9:23; Eph 3:16; Phil. 4:19), his grace (Eph. 1:7), his immeasurable kindness (Eph. 2:7), in the inheritance of the saints (Eph. 1:18), and are unsearchable (Eph. 3:8). In context, to be unsearchable is to be beyond comprehending the depth and breadth thereof. Jesus described the kingdom as a hidden treasure (Matt. 13:44). These are not future treasures; they are treasures and riches that the saints possess now, having come to know and understand Jesus Christ. So that you may possess these more fully, might you do so with complete assurance and not be deceived by the fading treasures of worldly desires.

On the other hand, there are the apparent riches in the things we can and do see in the world. These are the deceitful riches that choke the word and prove unfruitful (Matt. 13:22; Mark 4:19; Luke 8:4). Such riches are possessed with uncertainty and eventually decay (1 Tim. 6:17; Jas. 5:2). Paul directed us to the true riches that have a depth to them, indicating they have real substance and are not an illusion because they are in the wisdom and knowledge of God (Rom. 11:33).

Deception has many bedfellows among such behaviors as malice, envy, murder, strife, and evil (Rom. 1:29). Some may use deceitful schemes, composed of human cunning and craftiness, to lead people from the faith, especially those who are easily misled (Eph. 4:14). Such deceitful schemes may seem to be plausible arguments. Still, Paul encourages the saints to be fully assured of the truth and to recognize when it is being challenged so as not to be

> *"tossed to and fro by the waves and carried about by every wind of doctrine"* (Eph. 4:14 ESV).

Paul had a specific method of teaching about Christ and the Cross, which he expressed in 1 Corinthians 2:1-7. Paul taught new believers simply about Christ and the cross, avoiding plausible arguments and the wisdom of men so that their faith would rest *"in the power of God."* One could say Paul taught them *"the basic principles of the oracles of God"* (Heb. 5:12 ESV). But to the *"mature"* believers, people already grounded in the elements of the faith, he did *"impart a secret and hidden wisdom of God"* (1 Cor. 2:6-7 ESV). God's secret and hidden wisdom would be the solid food mentioned in Hebrews 5:14, by which, and through training and practice, the mature can *"distinguish good from evil"* (Heb. 5:14). Paul wants the Colossians to possess full assurance of the truth and maturity to avoid plausible arguments that lead people astray with various delusions.

The secret and hidden wisdom of God that Paul imparted to mature believers was "*decreed before the ages*" (1 Cor. 2:7). "*Before the ages*" is another way of expressing "*before the foundation of the world*," or pretemporally, as we encountered in the Ephesian passage we previously explored. It is the same wisdom that Paul presented in that passage about election, predestination, redemption, adoption as sons, and the incarnation and death of Jesus Christ. In this Corinthian passage, Paul explains that the imparting of God's secret and hidden wisdom was according to the Father's decree, specifically to whom, how, and when. Furthermore, in the Corinthian passage at hand, Paul brings us a bit further into God's pretemporal planning by disclosing there is more to this secret wisdom of God that we have not been told, that God has prepared things for those who love him that cannot even be imagined (1 Cor. 2:9). It is difficult to take all this in, especially that God's decree was for our glory (1 Cor. 2:7). These most certainly would be among the hidden treasures previously mentioned (Col. 2:3).

Verse 4 of Colossians Chapter 2 introduces further warnings that Paul will present as his letter progresses. This warning about being misled by plausible arguments is general, but it must be taken seriously. Furthermore, he will become more specific about the issues that the Colossians are facing.

Colossians 2:5

Paul's rejoicing

In verses 4 and 5, Paul outlines his hoped-for outcomes in response to the challenges faced by the Colossians. It is as if Paul had written that you are being tested, and in spirit, I am with you all the way, encouraging you on to your final victory in Christ. Paul affirms their victory in Christ with conviction and assurance that fills him with joy. Paul is not engaged in wishful thinking. He knows that not all who call themselves brothers are indeed brothers in the faith and will, in time, fall away. He also knows that those who have been called to Christ are united to him and will by any means come to the steadfastness of faith of which Paul rejoices. We must remember that there is power in the word of God, in Paul's epistle to the Colossians, that guards the hearts of saints. According to the verse, the saints receive grace to spiritually encourage and strengthen them, which will guard them against plausible arguments.

The warnings, if heeded, protect one's faith. Otherwise, they are recipes for spiritual disaster. The non-elect who profess to be brothers will, in time, fall away, for they do not have the capacity within themselves to heed the warnings. The elect brothers will, by the grace of God and the conviction of the Holy Spirit, properly heed the warnings of Scripture. It is in the character of their new nature to strive to be pleasing to God and to live godly lives.

COLOSSIANS 2:6-8
EXHORTATION AND WARNING

Because the Colossians' faith is firm and in good order (v. 5) and having received Christ as they were taught (vs. 6, 7), they can "*walk in him.*" The way we live our lives is important and has eternal consequences. If we live according to the flesh, our former nature, we will die, but if we live according to the Spirit, we will live (Rom. 8:5, 12-13). To guard us from walking as the world walks, Paul exhorts us to maintain an active defense against philosophy, deceit, human tradition, and the elemental principles of the world that are opposed to Christ, which would take us captive if allowed. Taking captive is to lead astray and perhaps shipwreck one's faith (1 Tim. 1:19).

Colossians 2:6
as you received Christ

"Therefore" connects what preceded as the logical reason for what comes next. Orthodoxy, followed by orthopraxy, is the usual persuasive argument for proper Christian conduct. Brotherly love, understanding in the knowledge of Jesus Christ, and the great riches in him are yours if and only if you have received Christ as Lord. And if you have received Christ as Lord, then the manner and conduct of your life are in Christ (Col. 3:3). Paul uses the phrase "*as you received Christ*" to affirm that they have indeed received Christ in truth and knowledge because he was taught to them by Epaphras (Col. 1:6-7). It was essential to confirm that the Colossians' faith was properly founded on the gospel's truth so that they could proceed in good order with Christian living.

This exhortation applies to all believers in Christ. There is a manner of life consistent with Christ's majestic glory, and it is only possible if we have received Christ aright, that is, if we have received the regenerating grace of the one true and glorious gospel of the Lord Jesus Christ. To live otherwise is to trivialize the great gift you have received and bear contempt for the one who held back nothing for your sake. Walk in a manner worthy of Christ that visibly distinguishes you from non-believers. Remaining focused on Christ is critical when the forces of darkness are contending for your attention.

Paul expanded on this argument in his letter to the Ephesian church, but with a different approach. He described the manner of the Ephesians' former lives as walking in the futility of their minds, separated from God, hard-hearted, callous, greedy, and sexually immoral. Then he told the Ephesians that this is not how they learned Christ. They should put off the old man of their former life and put on the new man that is created in righteousness and holiness after the image of God (Eph. 4:17-24). Peter also exhorted the saints to put off their former lives' passions and be holy in all their conduct, just as the Lord who called them is holy (1 Pet. 1:14-16). Living in righteousness and holiness is walking in Christ. Indeed, what Paul and Peter explained applies to all saints everywhere and at all times.

Many people believe that Jesus Christ must be offered and willingly accepted before a person can receive Christ and be saved. According to Scripture, the gospel and the kingdom are preached, proclaimed, and declared, but never offered. Christ, the gospel, and salvation are never offered in Scripture as a choice for people to accept or reject. Paul explained receiving Christ in his letter to the Romans. Those who receive Christ have received an abundance of grace, the free gift of righteousness, and will reign in life (Rom. 5:17). The grace that saves does not come in installments but in abundance and with power (1 Cor. 1:24, 2:5; 2 Cor. 4:7; Eph. 3:20; 1 Thess. 1:5; 2 Pet. 1:3), no offer is implied, no choice is enabled. Receiving Christ is entirely a matter of grace and divine power, not human will or choice (Rom. 11:6; 2 Tim. 1:9; Jas. 1:18). Our culture celebrates choice so much that it has imprinted itself on people's consciences to the extent that sin-free, autonomous human choice is a principle or a lens by which many saints read and interpret the Bible, and formulate their understanding of soteriology (the theology of salvation by Jesus Christ). However, they have unknowingly received Christ by grace alone, according to God's free and sovereign will. [In some English translations, the word "*offer*" appears along with the gospel and salvation in only a couple of verses that are misleading translations of the Greek text of these verses (1 Cor. 9:18 NASB & NIV; Titus 2:11 NIV biblehub.com).]

Colossians 2:7
rooted and built up in him

To be rooted in him has more than one significance. It means to be firmly attached, as a tree is to the ground, but it also means to be connected to the source of life, even as a tree draws its nourishment through its roots. One is built up in Christ by being rooted in Christ, and not in any other. The spiritual growth and development that proceeds from the moment we first believe takes on its proper form and vitality when not mingled with the world. Whoever is not rooted in Christ cannot be built up in Christ, for he has no connection with the source of God-pleasing spiritual life.

Peter describes the proper trajectory of an established faith. It enables the faithful, through self-examination, to confirm their calling and election (2 Pet. 1:5-7,10). This trajectory increasingly transforms us into the image of our Lord (Rom. 8:29). For our assurance, we note that God elected and predestined us for this purpose (Eph. 1:4-5; 1 Cor. 2:7; Rom. 8:29).

It is beneficial to have faith. It is a better thing to have faith in Jesus Christ. But faith, even faith in Christ, may have no eternal benefit until one is established in the faith. Occasionally, tiny words carry much weight. The definite article "*the*" precedes faith and specifies there is only one faith and one object of that faith, which is Jesus Christ, by which one must be saved (Acts 4:12). If truly established in that faith, all questions and doubts as to the nature and disposition of our souls ought to be laid to rest, provided we know that we received Christ by grace alone. If our faith rests on or with anything else, it rests on sinking sand (Matt. 7:26), and the assurance we believe we have is misconstrued.

All true saints have a faith that is precious (1 Pet. 1:7) and has equal standing (2 Pet. 1:1). When Jesus said that even the faith that was as small as a mustard seed could do impossible things (Matt. 17:20; Luke 17:6) he was speaking of an unwavering faith in himself (Jas. 1:6; Ps. 26:1; Heb. 10:23).

Paul confirmed to the Colossians that what they were first taught about Christ was indeed true. He placed his apostolic approval on what they heard of the gospel and salvation. There is but one gospel that saves (Gal. 1:7-9), one name under heaven by which we must be saved (Acts 4:12), one firm foundation (1 Cor. 3:11; 2 Tim 2:19) of which Christ is the cornerstone (Eph. 2:20). Abounding in thanksgiving rightly proceeds from being established in the faith for it is a great gift of unimaginable value to be saved such that recipients should live in constant gratitude.

Colossians 2:8
let nothing take you captive

Paul is interweaving two themes. The first is about the precious treasures you have received from God through Jesus Christ and the second deals with warnings about the things of this world that are warring against your soul. Previously, Paul mentioned plausible arguments because they are deceitfully misleading. Here, Paul is urging us to consider the established wisdom and practices of the world that stem from the fundamental principles of corruption and corruptive influences. Because the things of the world challenge your faith, you must be vigilant. Focus your mind on Christ. When you were first taught and learned of Christ, you became grounded and established in him by faith and were greatly thankful. In such a way, you received Christ and, by implication, all the treasures of knowledge and wisdom abiding in him (Col. 2:3). Walk in a way honoring and pleasing to Christ, which you now know how to do. Set your mind on Christ (Col. 3:2), or you may fail and be taken captive. Christ has no part in the elemental spirits of the world that give rise to human traditions and empty, deceitful philosophies (2 Cor. 6:14).

Paul did not oppose philosophy. Philosophy is a rational investigation of truth and a particular system of thought. Paul was addressing all systems of thought that do not conform to the gospel of Jesus Christ. The philosophies and empty deceit (Eph. 5:6; Titus 1:10)

Paul warned us about are according to human traditions (Matt. 15:6; Mark 7:8, 9, 13). That is, they find their source in the traditions of men, which vary from culture to culture and from time to time. Their philosophies are mere contrivances of men who think themselves wise in their own eyes and understanding (Prov. 3:5, 7, 12:15). Therefore, when people become entangled with such philosophies, they are led astray, and their minds become captive to them. Human tradition and philosophies are empty because they are devoid of value and truth; therefore, they are vain. They are deceitful because they are extolled as trustworthy. Paul did not oppose certain traditions and even advocated for them when they advanced righteousness and holiness, as taught in Christ according to the gospel (1 Cor. 11:2; 2 Thess. 2:15, 3:6).

A further source of deceit is the world's elementary principles (not spirits). These principles include things concocted in the minds of men, to which they assign spiritual value and meaning, which then enslave them (Gal. 4:3). Human traditions and vain philosophies arise from them. Faith and worship that is true and of the Spirit do not mix with the weak and worthless elements of the world (Gal. 4:9), the vain traditions of men, and what gives rise to them. By adding this for clarification, Paul was ensuring that we, and the Colossians, do not misunderstand and conclude that Paul was writing against all philosophy and all tradition (1 Cor. 11:2). But to be sure, Paul stated that anything that claims to be true and possesses spiritual value but is not according to the way the Colossians were taught Christ, is a deceitful lie and to be avoided.

These elementary principles of the world are addressed in other places, providing us with a deeper understanding of what we are dealing with. The elementary principles of the world hold all unbelievers in bondage to sin so that all the faculties of the soul, including the will, are in a state of inexorable corruption (Rom. 6:17, 19, 20; Gal. 4:9; Titus. 3:3; Eph. 2:3, 5:8; Col 1:3; 1 Pet. 2:9), by which all unbelievers are spiritually dead (Eph 2:1). That includes the elect before they received Christ. It took the power of God to liberate the saints from that bondage to corruption and darkness that held them captive (John 6:44; 1 Cor. 1:18, 24, 2:5, 6:14; 2 Cor. 4:7, 13:4; Eph. 1:19; 2 Thess. 1:11; Col. 2:12; 2 Pet. 1:3). But when the elect receive Christ and are born again, they are liberated from that bondage as they are delivered from the dominion of darkness by the Father (Col. 1:13). The saints rise to new life in Christ so that they are no longer spiritually dead (Rom. 6:4, 11; 1 Cor. 15:22; Eph 2:5,6; Col. 2:13, 3:1). Rising to new life is the beginning of eternal life since believers are dead to sin and can no longer succumb to spiritual death. That's because the elementary principles of the world have been put into captivity and restrained so that they have lost their power of death over the saints. They are only restrained for the saints and only so far as to be powerless to return them to their former death and bondage, but not so much that they continue to plague the saints with all manner of mischief if they are not diligent. A good translation of Ephesians 4:8 from NKJV explains this: "*Therefore He says: When He ascended on high, He led captivity captive, And gave gifts to men.*" Leading captivity captive is a way of expressing that the things that formerly enslaved the saints in sin, the elementary principles of the world, have henceforth been put into captivity or restraint. Thus, the saints have died to them, to the power of sin (Rom. 6:2, 7, 10). However, as we see in our Colossians verse, although these elementary principles are now in restraint, they are still present enough to afflict the saints. Yet, the world remains under the enslaving power of sin. There is an outcome the saints can look to with great hope and expectation on the day of the Lord. For a good translation of 2 Peter 3:10, we turn to NASB, *"But the day of the Lord will come like a thief, in which the heavens will pass away with a roar and the elements will be destroyed with intense heat, and the earth and its works will be discovered."* The elements that will be destroyed on the day of the Lord are the same elementary principles of the world from our Colossians passage, and are now only restrained. They will be utterly destroyed, and the saints will live in the new heavens and new earth where righteousness dwells (Matt. 13:41-43; 2 Pet. 3:13). This explains the three-part saying (1) in Adam the saints are not free to not sin, (2) in Christ the saints are free not to sin, and (3) in Glory the saints are not free to sin (source unknown).

COLOSSIANS 2:9-15
ALIVE IN CHRIST

These verses explain why philosophy, empty deceit, human tradition, and the elemental principles (not spirits) of the world are not in accordance with Christ, specifically Jesus Christ, and why we must not allow them, if they could, to once again take us captive. Paul will use this content in the next section to address some issues the Colossians are dealing with concerning Christian living and misleading influences within the Colossian church.

Colossians 2:9
the fullness of deity dwells bodily in Jesus Christ

Colossians 2:9 is the first of several verses discussed in Chapter 1. The "*him*" referred to is the Person Jesus Christ. Paul is drawing us to contemplate the Son's incarnation as man and that this Person is fully God, emphasizing that fullness. It is not a reference to Jesus' capacity to be filled. All that God is, including his aseity, permanently dwells within Jesus. Thus, Jesus is fully man and fully God in one divine Person of the Son. And so, it is proper to say Jesus Christ created all things because it is the divine Person who is the Creator, just as it is proper to say the Son died for our sins since this divine Person possesses a human nature and body. Verse 9 is similar to Colossians 1:19, with a significant addition: the reference to Jesus' body.

We must be careful about what Paul means when using the term "body". The verb "*dwells*" is in the present tense, active voice, and indicative mood (biblehub.com). It means that Paul is referring to Jesus' body, which is now in heaven, where the Son actively dwells, and that this is happening and is ongoing.

Let's reconsider Jesus' earthly ministry, "*In the days of his flesh*" (Heb. 5:7 ESV). Jesus was then, as he is now, fully man and fully God. During his earthly incarnation, Jesus' body was a physical body like ours. Many verses refer to Jesus being in the flesh (John 1:14; 6:51-56; Acts 2:31; Eph. 2:14; Col. 1:22; 1 Tim. 3:16; 1 Pet. 3:18, 4:1; Heb. 5:7, 10:20; 1 John 4:2; 2 John 1:7). Other verses refer to Jesus' physical body (Mark 6:9, 14:51; Luke 23:55, 24:23; John 19:38; 1 Pet. 2:24). Philippians 2:6-9 sheds a great deal of light on this. We see that Christ, being in the form of God, took upon himself human form and the form of a servant when he was born in the likeness of men. In Philippians 2:6, the word translated as "*form*" comes from μορφῇ (morphē). Quoting biblehub.com, this Greek term "describes the outward expression of an inward reality. The term implies more than just external appearance; it encompasses the true essence or nature of a being." Thus, his essential nature was that of God. Verse 7 states that Jesus emptied himself to take on the form of a servant. "*Emptied*" is translated from ἐκένωσεν (ekenōsen). This Greek word is used in several ways, including metaphorically. However, one way that biblebub.com explains this concept seems conducive to the circumstances of Jesus: "It can also imply the act of divesting oneself of status or privilege." Jesus, though in the essential form of God, divested himself of that status and privilege purposefully to assume the essential form (μορφὴν) of a servant. Verse 7 explains how this was done. "*Being born*" might not lead us to Paul's intended meaning. The Greek word from which this is translated, λαβὼν (labōn), is more often translated as "*having taken*" (biblehub.com). Digging deeper, we see that this leads to his divestment of status. So, let's look into what the Son took in verse 7. The word translated as "*likeness*" comes from ὁμοιώματι (homoiōmati), which, according to biblehub.com, does not necessarily mean an exact copy. The word translated as "*fashion*" or "*appearance*" comes from σχήματι (schēmati), which conveys the meaning of external appearance and form.

Being born vs having taken is not one or the other. Both are true. Paul intends to establish the sovereign will of God over the incarnation of Jesus, that it was by the Father's will that Mary was overshadowed (Luke 1:35). Thus, Jesus was conceived in her womb (Matt. 1:20). This aligns with the Father having sent his Son (Gal. 4:4). However, Jesus' substance, his human nature and physical body, are of the substance of Mary having been born by her (Gal. 4:4), yet without sin (Heb. 4:15).

What is most important in verse 8, and must be taken into account, is that Jesus took upon himself the likeness (ὁμοιώματι) and fashion or appearance (σχήματι) of man, but not the form (μορφῇ) of man. Being in the likeness and fashion of man means that Jesus is fully man, but a difference prevents him from being in the form (μορφῇ) of sinful man. The difference is that he is without sin, without a corrupt human nature, and is not of the darkness (2 Cor. 5:21; 1 Pet. 2:22; Heb. 4:15, 9:14; 1 Pet. 1:19). Although appearing as a man in the flesh and fully man, Jesus was and is essentially God. The incarnate Jesus Christ is inseparably fully man and God in the form of a servant. Still, he is a divine Person, not a human person, which is the difficult reality about Jesus that Paul is expressing.

Verse 8 takes us to the cross, where the reality of Jesus' physical body is most distinctly manifested in his death. Paul writes, "*even death on a cross*" to indicate that this was a cursed death (Deut. 21:23; Gal. 3:13). We also see that the Son did all of this in obedience to God, including physical death on a cross, as the divine Person, Jesus Christ. As a consequence of Christ's obedience, God highly exalted him (v. 9). This is subtle but consistent with Jesus' prayer that all that he had divested himself of by becoming the incarnate Jesus would be restored (John 17:5). This prayer is answered as he was exalted. But the likeness and fashion of man were not taken away. As verse 9 stipulates, Jesus is highly exalted as the Lord Jesus Christ. He continues as fully man and fully God as the divine Person Jesus Christ with the same body with which he was incarnate.

Following, or perhaps during, his ascension, Jesus' body was transformed into a glorious body (Phil. 3:21), as will our bodies when we rise to be with him (Phil 3:21; 1 John 3:2). Our glorious body will be a spiritual body (1 Cor. 15:44) and as such it will bear the image of the man of heaven, Jesus Christ (1 Cor. 15:49). We conclude that the body of the glorified Jesus that Paul is referring to is the same body in which he was incarnated but has been transformed into a spiritual body that is no longer flesh and blood (1 Cor. 15:50) and in that spiritual and glorious body Jesus is no less fully man than previously. To be clear, Jesus had and continues to have one and only one body, which at all times is in the likeness and fashion of man. Previously, it was physical, but now it is spiritual and glorious. "*In the days of his flesh*" is written in Hebrews 5:7, referring to Jesus' earthly ministry, the time between his birth and ascension. The verse indicates that Jesus is no longer "*in the flesh.*"

We've spent some time on Colossians 2:9 to explore what Paul meaningfully accomplishes with this short verse. The following verses of Chapter 2 review what Jesus has done and is doing for the saints. Before exploring these, Paul wants us to understand that while Jesus accomplishes these things, he is inseparably fully God and fully man at all times, both when on earth and, significantly, now in heaven. Jesus Christ is not a human person; he is a divine Person, and he is never a man apart from the divine nature of the Son of God. The ***hypostatic union*** of the human and divine natures is most significant when considering Jesus Christ's death on the cross.

Colossians 2:10
filled in Christ

Paul now begins the review of what the Colossians have received from Christ. They have been filled in him, which is to say they have received all the benefits and promises of Christ, the extraordinary riches previously mentioned. Through Christ, the saints have received everything necessary for life and godliness (2 Pet. 1:3). As fellow believers, we may include ourselves among those who have been filled in Christ. The meaning here of being filled is to be made complete, πεπληρωμένοι (peplērōmenoi) (biblehub.com). At the end of Jesus' sermon on the mount, he closes by saying, "*You therefore must be perfect, as your heavenly Father is perfect*" (Matt. 5:48 ESV). The Greek word translated as "*perfect*" may be better understood as "*complete,*" which is a more accurate way to interpret Matthew 5:48. As saints, we are complete only in Jesus Christ.

Paul brings us to a critical contemplation. Since we are already filled with all the treasures of Christ, to be complete as saints, what possible benefits might there be according to plausible arguments and vain philosophies that lead us from Christ? In their epistles, Paul and Peter used the expression "*being filled*" to orient the saints' thinking and response towards what they had received and to promote the proper mindset.

- Rom. 15:14 full of goodness, filled with all knowledge
- Eph. 13:19 you may be filled with all the fullness of God
- Phil. 1:11 filled with the fruit of righteousness

- Col. 1:9 may be filled with the knowledge of his will
- 1 Pet. 1:8 filled with glory

Being filled in Christ is to be made complete since, through Christ, we have received all things necessary as saints. There are other dimensions to explore. The list of how we are or will be filled in various ways indicates two things. The first is to our satisfaction. The knowledge of God, for example, and to seek that knowledge from him alone should fulfill our desire to the exclusion of that knowledge that is earthly (Jas. 3:15). Second, to be filled with the fruit of righteousness, for example, leaves no room for the fruit of unrighteousness. Being filled in Christ makes us complete as saints, fulfills our desires, and excludes all unrighteousness.

all rule and authority

As we consider Jesus Christ the head of all rule and authority, we realize this is about his glorified state with the Father. For the second time, Paul has elevated our thinking of Jesus in his glorified state (Col. 2:9).

Paul needed no further justification to make such a claim of Christ's authority since Jesus Christ is God (Col. 2:9), whose rule and authority are inferior and subject to nothing and to no one (1 Pet. 3:22). Thus, the saints should not seek fulfillment by any authority that opposes Christ's. Paul had written of Christ's power and authority to the Ephesians with much more detail and concerning being filled (Eph. 1:19-23) in which we are told of the greatness of his power and might, that he is seated in heaven at the right hand of the Father ruling with all authority, power, and dominion, that all things are under his feet. He is the head overall and fills all things. In the Ephesians passage context, Christ gives form, substance, meaning, and purpose to all things, without which nothing exists (Heb. 1:3, 2:10; 1 Cor. 8:6; Rev. 4:11).

During his trial before the Sanhedrin, Jesus told the high priest that he would see the Son of Man seated at the right hand of Power (Matt. 26:64). The Greek text does not capitalize the word "*power*." Still, the context of the verse indicates it refers to the Almighty, so it is capitalized. The Son of Man, as Jesus often referred to himself, would have been clearly understood by the high priest as a reference to Daniel's vision (Dan. 7:13-14). By this title, Jesus told the Sanhedrin precisely who he is. They understood, but then mocked him for his claim to be the Christ. Suppose the high priest reflected on Daniel's vision and the angel's explanation. In that case, he might have noticed the angel had changed the reference of the Son of Man to the Most High, equating Jesus with God (Dan. 7:27). The power, authority, and rule that Paul is writing about is that power prophesized by Daniel, claimed by Jesus, mocked by the Jews, and which is now at work on behalf of the saints from heaven by the divine Person Jesus Christ who is at the right hand of the Father.

Colossians 2:11
by the circumcision of Christ

Paul uses circumcision to amplify what he has been telling the Colossians about the great treasure they have in Christ and to expose the vanity of the Judaizers (Gal. 2:12). Do not suppose that the Hebrews, having the physical mark of circumcision, have anything to desire. Circumcision in the flesh was a type and a symbol of what was to come (Gen. 17:11). Now that the anti-type has come, the type has lost its principal value. The antitype is the circumcision of Christ, a circumcision made without hands. The circumcision made without hands is now the only circumcision of value (Phil. 3:3). Being filled in Christ and having the circumcision of Christ are of the same fullness. Therefore, the desire for something, in addition, is a matter of error, and the Colossian believers ought not to think that the Jews have something superior (Rom. 2:29). As he proceeds, Paul will maintain the connection with the concept that all the legal requirements of the law have been fulfilled in Christ.

This spiritual circumcision that is of Christ is the "*putting off of the body of the flesh.*" It has a substantial meaning. It is not one sin that must be put off, but the whole body or mass of sin that must be mortified. Paul describes elsewhere how the body of flesh is put off in the circumcision by Christ. Our old man, our former nature with its body of sin, was crucified with Christ (Gal. 5:24) so that we would no longer be slaves of sin, bringing the power of sin to nothing (Rom. 6:6). We will see further into Chapter 2 an interesting reason why Paul uses the phrase *body of flesh* rather than *body of sin*. He has an ulterior motive that will become clear in what follows.

Colossians 2:12
buried and raised

Paul continues to build his argument about what he means by the circumcision of Christ. In Chapter 1, he has already laid the foundation that Christ died and has risen. Being our redeemer, he paid the debt of death we owed to God (Col. 1:14), and he rose again as the firstborn from the dead (Col. 1:18). Thus, the mortification of the body of the flesh and the circumcision of the heart are realized in Christ. In explaining the circumcision of Christ, Paul writes that you have been buried with him and thus share in his death. Paul, therefore, connects the circumcision of Christ with being baptized into his death (Rom. 6:3). The baptism that saves is not the sacrament; it is the reality of being baptized into the death of Christ.

Paul does not leave us in a spiritual grave with a dead Lord. Instead, he establishes a great purpose for being buried with Christ so that we can be raised with him (1 Cor. 6:14). Paul is not referring to rising to meet the Lord in the air when he comes in glory. He means rising from spiritual death to spiritual life, which has occurred in every true saint. The saints, being at first spiritually dead in sin (Eph. 2:1) and alienated from God (Eph. 4:18; Col. 1:21), die to sin as they are buried with Christ (Rom. 6:10) and then rise with Christ to spiritual life in him (John 20:31; Rom. 5:17, 6:4, 23; Eph. 2:6).

There is no benefit to the forgiveness of sin if there is no life free of the power of sin that follows. Paul does not hesitate to remind us of the realization that we have been raised with Christ to a new life. He leaves us contemplating the mighty power of God that raised Christ bodily from the dead and that it is by this power of God that we also are raised to new life in Christ (1 Cor. 6:14, Eph. 2:6). Hence, this same power guards us through faith until that day when we meet Christ in the air (1 Cor. 15:43; 1 Pet. 1:5).

Paul had exhorted the Colossians to remain focused on Christ and the great treasure they have in him so that vain philosophies would not delude them. We can see in verse 12 that Paul continues accomplishing several things to that end. The very same power of God that raised Jesus from the dead is at work in us through faith and which is guarding us (1 Pet. 1:5). For God has circumcised you in Christ by putting off the body of the flesh, which is sin, and baptized you into his death so that you have thus risen to newness of life in Christ (Rom. 6:8).

circumcision and baptism

The current and the previous verses connect the circumcision made without hands and being buried with Christ. Although no water is involved in this burial, it is nonetheless referred to as a baptism. These two verses mean that having been buried with Christ in baptism, one is circumcised with the circumcision made without hands, thus equating the significant meaning of the sacraments of baptism and circumcision. The associated sacraments have noticeable physical and administrative differences but share essential realities. Both are signs of the same reality, described in two ways: one by putting off the body of sin and the other by dying to the power of sin, which occurs when we are buried with Christ in baptism. In other words, circumcision and baptism are sacraments of the same reality, administered under different forms. The sacraments of circumcision and baptism are analogous in that they are signs of the same covenant of grace with its promises of grace to believers and their children fulfilled in Christ (Gen. 17:9; Acts 2:39). The difference between these sacraments is that the promise signified in circumcision was looked to by faith for future fulfillment whereas in baptism it is regarded by faith as a promise fulfilled.

God established his covenant with the Hebrew people to be God to them and that circumcision would be a sign of that covenant to them and their descendants for all generations (Gen. 17:7, 10). Every male from eight days old was to be circumcised (Gen. 17:12). The sacrament of circumcision was a sign of the covenant and a seal of righteousness, which is by faith (Rom. 4:11), including faith in God's promises. The Jews, as they practiced circumcision, looked forward to the fulfillment of the promise that would occur with the coming of the Messiah. The circumcision of an eight-day-old child was a sign of God's covenantal promises and a seal of the parents' righteousness by faith in the promise that God would be a God to them and their children. Confirmation of the promise has come in the person of Jesus Christ. The saints, Jews, and Gentiles alike have redemption in Christ, the forgiveness of sin (Rom. 8:15), and the fulfillment of the promise. The circumcision of Christ, the circumcision made without hands, is the fulfillment of what the sacrament of circumcision signified in a type and anti-type relation. Now that the antitype has come, the type is no longer necessary. That type was circumcision, but the covenant to which it attested was everlasting (Gen. 17:13). Now that the anti-type has appeared, the death, burial, and resurrection of Christ, what the two sacraments signify, has been accomplished. Baptism that attests to it is administered in continuity with the commandment as the replacement of circumcision. Verses 11 and 12 establish this connection and seal the continuity of the reality signified by the sacraments.

The sacrament of baptism was instituted by Jesus Christ when he sent out his disciples to make disciples in all nations and baptize them in the name of the Father, the Son, and the Holy Spirit (Matt. 28:19). What baptism signifies has two parts. The first part signifies what circumcision did: the remission of sin, putting off the body of flesh, and dying to sin. What circumcision looked forward to, baptism regards as fulfilled. However, both are signs of the covenantal promises of God, to be our God and our children's God (Acts 2:39). The second part of baptism signifies rising to new life in Christ. More can be said about baptism, so I refer readers to the Westminster Confession of Faith, Chapter 28, "Of Baptism," and the London Baptist Confession of 1689, Chapter 29, "Of Baptism."

Serious divisions exist in the church over the sacrament of baptism. The main divide is whether or not to baptize the children of believing parents. Within that division, churches that baptize infants are further divided. Some believe that the sacrament of baptism confers salvation and unites the person baptized to Christ. Others who practice infant baptism regard it as a sign and a seal of the covenant of grace, as well as an entry into the covenantal community, the church. There are Reformed churches that practice infant baptism and some that don't. There are Arminian churches that practice infant baptism and some that don't. What is most disagreeable to Scripture is the practice of any alleged sacrament that purports to confer salvation, remission of sin, and union with Christ. The only baptism that saves is dying with Christ and rising to new life in him.

the biblical case for infant baptism

Buried with Christ in baptism is the circumcision of Christ (Col. 2:11-12). The fundamental issue of the spiritual realities of circumcision and baptism is resolved by verses 11 and 12. The sacraments of baptism and circumcision are signs of the same reality, the covenantal promises of God. Each of the following points has strengths toward understanding infant baptism as a biblical practice and ordinance of the covenant. Collectively, they form a body of evidence which, by a good and necessary consequence of Scripture, the analogy of faith, establishes that the baptism of children is an essential practice of believing parents. Unfortunately, not all agree. Therefore, these points are presented for consideration, in the hope that they will be edifying to all and to God's glory.

1. It is already clear that Colossians 2:11-12 equates the realities of what the sacraments of circumcision and baptism signify. Their union forms a continuous signage of God's eternal covenantal promises given to believers and their children. The sacrament of baptism is, in part, a sign of being buried with Christ, which is being circumcised with Christ and formerly signified by the sacrament of circumcision, which was given to Abraham as an everlasting ordinance of the covenant. Note that the sign is an ordinance of an everlasting covenant.

2. God established his covenant with Abraham and his offspring for all generations as an everlasting covenant (Gen. 17:7). Note that God established his covenant with future generations, which necessarily includes us. God instructed Abraham and his offspring for all generations to keep his covenant (Gen. 17:9). Then God commanded that his covenant was to be kept by circumcising all males among Abraham as a sign of the covenant (Gen. 17: 10:11). The males required to be circumcised included all male children eight days old and servants, whether Jewish or not (Gen. 17:12-13). Any male who was not circumcised was then a covenant breaker and was to be cut off from his people (Gen. 17:14). By this, God commanded his covenant to be kept

throughout all generations and established a sign of the covenant and commanded as a condition of keeping the covenant rules for its administration. All males in the community, including infants eight days old, were to receive the sign. Additionally, at that time, God appointed circumcision as the sign of the covenant and covenant keeping. The seriousness of covenant keeping was presented to us when Moses delayed circumcising his son. God was furious with him and threatened to kill him as a covenant breaker until his wife quickly circumcised their son (Exod. 4:24-25).

3. The command to circumcise male infants originates with the covenant and is a matter of keeping or breaking the covenant. It is a mistake to think the command given in Genesis 17 was exclusively tied to the sign of circumcision given at that time. In its basic form, keeping the covenant is applying the sign of the covenant to whomever it is due.

4. Since the command is a matter of keeping the everlasting covenant and not tied to the sign itself, God does not have to issue a second command to baptize infants of Christian parents, as that command already exists in Genesis 17:12. Furthermore, giving the sign to covenant children never depended on their faith. It depended on their parents' faith in the covenantal promises and their duties under covenantal obligation. When a Jewish child is circumcised or when a Christian child is baptized, the parents are making a public profession of their trustful faith in God's covenantal promises to themselves and their children, as well as fulfilling covenantal obligations.

5. With the advent of Christ, the nations were brought into the covenant community and included in the covenantal blessings and promises. Before Christ's advent, only Jewish males received the sign of the covenant, circumcision. Following the advent, the sign of the covenant, baptism, was also administered to women and Gentiles. Following Christ's

institution of the Lord's Supper, with no command to include women and no biblical record of their participation, the church universally included women as a good and necessary consequence of Scripture. The sacraments were not withheld from those to whom they were due with the blessing of grace therein. As the sign of the covenant of grace and its promises were not withheld from Jewish children, so should it not be withheld from Christian children. Doing so restricts the grace inherent to the sacrament at a time when the covenant community has become more inclusive. It also creates an asymmetry in grace between the Testaments. Jewish children possessed the sign of the covenant with its promises and were included in the covenant community. However, children of Christian families who are not baptized are not recognized as members of the covenant community and do not receive the grace otherwise offered in the sacrament. Jewish children who were circumcised possessed the sign of the covenant with no more faith than baptized Christian children.

6. Jesus spoke against the developing notion that he was abrogating the Law or the Prophets (Matt. 5:17), which, if unchecked, would develop into a form of antinomianism. The phrase "*Law or the Prophets*" is understood to encompass the entire Old Testament. In the discourse of the ensuing verses, Jesus' address is inclined toward the Mosaic Law but returns to a more general application. There is no point of law made in the Old Testament that Jesus abrogates, though some are expanded or fulfilled, but not abrogated. Matthew 5:17 is a compelling confirmation that the sign of baptism now administers the covenantal ordinance that established the sign of circumcision according to that same ordinance. The covenant of grace is the foundational covenant from which all other covenants derive. From covenant to covenant, there is an unfolding of greater and greater revelation, leading to Christ. The sacrament of baptism is a sign of putting off the old nature and rising to new life in Christ, a more thorough sign of the saving grace found in Christ, and a reflection of the

eschatological promises made to believing parents and their children, rather than circumcision.

Jesus was addressing the foundations of righteousness found in the Old Testament that align with the Law and the Prophets and entrance into the kingdom of heaven (Matt. 5:20). Failure to administer the sign of the covenant would result in being cut off from the covenantal community and access to all blessing from that fellowship as a covenant breaker (Exod. 17:14). This malediction has not been abrogated.

7. The children of one believing parent are holy (1 Cor. 7:14). The same Greek adjective translated as holy, ἁγία (hagia) (biblehub.com), is also used to describe the prophets and the apostles (2 Peter 3:2; Eph. 3:5). These examples express it as an adjective attached to plural nouns, children, prophets, and apostles. The same word is used for the Holy Ghost (Luke 1:41), the holy covenant (Luke 1:72), and our holy calling (2 Tim. 1:9), but in the form attached to singular nouns. Being holy means being set apart, yet when baptism is withheld from children, they are being treated as if there is no distinction between them and the unholy children of unbelievers.

8. In the New Testament, three entire households were baptized (Acts 16:15, 33, 1 Cor. 1:16). In the case of Lydia's household, only Lydia is presented as having faith. In the jailer's household account, although the gospel was preached to all and all were baptized, only the jailer is mentioned as believing in God. In the case of Stephanas, Paul informs us that those in Stephanas' household were the first converts in Achaia, but does not explain when they became converts (1 Cor. 16:15). The text does not specify whether these conversions took place before or after the baptisms occurred, specifying when is just an assumption. These three baptism examples of household members depended solely on the heads of the households having faith before these baptisms. The text also does not specify whether children were present

in these households; assuming they were not present is another assumption. The problem with these assumptions is that they are speculative and can result in an eisegetical (imposed) interpretation (1 Tim. 1:4). When understood this way, it is possible to grasp the similarity between households being baptized and Old Testament Jewish families being circumcised, which included non-Jewish servants (Gen. 17:12-13).

9. There is no record in Scripture of any individual raised in a Christian home being baptized as an adult later in life. Consider Timothy, for example. He was raised in the faith from childhood by his believing mother and grandmother, and began traveling with Paul as an adult. We have no record of his baptism as an adult like we do of his adult circumcision. A likely reason, consistent with all that has been written above, is that Timothy was baptized as a child, a historically known practice of the early church. Later, as the movement toward believer-only baptism emerged, many of the earliest baptized adult followers had grown up in Christian homes. They became known as Anabaptists, a title not meant to be complimentary. The prefix *ana* means *again* or *in repetition* because the earliest Anabaptists had already been baptized as infants, adding further credibility to the claim that infant baptism was an Apostolic practice.

It is helpful to examine the relevant differences between two confessions of faith on the issue of baptism, the Westminster Confession of 1647, Chapter 28, and the London Baptist Confession of 1689, Chapter 29.

According to the Westminster Confession, Baptism is a sacrament of the New Testament administered under the same ordinance as was circumcision. It is a sign and seal of the covenant of grace, marking admission into the visible church. It is to be administered to those professing faith in Christ and to their infant children. Water is the outward element to be used, but immersion is not required.

According to the London Baptist Confession, Baptism is an ordinance of the New Testament that marks one's acceptance into fellowship. Only those professing faith in Christ can be baptized, and then by water immersion.

The differences are fairly clear. The Westminster Confession holds that the administration of baptism complies with the original ordinance contained in the covenant of grace. Those professing faith in Christ and their infant children are to be baptized and admitted to the covenant community, the visible church. The London Baptist Confession regards baptism as being under an entirely new ordinance that is not annexed to the covenant of grace. It bars infant children of believing parents from being baptized as well as acceptance into the covenant community, the visible church (or visible saints in this case).

The sacrament of baptism, or previously circumcision, is an ordinance of the covenant of grace, as stated to Abraham. The sacrament marks entry and acceptance into the covenant community in the Old and New Testament times and holds forth the covenantal promises. These promises include ingrafting into Christ, regeneration, and remission of sins, which form the Covenant of grace. As stated in the Westminster Confession of Faith in Chapter 28.5, grace and salvation are not inseparably annexed to it. The sacrament's effectiveness lies in God's free and sovereign will to confer the promised grace and exhibit it at his appointed time (WCF 28.6). The sacrament does not unite any individual to Christ; neither does it regenerate, justify, nor confer salvific grace to its recipients, whether infant or adult.

Colossians 2:13

dead in sin:

Paul realized there were missing details to fill in. Although the Colossians, and for that matter, all believers, have died with Christ, they were previously already dead in a different way. They were spiritually dead to God because they lived in trespasses against God (Eph. 2:1). This detail was mentioned in the exposition of the previous verse.

There is a difference between trespasses and sins. All trespasses are sins, but not all sins are trespasses. Trespasses are sins that occur intentionally or unintentionally, but the person is unaware that he is sinning. Not knowing you are sinning is not an excuse, so you are just as dead in trespasses as in sins. The apostles often refer to trespasses, which by human standards may seem a lesser offense, to establish that we are dead, even if we are unaware that we have ever offended God, for no one can say they know they have never sinned because they are unaware of any. Indeed, this is depravity, as we sin even when we aren't aware.

When they had not yet received the circumcision of Christ, the Colossians were dead in their uncircumcision, being ruled by the desires of their flesh, which means the same as dead in trespasses, as were all believers before receiving Christ. We see here that the circumcision that is of Christ puts off this body of the flesh; that is, it puts off its power to rule over us. This circumcision or baptism into Christ's death, that is, our sharing in his death, mortifies the power of the flesh to rule over us, and as we rise with Christ, we rise to a new life so that we may live to God. God made us alive together with Christ (Eph. 2:5) and has forgiven all our trespasses.

made alive with Christ

While it is true that the saints were made alive by Christ, in the Greek text of this verse the saints were made alive *together with* Christ (biblehub.com), emphasizing there is no separation or distinction between us and Christ in being made alive, as in Ephesians 2:5. It forces us to realize that before being made alive, neither the saints nor Christ were alive.

In the exposition of Colossians 1:14, the section "*What were the nature and circumstances of Jesus' offering that made it acceptable?*" states that Christ died spiritually at some time after the guilt of the elect's sin was imputed to him and before his physical death. Some people mistakenly think that would mean he was damned to hell and have a most extreme objection. It is an ill-founded objection since all believers were previously dead in their sins and trespasses (Eph. 2:1, 2:5, Col. 2:13), alienated from God (Eph. 2:12, 4:18; Col. 1:21), and that death was spiritual death, not eternal death in hell.

To be raised *with* Christ, he must be raised from the same condition, separated from the Father as we were. When Jesus was nailed to the cross, he was guilty of our sins, but when he rose from the grave, he was no longer guilty. His guilt had been forgiven, but until it was, he was separated from the Father, spiritually dead. When we were buried *with* Christ, we were still under the power of sin, but when we rose *with* Christ, sin had lost its power over us, and we, together with Christ, rose to spiritual life. We were no longer guilty of sin, freed from its power to enslave us, and we could live a new life to God in Christ, our federal head.

forgiven

Paul has been conveying to us what is involved in the working out of the Father's eternal decree in human history (Eph. 1:3-10). Verse 13 states that the saints were once dead in trespasses, which is to say they were under the dominion of darkness (Col. 1:13). Then, God made the saints alive together with Jesus, which is to say that the Father transferred the saints to the kingdom of his beloved Son (Col. 1:13). Verse 13 states that God also forgave all the saints' trespasses. Forgiveness of sin is redemption by the blood of Jesus Christ according to the Father's grace (Eph. 1:7; Col. 1:14).

Colossians 2:14

nailed to the cross

In our state of uncircumcision, being ruled by the desires of the flesh, we amassed a record of debt that stood against us. Thus, during our former life, we were children of wrath, like the rest of the world (Eph. 2:3). That debt had a legal demand to be paid, a payment that required the death of the one who owed it. The death that is required has three stages: spiritual, physical, and eternal. What became of this record of debt? God nailed it to the cross. In so doing, he canceled it and legally set it aside. Of course, it was Jesus Christ who was nailed to the cross, but we see here that it was God who nailed him there (Gal. 3:13), and we see that it was to cancel our debt. Thus, we are reconciled to God (Rom. 5:10; 2 Cor. 5:18), and we are redeemed by Christ, who paid the debt we owed. Christ's incarnation, crucifixion, and shedding of blood had been the Father's plan from all eternity for our redemption (Eph. 1:7).

Chapter 1 discussed how Jesus' death on the cross redeemed us from the curse of the law. The guilt of our sin in full was imputed to Jesus sometime before his crucifixion. The terms "imputing" or "imputation" are easily confused with "imparting" and "impartation." Both involve an actual transfer from a source to a receiver. Imputation involves only a legal transfer of obligation and standing. Impartation also changes the nature of the receiver to be like that of the source. When the quilt of the saints' sin was imputed to Jesus, he became legally guilty of sin under the law, but not a sinner himself. When Jesus' forensic righteousness is imputed to the saints, they become forensically righteous before God but not righteous in themselves. When we talk about ***double imputation***, we mean that an exchange took place in which Jesus' imputed guilt was an external guilt, and our imputed righteousness is an external righteousness (2 Cor. 5:21). Our guilt was not imparted to Jesus, for if it had been imparted it would have constituted him a sinner and thus disqualified him as our redeemer and savior. Impartation alters the nature of the receiver and their legal standing. As saints are sanctified and grow in grace, righteousness is imparted to them, and they are changed to be like Christ more and more.

In the context of circumcision and baptism in Christ, impartation is vital. Christ's death was imparted to us; we died to sin both legally and in substance. When Christ rose from the dead, his rising was imparted to us. We rose to new life in Christ with new abilities of the soul, such as saving faith. While double imputation of guilt and righteousness does occur, as described, impartation occurs only from Christ to the saints.

Roman Catholics reject the imputation of Christ's forensic (legal) righteousness and teach that justification and sanctification are imparted through the sacraments of the RC church. Sadly, believers in this doctrine can never have full assurance of their legal standing with God and are inexorably bound to the traditions of their church, always hoping that by some means they may be saved.

record of debt canceled

Before being redeemed, we bore the burden of our own sin. There seems to be a sort of peace inherent in spiritual death since it prevents one from realizing the burden of debt they owe. Only eternal damnation can pay such a debt. But now that we have been redeemed, we realize that the suffering of our Lord was necessary to redeem us from that debt. There is indeed a record of debt against all sinners, but for the elect, it was nailed to the cross, having been imputed to Jesus. It was Jesus nailed to the cross in legal possession of our debt and subject to impending eternal death. He took the record of our debt, together with his shed blood, to the Father, and the Father counted it as payment in full by him. It is now as if the books of the record of our debt had our names stricken and replaced by the name Jesus, and when opened, the pages once full of the deeds of our sins have been wiped clean by the Savior's blood.

Our English translation doesn't do justice to the Greek text. First, the record of our debt was not only canceled but blotted out or obliterated (Ps. 103:12; Isa. 38:17; Mic. 7:19). When the guilt of our sin was imputed to Jesus, that decree of debt, which is eternal death, fell upon Jesus, whose suffering and physical death had to make full satisfaction for. Our debt had been canceled, and the record of it was removed, not just set aside, but because it had been paid. [See biblehub.com] Do not think it was a light thing for the Father to have crucified his beloved Son to cancel the record of your debt.

Colossians 2:15
the Father's triumph

Paul appears to have taken a step away from his argument about our treasures in Christ, which we place at risk when we allow ourselves to be led astray by plausible arguments and other things not of Christ. When Jesus was arrested, tortured, and crucified, it was by the hands of lawless men, the rulers and authorities that existed in Jerusalem at that time. When Jesus rose triumphantly over death and the grave, the same people who had crucified him came to a deeper understanding of what they had done and who Jesus was, although some of them already knew. Not only had they endeavored to put Jesus to death, they meant to eradicate all that he had taught, the knowledge of who he was, and blot out expectations of his coming kingdom. Of course, when Jesus arose, they realized their failure. Even in the face of failure and shame, such persons as Paul continued their efforts against Jesus and the faith. In Paul's case, he continued until he journeyed to Damascus and was confronted by the glorified Jesus. Paul's transformation was quite profound, from being a murderous persecutor of the church to a great evangelist who surrendered the remainder of his life to Christ and the church.

However, Paul states that this is the Father's triumph in and through Jesus Christ because all that Jesus did was in accordance with the Father's will. The following comprehensive list of verses from the Gospels portrays Jesus as the apostle of our confession sent from the Father (Heb. 3:1-2). These establish beyond all doubt that Jesus accomplished all things on behalf of the Father who had sent him. These verses are Jesus' testimony that he was sent by his Father to do his Father's will and to accomplish all that his Father had given him to do by authority and power from the Father. They also testify to the union of the Father, Son, and Holy Spirit.

Matthew:	7:21
	11:27, 20:23
Mark	8:38
Luke	10:22,
	22:29
John	3:35
	5:19-23, 26, 36-37, 43
	6:27, 32, 37,40, 44, 45, 57, 65
	8:16, 28, 54
	10:17-18, 25, 29-30, 32, 37-38
	12:49-50
	13:3
	14:6, 9-11, 13, 20, 24, 28, 31
	15:8, 10, 15, 26
	16:16, 28
	17:5, 21
	20:21

The gospel is truly a story of the Father's triumph through Jesus Christ. From his humiliation as a helpless baby born in a stall, Jesus grew to triumph over temptation and Satan, to triumph in obedience under the law, surrendering to the wrath of God, making satisfaction to divine justice by his blood, defeating death and the grave, destroying the power of sin, redeeming the elect, and ascending in glory to the Father. Even now, he possesses a name above all names, at the sound of which all knees will bend, and every tongue will confess that Jesus Christ is Lord of lords and King of kings. As

Paul reminds us, all this was and is according to the will and purpose of the Father, as decreed before the world began (Eph. 1:3-10; 1 Cor. 2:7).

Paul maintains the continuity of his argument. By momentarily having us contemplate what seemed to be a new theme, we realize its more considerable significance and relevance. The triumph of the Father through Jesus Christ is everything to us. Since his triumph is over all things that seem to have power and authority in this world, he has brought them to nothing, and we may see them for what they are: shameful things.

We must see that in triumphing over the rulers and authorities of this world, they have been disarmed. For the elect saints, no power can separate them from Christ (Rom. 8:37-39). Although they may stray for a time, like a lost sheep, they will be found (Matt. 18:12-14). The Father's decree has disarmed the powers of sin and darkness and triumphed over them (Col. 1:13) so that no elect saint may perish (Phill. 1:6; Matt. 18:14). But though the saints may never perish, they can be led astray if they do not heed the warnings written by the apostles and remain steadfast in all things of Christ.

COLOSSIANS 2:16-19
LET NO ONE DISQUALIFY YOU, PART 1

Paul encourages the Colossians to be steadfast in their faith and to hold fast to Jesus Christ, the Head. He had previously warned them not to be deluded by plausible arguments. We see here that being criticized and judged about certain things may be perceived as plausible arguments, along with other things insisted on that can, if allowed, lead to various problems of faith, particularly if they espouse a false gospel.

Colossians 2:16
let no one pass judgment on you

The tenor of this section leans toward exposing attempts to impose Jewish ordinances on the Colossian saints. We should not assume this is the only pressure on the Colossian saints who have emerged from the pagan practices in that region. In his first epistle,

Peter mentioned one potential influence to avoid: former acquaintances are surprised when you do not join their debauchery (1 Pet. 4:4). Paul wrote about the influence fellow saints might have concerning the consumption of particular foods and differences of opinion at length in Romans Chapter 14 and 1 Corinthians Chapter 8. These sources of influence need to be considered and understood.

Paul was writing to a primarily Gentile audience who may have some familiarity with Jewish customs and contact with Jews. He has already established that Gentile believers have received Christ and have been circumcised with the circumcision made without hands, the putting off of the body of flesh, which is sin. By this, the Gentiles are told they have the substance of what was foreshadowed by the sign of physical circumcision, so as not to desire what may be advocated by certain men. This exemplifies what Paul had previously told the Colossians about plausible arguments, vain philosophies, empty deceit, and human traditions so that they would not be captivated by them. Paul has told the Colossian believers that they have received everything from Christ and are now filled in him. To desire more or something else is to pursue error and to be led astray. More importantly, the Colossians, and all saints by extension, already possess the fullness of Christ by faith and need not pursue or perform some act or ritual to qualify, which would be of the nature of a false gospel.

Many ordinances related to food, days, and other matters were still observed by the Jews, but not by the Gentiles. They have become questionable things left to the liberty of conscience for each individual to resolve freely. Therefore, do not forfeit this freedom by succumbing to threats and judgments about sin in these matters. Since Christ has canceled our debt of sin and disarmed all the authorities that stood against us, what Paul wrote in Romans applies. The saints are no longer under condemnation, and no accusation can be brought against them (Rom. 8:1, 33). Therefore, let no one accuse or judge you regarding food and festivals as if there is a lack of faith or sin.

Letting no one judge you does not mean that saints can do whatever they please without question. Men called overseers within the church must be listened to, with proper consideration, when they issue correction and discipline in the name of Christ. Accept correction when it is due. But that isn't Paul's point. Paul's context is more about matters that have become of little consequence in and of themselves, even if they were previous ordinances. There is a reason he singles out food questions and observances of days. Such things can become serious problems when someone or a group tries to press them into issues of faith and Christian conduct as if they are inherent to the gospel.

Paul did not contradict what he wrote about food in his letter to the Romans. We should consider what we eat or don't eat so as not to injure the faith of other brothers (Rom. 14:20). That has to do with brotherly affection and building one another up. In Colossians, Paul warns us about those who would impose false rules on the church if given the opportunity. It might be like someone insisting, as a matter of faith, that Wednesday is Prince Spaghetti Day and holding the saints to it. However, Paul's reasoning has more to do with Jewish ordinances, as we will see, and those of other creeds.

Colossians 2:17
shadows

We all know very well that food and drink are real things. Paul is not writing about what they are in substance but about what they represent and the religious ordinances associated with them. As he writes, they represented something that was to come. That substance has now come, and that substance is Jesus Christ. Paul's logic is unavoidable. You have the substance of what was foreshadowed; therefore, you no longer live according to the shadows but live according to the true substance of Christ. The ordinances, once in force, have been fulfilled and are no longer in force.

Gentile believers find themselves pitted against Jews who continue to hold to the old ordinances of food and days. The Gentile Believers' observance of food and days differs. To the Jews, these things and ordinances remain the substance of their religion, even though they prefigured what has already come and for which they now vainly wait. But what the Jew waits for has been revealed to the Gentiles. All that had been foreshadowed is now fulfilled and realized in Jesus Christ. Denial of Christ's fulfillment explains why the Jews cast judgments against the Gentiles for the things they eat and what they observe (v. 16). Giving in to the Jews and their criticisms would burden the Colossians with ordinances that have been cast aside and weaken their faith, if not derail it.

Colossians 2:18-19
avoid legalisms

Paul addresses a critical problem in these verses. Before explaining the problem, he instructs the Colossians on how to address it. If you remain focused on Christ, rooted and grounded in him, as you were first taught, then let no one tell you otherwise to cause you to doubt and deviate to find fulfillment elsewhere.

The English translations of the beginning of verse 18 vary, but the ESV and NASB represent the Greek text most closely and lead us to Paul's intended meaning. The word "*disqualify*" comes from the Greek καταβραβευέτω (katabrabeuetō), which, according to biblehub.com, generally means to judge against. We may say, "Let no one judge against you to make you think you are not qualified to be among the saints unless you concede to whatever they tell you," with examples following.

Paul then draws our attention to people who insist we do, practice, and believe certain things outside the gospel. It's these people we must not give credence to. We will stray if we yield to their judgments against us and comply with whatever they insist we do. Paul warns us against following those who establish and impose legalisms, claiming they are necessary for salvation, but which are man-made.

Paul began by establishing, as a matter of faith, that indulging in past adherence to the shadows of things to come is no longer necessary and should be avoided as a form of legalism. He then builds on that to man-made legalisms that can shipwreck your faith. He warns the Colossians by beginning verse 18, *"let no one disqualify you."* As we consider this, it may prompt us to think of running a race. Paul has made a few references to running in a race elsewhere. Hebrews 12:1 also does. That analogy plays well here. As we run towards the goal, people along the track attempt to hinder our progress by turning us off course. Therefore, we must proceed steadfastly, focusing on the true goal and seeking our fulfillment in Christ alone, to obtain the imperishable crown of righteousness (1 Cor. 9:24-25; 2 Tim. 4:7-8).

Once a person rises to spiritual life with Christ, their soul has received eternal life (John 10:27-29). All those who are born of the Spirit will be raised to glory with Christ on the last day (John 6:44). If you hold on to that fact, then whatever someone tells you to do, practice, or believe as a matter of faith and obedience that is contrary to the one true gospel should not make you feel or think you could be lost. No matter how they judge you for resisting them, do not believe them.

asceticism and Gnosticism

Paul's warning also concerns the source of these legalisms—man-made religions. His list contains practices and beliefs likely prevalent in that time and region, but the principle at the heart of his warning remains essential, and we must not fail to grasp it. Today, the practices and beliefs contrary to the gospel have evolved, but they remain man-made and deceptive, leading believers astray from the true gospel if they allow themselves to be misled by them. Paul mentions asceticism first. Asceticism is the belief that the physical body is evil, which must be purged by self-deprecation through the denial of all physical pleasure. Paul's warning concerns those who insist on its practice, a legalism, and, more importantly, that we should not fall prey to their judgments against us for not practicing it.

There is a stark contrast between the works of the body and the fruits of the Spirit. Of the body, they are *"sexual immorality, impurity, sensuality, idolatry, sorcery, enmity, strife, jealousy, fits of anger, rivalries, dissensions, divisions, envy, drunkenness, orgies, and things like these"* (Gal. 5:19-20 ESV). Of the Spirit, they are "*love, joy, peace, patience, kindness, goodness, faithfulness, gentleness, self-control*" (Gal. 5:22-23, ESV). While advocates of asceticism claim it suppresses the works of the flesh, its only success is external by suppressing the act but not the desires from within or their consequences. Paul made his point in his letter to the Galatians: "*And those who belong to Christ Jesus have crucified the flesh with its passions and desires*" (Gal. 5:24 ESV). The internal desires of the flesh have already been dealt with when you came to Christ, when you died to the powers of sin. Although sin cannot again separate you from God, its presence lingers, and that is why Paul also wrote, *"But put on the Lord Jesus Christ, and make no provision for the flesh, to gratify its desires"* (Rom. 13:14 ESV). Making provisions for the flesh is to seek opportunities for its gratification, actions that align with living in its desires rather than living in the Spirit. Paul knows that we struggle against these desires, but if we are in Christ and focus on him, we will be more able to avoid yielding to the desires of the flesh. However, Christ took our failures to the cross, and we no longer bear them.

Earlier in this chapter, Paul explained that the circumcision of Christ was the "*putting off of the body of flesh*" as opposed to the "*body of sin*." While either phrasing means the same thing, Paul's objective is to draw our attention consistently to the fact that Christ has indeed dealt with all concerns the saints might have about the sinful desires of the flesh and thus refrain from indulging unfruitful practices.

The worship of angels and visions seems to go together into what would today be called Gnosticism. Gnosticism was a diverse set of religious ideas that gained prevalence during that period. At the heart of Gnosticism is the belief that man's chief problem is ignorance, not sin. To remedy that problem and be saved, a person needs some special knowledge (gnosis) obtained through worshiping various spiritual beings besides God and visions. It is unlikely that Paul refers to the holy angels who occupy heaven and serve as messengers of God. While the term angels used here comes from the usual word for angel, it is unlikely that Paul refers to the actual holy angels. In all encounters between men in the Bible and angels from heaven, the angels refused to allow men to worship them. The worship Paul refers to is either a delusion of the mind or a spiritual impostor masquerading as an angel from heaven. It seems this is what Paul warns us about when people insist on it and judge us.

The prophets and apostles had visions, as recorded in the Bible. That did not make them Gnostics. Their visions were initiated under God's sovereign authority and conducted for his purposes and our benefit. Many people in the Bible, such as the prophets, lived very austere lives that would be considered ascetic. While they lived that way, none of them taught or preached asceticism. Arguments still abound that push certain verses in the Bible to the extreme to advance the practices of asceticism. When a person experiences the new birth by the Holy Spirit, they have a spiritual encounter and undergo a spiritual transformation. When a saint experiences the joy in Christ that is inexpressible and peace that surpasses understanding, they are experiencing something that is outside the ordinary and natural. All this falls under the general umbrella term of Christian mysticism.

However, the umbrella term Christian mysticism harbors more than what is Biblically sound and consistent with the Christian faith. Within the broader scope of Christian mysticism are other mystical practices and experiences that retain only the trappings of Christianity, yet remain distinct from it. These include visions of departed saints, transcending physical reality, reaching union with God, the belief that all religions are united on a spiritually transcendent level, and the understanding that Christ's crucifixion was only a metaphor. The thrust of these practices and beliefs, under the banner of Christian mysticism, is to achieve spiritual growth and union with God. However, it is only God who grants spiritual growth through Jesus Christ, and it is only through Jesus Christ that one is brought to the Father. You might be led to this, or something like it, if you don't heed Paul's warning about false worship and pursue visions.

puffed up without reason, not holding to Christ

Paul writes of those insisting on these things as being puffed up without reason, thinking more highly of themselves than they should, thereby helping us identify who they might be. Their reasoning is based on a self-appointed status, by which they claim any argument of theirs deserves our attention and compliance. They insist on various beliefs and are judgmental of others (v. 16) because they reason and make decisions with sensuous minds that are fixed on the physical body, flesh, and human nature.

The root cause of their being puffed up in themselves and insisting we submit to their legalisms is that they do not hold to Christ as their source of spiritual nourishment and fulfillment. They seek to be nourished and filled elsewhere. In their search for fulfillment, they are driven by various winds of doctrine, even leading them to offer worship and glory to created things that belong only to God. All that they judgmentally accuse the saints of not participating in is counter-productive to the nourishment and growth that is by God. Any perceived benefits they claim are delusions.

Paul reminds the Colossians that Christ is the head of the Church, an office he alone holds. He goes on to explain how the church is filled with Christ. From Christ, the Head, the whole body is

- nourished - spiritually fed with truth, knowledge, understanding, and wisdom (John 6:54-58; 1 Cor. 12:8; Eph. 1:17; Col. 1:9, 2:3; 2 Tim. 2:7; 1 John 5:20)
- knit together - refers to the communion of the saints, fellowship, bond of unity (Col. 2:2; Eph. 2:22, 4:3; 1 Pet. 2:5)
- grown - both in number, maturity, and sanctification (1 Cor. 2:6, 14:20; Eph 4:13; Col. 1:28; Heb. 5:14; John 17:17, 19; Acts 26:17; Rom. 6:22; 1 Cor. 1:2, 30, 6:11; 1 Thess. 4:3; 2 Thess. 2:13; Heb. 2:11)
- growth - is according to God's plan, action, and power. (Acts 17:28; 1 Cor. 3:6, 7, 6:14; Eph. 1:19, 3:7; Phil. 3:21; 2 Thess. 1:11; 2 Pet. 1:3)

God nourishes and grows the church through Jesus Christ, who is the head of the church. A second time, Paul uses the term *"knit together"* to express how the saints are unified in one body. "*Joints and ligaments*" are metaphors for the different roles, duties, and callings believers have among the saints (Eph. 4:11-12) to build up the body of Christ. Others who claim they have something else to offer or that is required are not speaking from God and have a different purpose. The "nourishment" they offer is potentially poisonous. As Paul says, these are people who do not regard Christ as their Head so much as they should and are therefore susceptible to being driven by every wind of doctrine (Eph. 4:14). Anyone who would seek some other source than Christ for spiritual fulfillment and eternal bliss, especially someone from within the church, and leads others into this delusion ought to be, as Calvin states, bid farewell. Calvin's advice aligns with the exhortation to avoid fellowship with nonbelievers (2 Cor. 6:14-18). This 2 Corinthians passage is an exhortation to keep yourself and the church free from those who use the guise of fellowship to lead you, if not the whole church, into their faithlessness.

Wherever beliefs and practices in churches today stand in opposition to the gospel or claim to be alongside it, there are likely associated legalisms that members are required to conform to. Paul's exhortation is still relevant, should you be criticized or your faith called into question for not conceding to such legalisms. Take their judgments for what they are worth; they are the railings of deluded people, puffed up with themselves who think they can modify the gospel and hold you accountable to it (Gal. 1:8-9; Jude 1:3).

COLOSSIANS 2:20-23
LET NO ONE DISQUALIFY YOU, PART 2

It appears that Paul has been addressing an existing problem among the saints in Colossae and the surrounding region. A dimension of this problem appears to be that the saints do not fully trust that they have been delivered from the power of sin and are reverting to legalistic practices that are detrimental to their faith. For us, this remains just as real a problem today as it was then: people seeking a means to accommodate themselves to God and pursuing a merit-based salvation rather than faith in the free and pure grace of the gospel. People come to the Father through faith in Jesus Christ, not by works, and primarily not through self-initiated spiritual experiences, visions of departed saints, or transcending the physical realm. Concepts that stand out and demand consideration are: human precepts and traditions, appearance of wisdom, and self-made religion.

Colossians 2:20
the power of sin

It is central to Christianity that there are two categories of people (John 3:16,18), those elected for glory (Matt. 24:31; Mark 13:27; Rom. 9:23; Eph. 1:4; Acts 13:48, 1 Thess. 5:9; Heb. 2:10) and those appointed to destruction (Rom. 2:12, 9:22; 1 Cor. 1:18; 2 Cor. 4:3; 2 Thess. 2:10; 1 Peter 2:8). Jesus made this clear with the parable of the wheat and weeds (Matt. 13:24-30, 36-43). One type of seed produces wheat that represents the sons of the kingdom. The other type produces weeds that represent lawbreakers who are doomed to perish.

There is another way to approach the central concept of only two types of people in the world. Colossians 1:13-14 tells us that the Father delivered some people from the dominion of darkness, and 2 Peter 1:3-4 tells us that by the Father's divine power, some people have escaped the corruption in the world. Those who have been delivered and those who have escaped are the saints. They are no longer in darkness or corruption. Yet others remain in darkness and corruption.

Paul is not questioning the Colossians' salvation, just as if he had begun verse 20 with, "since with Christ you died…" At the same time, he's not confirming it either. What Paul accomplishes by using this conditional approach forces the Colossians and us to consider our actual condition more deeply, with the realization that not everyone has died with Christ. There are only two conditional outcomes, each with different consequences. Either we have died with Christ and to the power of sin, or we have not died with Christ and remain under sin's domination.

If we are living according to legalisms and not by faith, our life testifies against us - that we may not have died with Christ. Dying with Christ is dying to the power of sin; it is our deliverance from darkness and our escape from corruption, but if we are not living by faith according to that truth, then our testimony betrays who we may be. The little word "*if*" that Paul begins verse 20 with is a matter of life and death.

Assuming you have died with Christ, then the elementary spirits in the world, that is, sin and all its causes, would have no power over you. You would have died to the power of darkness and corruption. There would then be no reason to live as though that were untrue. However, here we have the Colossians, claiming to be believers in Christ and all that entails, yet living under regulations as if they were still in the darkness and corruption of the world, endeavoring to be freed by their own merit through obedience to these regulations. Paul spotlights the contradiction between their profession and practice.

Something in verse 20 may pass us by without being properly noticed. The saints died with Christ. And the saints died to the power of sin. But the verse states that these two things happen together, inseparably. Both Christ and the saints, together, died to the power of sin (Rom. 6:10). The guilt of the elect's sin that was imputed to Jesus (Col. 2:14) possessed the power to impose upon Jesus the legal sentence of death (Rom. 6:23). It was then legal and just for the Father to put him to physical death on the cross (Acts 2:23; Gal. 1:4). Jesus' body went to the grave and his soul brought his blood before the Father as a sacrificial offering for sin (Heb. 9:12). Having endured through protracted suffering the equivalent of eternal death, his sacrifice was counted redemptive (Col 1:14) and propitiatory (Rom. 3:25; Heb. 2:17; 1 John 2:2, 4:10) for himself and the elect as their high priest (Heb. 5:5, 10) and federal head (Rom. 5:15-17; 1 Cor. 15:45). The Father's acceptance of Jesus' sacrifice explains how Jesus went to the cross guilty and rose not guilty. By his sacrifice, Jesus destroyed the power of sin and its legal demand over himself and the elect. Spiritual death no longer had any claim over the elect, so with Christ, the elect rose to spiritual life (Rom. 6:4, 10, 8:11). This lies at the very foundation of Paul's wonderful declaration that there is no condemnation for those who are in Christ (Rom. 8:1). The power of sin with its legal demands can no longer impose the sentence of death on those who are in Christ, nor on Christ. Therefore, the crucifixion of Jesus Christ was a one-time only sacrifice for sin, and the writer of Hebrews and Paul can declare with certainty that Jesus died once and for all (Heb. 7:27, 9:12, 26; Rom. 6:10).

Colossians 2:21-22
human precepts and teachings

Paul becomes more specific about the general reference to regulations in verse 20. "*Do not handle*" refers to not taking hold of something, such as embracing or clinging to it. "*Do not taste*" means not to experience. This word was used by Peter when referring to having experienced Christ (1 Pet. 2:3). "*Do not touch*" is a command to refrain from physical contact. Collectively, these refer to sensuous physical activities that align with the principles of asceticism. As Paul mentioned, asceticism becomes a body of human precepts, rules, and regulations when practiced for spiritual and sanctifying fulfillment. Its source, however, is only a product of human reason and teaching. The ESV, NASB, KJV, and others translate φθοράν (phthoran) as "*perish*" in verse 22. Perish isn't a wrong translation, but it makes the verse's meaning more difficult to deduce. Remember that Paul is discussing regulations produced by human reason and teaching. It isn't the handling, tasting, and touching that are supposedly perishing by use, but rather that, according to human reason, the physical senses of the user are being corrupted by using them. "*Corruption*" is a better translation of the Greek word because it aligns with Paul's context. According to human precepts and teachings, using the physical senses of touch, taste, and handling leads to corruption and should, therefore, be altogether avoided for sanctification. That is precisely what Paul denies and admonishes the Colossians for, and exhorts them not to submit to such human teaching and their regulations.

Colossians 2:23
the appearance of wisdom

There is a wisdom that is from God that appears to the world as folly (1 Cor. 1:18, 3:19). It is a wisdom from God that is manifested through the church (Eph. 3:10). It is realized through Jesus Christ with power (Eph. 3:11, 1 Cor. 1:24) to call the elect to salvation (1 Cor. 1:18). It is this wisdom that Paul has been writing about up to this point. In Colossians 1:9, Paul asked that the Colossians be "*filled with the knowledge of his will in all spiritual wisdom and understanding*" (ESV). In verse 1:28, Paul explained that he proclaimed and taught Christ in all wisdom. In verse 2:3, he explained that "*all the treasures of wisdom and knowledge*" (ESV) are hidden in Christ. Peter confirms that Paul wrote according to the wisdom given to him from God (2 Pet. 3:15). James, in a manner, sets the stage for our understanding. There is a wisdom, he says, that is from above, which is from heaven and thus from God. Its attributes of purity, peace, mercy, and so on are reflections of the divine nature and the new abilities of the risen saints (Jas. 2:17). This is the wisdom that calls with the power to save. But James continues to say there is also an earthly wisdom. Earthly wisdom is unspiritual and even demonic (Jas 3:15).

The wisdom Paul is now writing about only appears to be from above, from God, but it is earthly, with the power to deceive, making one believe it contains spiritual nourishment when, in fact, it does not. Paul recognized that this deceptive power can hold out the promise of the cross and yet have no saving grace in it. That is why he preached Christ with simplicity, not earthly wisdom (2 Cor. 1:12). Paul knew and was telling the Colossians that salvation is by grace alone through the power of God, and it does not abide in the wisdom of men (1 Cor. 2:5).

Specifically, the human precepts and teachings mentioned in the previous verse only appear as wisdom. Although Paul is addressing the situation in Colossae, it is part of a more significant problem facing believers everywhere and at all times. Someone always presents a scheme that is claimed as an essential part of biblical Christianity. The way to counter them is to know the truth as the Holy Spirit delivered it through the prophets and apostles of God (2 Pet. 1:21, 3:2) and to be steadfast in it. If you are filled with the knowledge of Christ and understanding, as Paul prayed, it will prevent you from being deluded by plausible arguments that have only the appearance of wisdom (Col. 2:4).

self-made religion, humility, and severity to the body

The false wisdom Paul is writing about, he says, promotes three things. In this verse, the ESV creates a tautology by listing these as self-made religion, asceticism, and bodily severity. Asceticism and self-denial are essentially the same. The Greek word that the ESV translates as "*asceticism*" is ἐθελοθρησκίᾳ (ethelothrēskia), which is more accurately translated as "*humility*." Thus, the three things promoted by false wisdom are self-made religion, humility, and severity to the body.

Self-made religion stands in opposition to that which is acceptable to God. Other translations render this as "*will worship*" and "s*elf-imposed worship*." Its source lies within the individual, having been deceived and deluded by a mere appearance of wisdom. Although the individual believes he is on the right path, his worship is idolatrous.

Humility is encouraged and taught as a Christian virtue by the apostles (Eph. 4:2; Phil. 2:3; Col. 3:12; 1 Pet. 5:5) to follow after Christ, to be a good witness, and so forth. However, the humility Paul lists in verse 2:23 is not rooted in the faith that sanctifies. Therefore, any humility derived from a worthless practice has no value. Indeed, many humble persons are not Christians. Their humility is recognized, but it does not confer any spiritual benefit in Christ. That is the humility mentioned in verse 23.

Paul has previously discussed asceticism and advised the Colossians not to submit to it as a form of regulation or legalism. He said this can separate the non-faithful from the faithful if they delve deeply into this practice and find they were never in Christ (Col. 2:18-19). In other translations of verse 23, we find "*neglecting the body*", "*severe treatment of the body*", and "*harsh treatment of the body*". Asceticism lies at the heart of this approach to the body. It has no spiritual value when rooted in legalism or being deceived by human precepts and teachings.

CHAPTER 2
SUMMARY

the hidden treasures in Christ revealed to the saints

Chapter 2 contrasts the riches of the saints' treasures in Christ against the delusions of vain philosophies, plausible arguments, human traditions, and self-made religion. Paul has us look heavenward to behold Jesus Christ in his divine glory, to see the indwelling fullness of God, his supreme authority, and his headship over the church. It is Jesus Christ to whom we have come, receiving all the hidden treasures of wisdom and knowledge in him.

With the love of Christ in our hearts, Paul bids us to love one another with brotherly affection as a family striving together for the faith with a shared and steadfast concern for each other's souls.

Christ, our Redeemer, bore our sins on the cross. Having been united to Christ by the Father's eternal decree, we died with Christ to the power of sin and rose with him to new life. Coming to Christ is the circumcision made without hands and the baptism that saves. The Father blotted out the record of sin that stood against us and counted our debt paid by the blood of Jesus Christ.

Christ, the mystery hidden from the world, has been revealed to the saints with all knowledge and understanding that they may have the full assurance that they are secure in him. There is, therefore, no reason to follow human traditions, plausible arguments, or regulations that have no value or might lead one astray, if not into spiritual ruin.

safeguarding the gospel

Paul's effort was to preserve the purity of the gospel by protecting it from elements foreign to the Christian faith and the true gospel of grace. He did not approach this by addressing all external influences on the saints that might lead them astray, though there were many in the first century, as there are today. The one true gospel that saves is found in the Bible. In Acts 20:24, when speaking to the elders from Ephesus, Paul calls this gospel "*the gospel of the grace of God*," a monergism of grace alone. It is not called the gospel of grace plus human effort, but such synergisms (cooperative means or efforts) have crept into the Christian mindset and have displaced the gospel of grace. In his speech to the Ephesian elders, Paul warned them that from within their own ranks, there would come men who twist things to draw the saints away from Christ. It was an issue in Paul's heart that people find it challenging to believe that salvation is a matter of God's decreed will, that he will save whom he freely and sovereignly chooses to save, freely by grace alone through Jesus Christ alone. He needed to address this with the Colossians and us. Thus, Paul wrote about legalism, circumcision, asceticism, and Gnosticism, which the saints sought as a means of merit-based salvation —a practice that, even today, many beloved saints have reverted to.

God's eternal plan and mystery

To expand on what Paul meant by God's mystery, Ephesians 1:3-10 was explored in detail to establish what God's eternal plan entails, how Jesus Christ is a part of it, and how the saints fit into it. The details brought to light involve election and predestination of the saints, their adoption as sons, the appointment of Jesus Christ, the ordering of Adam's fall, and the free and sovereign mercy of the Father.

infant baptism

In verses 2:11 and 12, the occasion was used to outline the reasons for baptizing the children of believing parents. The primary justification for infant baptism is that the ordinance to circumcise infant sons was not attached to the sign of circumcision but to the everlasting covenant. Thus, the ordinance remains in force, although the sign has been changed to baptism. The sacrament of baptism marks an individual's acceptance into the covenantal community and conveys certain blessings consistent with the covenant; it does not save or unite the individual to Christ.

A key passage in chapter 2:

> *Therefore, as you received Christ Jesus the Lord, so walk in him, rooted and built up in him and established in the faith, just as you were taught, abounding in thanksgiving.* (Col. 2:6-7 ESV)

CHAPTER 3 THE OLD SELF AND THE NEW SELF

INTRODUCTION

Paul has laid a foundation in the knowledge of Christ, concerning his preeminence, glory, rule, and authority, as well as the treasures that the Colossians possess in Christ. Christ has been presented as their creator, redeemer, propitiator, and head of the church to which they have been called.

With gentle yet firm loving kindness, Paul exposed the false beliefs, practices, and teachings circulating among them, threatening to shipwreck their witness and faith.

Based on that strong foundation, what they had been properly taught, and their false practices, the Colossians are called in Chapter 3 to consider their spiritual lives. Paul directs them in the practices of Christian living and spiritual growth. He directs them to what they should set their minds upon and seek after, what they should avoid, and, importantly, what is entailed by living in Christ with a new nature.

Paul touches on topics that lead the reader to delve deeper into understanding God's wrath and man's nature.

The Chapter opens with a conditional phrase that sets the mood of the Chapter, "*If you have been raised with Christ*," Then believers are wonderfully encouraged by the realization of being renewed in the image of their creator.

The second half of the Chapter continues with exhortations regarding Christian conduct in general and within specific relationships, primarily within the family. The instructions on relationships coincide with similar instructions in Paul's letter to the Ephesians and Peter's first letter.

We will encounter an issue related to translation. The phrases "*old self*" and "*new self*" appear throughout the ESV bible. However, the Greek words from which these come are παλαιόν ἄνθρωπον (palaion anthrōpon), properly translated as "*old man*". Also, καινὸν ἄνθρωπον (kainon anthrōpon) is properly translated as "*new man*" (biblehub.com). Changing *man* to *self* forfeits the generality of what is meant by *man*. The meaning is to get at the general condition of man, both before and after regeneration. It is potentially lost when referring to the self. This issue is most evident in Ephesians 2:15. The context of the verse is the mystery of the Gentiles being brought into the covenant of grace and being unified with Jews with peace between them. The verse claims they have been made one new man in the place of the two. In Greek, one new man is ἕνα καινὸν ἄνθρωπον (hena kainon anthrōpon). The verse would make no sense if it were to say they have been made one new self in the place of the two. The ESV translators recognized the general condition of what was being referred to in Greek, but where they thought it was possible, they changed it to *self* in preference to being gender-neutral. Where does this leave us? For this commentary, the word *"self"* will be used to maintain continuity with the ESV in quotes of verses and headings. In the commentary, *man* will be used instead of self to maintain the original meaning of the text.

COLOSSIANS 3:1-4
HIDDEN WITH CHRIST

These verses establish that those called to Christ live in an in-between period of life. Paul makes three points. (1) Having risen with Christ, we should seek things above. Only the saints risen with Christ can do this (Rom. 3:11). (2) Your life, both now and in its eternal state, is currently hidden from you in Christ; that is, you do not fully know what your life is in Christ or what it will be. (3) When Christ appears, your life in him will be fully revealed. We discover wonderful truths to contemplate as we explore these four verses.

Colossians 3:1

risen with Christ

Paul is engaging the Colossians in a sort of trial, like a prosecutor. He began in Chapter 1 by introducing the chief magistrate in the case, Christ. Paul laid out Christ's preeminence in all things, his glory, deity, rule, and authority. Furthermore, he established the immeasurable treasures of being in Christ. In Chapter 2, Paul presented the case against the Colossians. They were following the contrivances of men, vain philosophies, asceticism as a list of ordinances, and dabbling in Gnosticism. Although they possessed the truth of the gospel as brought to them by Epaphras, they were placing their faith in jeopardy by pursuing practices that were not of Christ. Paul has made two critical and soul-searching hypothetical remarks to the Colossians. The first is *If with Christ you died to the elemental spirits of the world*, (Col. 2:20). The second is *If then you have been raised with Christ*, (Col. 3:1). The second of these hypotheticals is conditional on the first; thus, the inclusion of the word "then" in the verse. You can only rise with Christ if you have first been buried, that is, died with Christ. In a way, Paul calls you to the witness stand and asks you to explain the nature of your life, leaving you to draw your own conclusion.

These hypothetical comments have eternal consequences. Someone claiming to be a Christian should know they have both died and been raised with Christ. If a person lives like he has not died with Christ and like he has not been raised with Christ, on what, then, does he base his claim that he is in Christ? Paul does not confront the Colossians by making such a stark accusation. Rather, he leads them to weigh these hypothetical statements and draw their conclusions about how they have been living in relation to the one true faith in Christ and what they have placed at risk. Of course, if this were an actual trial, the Colossians would have to plead guilty, if not by commission, then certainly by tolerating the false practices and teachings that have become prolific among them.

The whole of the believer's experience of and in Christ begins with and hinges upon being raised to new life with Christ. Barring that, there is nothing to be gained in Christ. The certainty of eternal death, as the legal and inevitable penalty for one's sins, remains upon our souls and consciences if we are not raised with Christ. Being raised with Christ is the beginning of living a new life without the power and penalty of sin hanging upon us, in which we live to God and please him. Being raised with Christ is the source of all holiness and true happiness.

seek what is above

The Apostle exhorts those raised with Christ to "s*eek*." It is far from an invitation and not merely an encouragement. Instead, Paul is prompting believers to exercise their new abilities, for it is in the nature of those who have been raised with Christ to seek them. And we may conclude that there are significant benefits for believers who seek. This exhortation to seek things above is directed to those raised with Christ, for only they can do so.

Why does Paul exhort only those raised with Christ to seek things above, where Christ is, and not everyone? The answer lies with what John quoted from Jesus in John 6:44,

> "*No one can come to me unless the Father who sent me draws him. And I will raise him up on the last day"* (ESV).

The Father has drawn to Jesus those raised with Jesus, who now have the capacity and desire to seek heavenly things. Having been raised with Christ, believers are no longer under sin but under grace (Rom. 6:14) and can discern spiritual things. But everyone who remains under the bondage of sin is unable and unwilling to seek God (Rom 3:10-11) and cannot discern spiritual things (1 Cor. 2:14). The bottom line is that unless and until you are buried and raised with Christ, you will never seek heavenly things, including your own salvation. Even those raised with Christ must be reminded that they can, should, and must seek what is above.

Believers are to seek the things that are above and to do so by nature. We are told to seek things above, "*above*" where there is no physical way to reach them. There is no direct access to them. Things "*above*" have a special status; they are in a special category because they are "*above*." They have been set apart or separated from things that are not "*above*" and do not mingle with them. But where is "*above*?" "Above" is where Christ is. We are to seek the things where Christ is. And where is Christ? Christ is seated at the right hand of God. We are to seek the things that are in the very presence of God and are, therefore, holy things. We may even conclude that the Apostle is directing us to seek the very presence of God, which is to seek holiness itself and to strive for the kingdom to which God has transferred us (Col. 1-13).

It may seem that there is a contradiction about seeking and who can seek things about Jesus. If no natural person seeks after God (Rom. 3:11) or can come to Christ (John 6:44), how is it that Jesus calls people to come to him (Matt. 11:28)? Isn't that seeking God? Let's examine the verse.

> *"Come to me, all who labor and are heavy laden, and I will give you rest"* (Matt. 11:28 ESV).

It's not a general invitation. It's addressed to specific people who labor under a heavy burden. It is a welcoming call to those whom God has made aware of the burden of sin and guilt they bear as he draws them to Christ. It is Jesus' pledge that in him they will find rest, the forgiveness of their sin, the removal of their burden, and peace that surpasses understanding. Although they may not yet be aware, those who can come to Jesus have already been given to him by the Father (John 17:2). The Father's drawing people to Jesus, as mentioned in John 6:44, is accomplished in various ways. This is just one of them.

Christ is seated

Paul has previously laid the foundation of our faith, that is, Christ. God has created all things through Christ (Col. 1:16), he is the firstborn over all creation (Col 1:15), the firstborn from the dead (Col.1:18), the head of the church (Col. 1:18), the head of all authority and power (Col. 1:16, 2:10), in him the whole fullness of deity dwells bodily (Col. 1:19, 2:9), he physically died (Col. 1:22) and rose again from among the dead (Col. 1:15). And we have both died with Christ and have been raised with Christ (Col. 2:12). Now Paul brings our minds into the very throne room of God where Christ is seated at God's right hand. Attributing a right side to God, or a right hand, is an anthropomorphism. It is used to explain that Christ has the highest honor and position.

There are complexities we may never fully understand. The fact that Jesus Christ died on the cross as both man and God is one such complexity. We know it was a physical body that died, and it was the human part that possessed the capacity for death, yet the divine essence, the whole fullness of deity, was never separated from the human part. Likewise, as Paul writes of Christ seated at the right hand of God, we understand this is a position of equality with God, which must be attributed to Christ's divine essence. Yet, human nature is ever-present in the divine Person of Jesus Christ since the incarnation.

It is also challenging to ascribe nuances to how Christ is referred to in Scripture. Sometimes, it is either Christ, Jesus Christ, Christ Jesus, or Jesus. Sometimes, the word Lord is included. In verse 1, Paul writes "Christ," which I believe is meant to lead us to his divine nature seated at God's right hand. Which, in addition, should not be taken literally as being seated. It's a metaphor and another anthropomorphism. Paul is not suggesting that this is a new development between the Father and the Son, nor implying that the Son is only now on the right side of God since he has risen as Jesus Christ. It is an eternal position of relationship between the Father and the Son. Even during his earthly ministry, the divine nature of the Son, Christ, was on the right side of God. It's a statement about relationship and equality, not limiting Christ's immanence.

The metaphor regards being seated. Sitting indicates a particular and lesser state or degree of action, but not necessarily inaction. As the head of the church, Christ became Jesus Christ (Phil 2:8). Having completed the work of his earthly ministry, Christ can now be seated. Nevertheless, Christ mediates between God and man and holds all things together (Col. 1-17).

Colossians 3:2

set your mind on the right things

Paul concludes by using hypotheticals to prompt the Colossians to reflect on how they live in light of their profession of faith in Christ. He now addresses them as though they have died and been raised with Christ and proceeds to instruct them on how their lives in Christ are to be ordered.

To set their minds on things above is to contemplate the presence of God and the blessedness of being in his presence. The more we dwell in thought upon heavenly things, the less precious earthly things become to us. It is now your nature, having died with Christ, to be dead to the things of this world. The old nature sought after the things of the earth that appealed to the flesh. Although we remain in the world, we are no longer of the world. James also exhorted us to keep from being polluted by the world (Jas. 1:27). Things above are holy because they are with God. Things on earth are earthly and pass away. We cannot hold onto things that pass away, but the things that remain are those that are above. While earthly treasures eventually pass away, treasures in heaven do not (Matt. 6:19-20).

For a moment, let us examine this verse in the context of the two verses that follow. Since our life is hidden with Christ, it behooves us to contemplate whatever we can concerning that life. We know Christ will appear on the last day to judge the world and assemble the saints. We will then appear among the saints with Christ in glory, see him face to face, and know fully what we are (1 Cor. 13:12; 1 John 3:2). Certainly, that includes being revealed to all creation as the sons of God. Our blessed hope is to meet Christ in the air, be changed into his likeness, made complete, presented to the Father holy and blameless, and receive the crown of life, an eternal kingdom, and an imperishable inheritance. Though our life is hidden with Christ, we can perceive it dimly now and, in so doing, elevate our minds from the earthly to things above (1 Cor. 13:12).

The things we set our hope on result from the condition of our hearts. Paul is elevating our hope to things in heaven, to eternal things, to a life with Christ that we can only see now in part. But suppose our hope in Christ is fixated on this earthly life. In that case, if we don't perceive the benefits of Christ beyond our current situation and expect all the benefits of Christ to be poured out on us today to secure all happiness now, we reduce ourselves to someone more like a prodigal son than a saint. We must set our hope on a future resurrection, not on this earthly life, and live for that day and the inheritance now being kept in heaven (1 Pet. 1:4).

Peter and Paul agree that believers should maintain a sober mind in all things (e.g., 2 Tim. 4:5;1 Pet. 1:13). Having a sober mind encompasses being mindful of eternal things, things above, and the coming revelation of Jesus Christ. 2 Timothy 1:7 may be translated as in the ESV.

> *for God gave us a spirit not of fear but of power and love and self-control (sound mind)* (ESV).

Where *sound mind* has been shown as an alternate translation of σωφρονισμοῦ (sōphronismou) (biblehub.com), the ESV renders it as *self-control*. That is a valid literal translation, but it seems to miss the proper context of the Timothy Chapter. The context of 2 Timothy Chapter 1 is Paul's instructions and encouragement to Timothy regarding his faith, the ministry of proclaiming the gospel truth, and a brief review of the fundamentals of the faith. It seems that *"sound mind"* as rendered in the KJV is a better-suited translation in this instance than *"self-control"*, concerning context. When considering 2 Timothy 1:7 in this way, we can begin to understand how God gives us a spirit possessing a sound mind by first directing us on what to think about. The one who heeds what is written in Colossians 3:1-2 would be more apt to possess a spiritually sound mind in time.

Verses 1 and 2 of this Chapter direct us to think heavenward. Certainly, anyone can think about the concept of heaven, but Paul has presented specific things for believers to set their minds on, things nonbelievers may only scoff at. Among the consequences of having risen with Christ is a changed mind. Formerly, we walked in the futility of our minds (Eph. 4:17), unable to discern spiritual things (1 Cor. 2:14), such as contemplating things above. But now we have the mind of Christ (1 Cor. 2:16). Having such a mind, we can not only think about things where Christ is, but hope in them with full assurance and grow into spiritual maturity. To that end, Paul has also written to let our thinking be mature (perfect or complete) (1 Cor. 14:20).

Colossians 3:3
hidden with Christ

Verse 3 is wonderful, but none of the main English Bibles render the verb correctly when translating the Greek text. From biblehub.com, the interlinear verse is

> *"You have died for and the life of you has been hidden with [the] Christ in [the] God"*

The two definite articles have been included above because they appear in the Greek text but not in the interlinear English. "*You have died*" specifies a factual, singular action completed at some past time. The "*you*" is plural, indicating all believers. Thus, the phrase can be understood as *"the saints have died with Christ*." The word *"for*" connects this verse to why the saints can and should set their minds on things above. Verses 2 and 3 go together as if they were one sentence.

There are four persons referred to in this text. They are you (plural), Christ, God the Father, and the writer of the verse. The verb "*has been hidden*" denotes a present and ongoing action initiated in the past. The saints' lives are the object of the action, but Christ and God perform and receive the action. It is correct to say that the saints' lives are hidden with Christ, but this has always been the case. In particular, the word translated as *"in*" introduces the concept of instrumentality, meaning that Christ is the means by which the action is carried out on behalf of the Father. Finally, the verb indicates that this is the perspective of the one who wrote this statement, Paul, via the Holy Spirit.

"*You have died*" is true only of the elect who have been born again. Paul is being gracious and is not confirming election or salvation. The remainder of the verse is also valid for only the elect. We may consider the question: when were the saints' lives hidden in Christ? Previously, we saw that the Father has elected and predestined all those who are to be adopted as sons through Jesus Christ. Thus, the elect and Christ have been united from all eternity by decree. The elect were to be made blameless and holy and, through Jesus Christ, redeemed by his blood, which is the forgiveness of sin.

Thus, Paul can say their lives have been hidden with Christ because they have been united to him pretemporally. Let's note that the elect's lives are not hidden in Christ; they are hidden with Christ. We know Christ is God's mystery, and it is to be revealed when and to whom God chooses. And what we will be in Christ has yet to be revealed until Christ is revealed in all glory (1 John 3:2). But make no mistake, you may consider this applies to you only if you have died with Christ. Even our life with Christ is, to some degree, a mystery (1 Cor. 15:51). If you are still, as you are reading this, a nonbeliever, perhaps you are among the elect. Then, your life is hidden with Christ, and a day will dawn, during which you will supernaturally die and rise in Christ to be born again by the grace and power of God.

There are consequences to consider. Since our true life is hidden with Christ, why would we seek life elsewhere? We are told that our life is with the author of life, who gives life abundantly (John 10:10). If we do not recognize the importance and implications of that, we will be susceptible to searching for life through things that have no life in them, like human precepts, traditions of men, vain philosophies, asceticism, and Gnosticism. Keep this in mind, as it offers great assurance. Paul did not tell us that our lives might be or could be hidden with Christ; they were hidden with Christ when the Father freely and sovereignly, by decree, predestined the saints to be adopted as sons to himself through Jesus Christ (Eph. 1:5).

Colossians 3:4

when Christ appears

Your life now, being hidden with Christ in God, is spiritual, and you live according to the Spirit. But there is more to be said about verse 3 as it leads us into verse 4. What do we know about this life that is hidden with Christ? Very little. The Apostle John tells us that what we will be has not been revealed except that when Christ appears, we will be like him. He gives us a reason for what we will become: we will see Jesus Christ as he is. Just seeing Jesus as he is, unveiled, will transform the saints into his likeness. Until then, it remains hidden. (1 John 3:2).

Paul is portraying our present state as an in-between state. We are dead to the life we once lived. Now, we live to God in this present state. But our eternal state, that which has not been revealed, is hidden as a mystery with Christ in much the same way Christ himself is a mystery, even to us, until we see him as he is, as John informs us. Like John, Paul provides a glimpse into this in verse 4. Paul tells us that Christ is our life, but he means this in a different sense. Whatever there is of life in us is of Christ, by Christ, for Christ, and for his glory. The life that will be revealed is that kind of life, but in abundance. He amplified this in 1 Corinthians Chapter 13:10-12. We are incomplete now, but will be complete and perfect (Matt. 5:48). What we see of our lives in Christ now is likened to seeing ourselves in a mirror. It is our faces that we see, which are still parts of physical bodies of flesh and blood. Our bodies will change when we see Christ face-to-face. What we know now of our lives in Christ is merely a part of its whole reality, but then we will know our lives in Christ even as our lives are already known by Christ, and we will not need a mirror to understand that we are no longer flesh and blood.

As we have said before, our physical bodies will also be changed, even as our souls have already been changed. In another place, Paul told us there would be changes to our bodies before we receive our inheritance. Our bodies will cease to be of flesh and blood and become imperishable spiritual bodies raised in glory and power (1 Cor. 15:42-44, 50). When Christ's glory is revealed (1 Pet. 4:13), we will appear or be revealed with Christ as the sons of God. (Rom. 8:19, 1 Pet. 5:1). This seems to be as far as we can delve into what lies ahead, for what lies ahead is hidden with Christ in God. But we can be sure of this; it is fixed and certain. Because we have died to this world and live to God in Christ, we should set our minds on things above and seek what is holy. The following section will further instruct us in this matter by enumerating how this applies to our daily lives.

COLOSSIANS 3:5-7
THE OLD SELF AND THE NEW SELF – PART 1

Paul connects the previous content of his letter with the present. He has just written the underlying principle and logical reason for the exhortation he is about to make. Paul does not use the argument, "Do this because I, an Apostle of Christ, say so." Instead, he leads us to Christ, the head of all authority, power, and wisdom, and makes his case before Christ. Paul then turns to us and invites us, as it were, to deny the validity of his argument. We cannot. Our thoughts and emotions have been drawn to Christ, and the longing of our hearts now is to live according to that which pleases our beloved Redeemer. The source of this ability is embedded in the case Paul has just made. Christ is the source of such ability. We can heed Paul's exhortation if we have died and been raised with Christ. If so, then our lives are hidden with Christ. It is a fallacy to think someone could please God otherwise. It boils down to this: the repudiation of Paul's forthcoming exhortation is a repudiation of Christ and an affirmation that we have no part in him.

Paul has already established that there are things above and on earth. The things above are in the very presence of God, and we are to set our minds on them and seek them. Here, Paul is presenting how this is accomplished. It begins by realizing that we have become contaminated by earthly things enumerated in verse 5. They are not merely external influences but reside within us as members of our bodies. We should regard this list as a list of categories, perhaps not a complete one. Mortify, which means to subdue, is actually "*put to death*" in the original Greek.

These verses reflect our former lives, but they are more than mere reflections; they present a list of temptations that will trouble us as long as we remain in the flesh. They are why God's wrath will come at the appointed time. But to the praise and glory of God, we no longer walk and live in them. We are greatly comforted by the acknowledgment that the wrath of God is no longer for those who live by the Spirit and have put off the deeds of their former lives (Rom. 8:3; Gal. 5:25).

Colossians 3:5

one new nature, the old has passed away

Here, contradictory concepts of the old nature emerge. Regarding the old nature, the nature of the natural man, there are two points of view. (1) The old nature is dead and no longer exists. (2) The old nature is only weakened, and our new nature must kill it and take its place.

The confusion arises because we tend to think of human nature as a thing. Paul even metaphorically describes putting off the old man and putting on the new man, much like changing a garment (Eph. 4:20-23, Col. 3:9-10). In the Ephesians passage, Paul specifies that the old man refers to one's former way of living, while the new man was created in the likeness of God, in righteousness and holiness. Paul repeats this metaphor in Colossians 3:9-10, which we will get to in a moment.

It is more appropriate to consider human nature as a manner of living derived from the faculties of the soul. As humans, we have both physical and spiritual limitations and abilities. An unregenerate man, by nature, is wholly disposed only to sin until he is born again (Rom. 6:6; Gal. 4:3, 8; Eph. 4:22). His manner of living, by nature, is to do evil all the time and to be subject to the wrath of God (Rom. 2:5, 5:9). His soul is so influenced by the desires of the flesh that it succumbs to them. Likewise, the natural man's will is enslaved to sin as much as the rest of him (Col. 1:21; 3 John 1:11). Paul bluntly states that before an elect person is drawn by the Father to Christ they lived, according to their nature at that time, in the passions of the flesh and the desires of the body and mind (will) such that they were children of wrath (Eph. 2:3). In other words, our unregenerate souls were in submission to the desires of the flesh and we "*lived in the passions of our flesh*." Living in the passions of our flesh was our old nature. The natural man exists in contrast to the spiritual man (1 Cor. 2:14-15).

When a person is born again, a spiritual transformation occurs to the degree that they may be called a new creation (2 Cor. 5:17). The old nature is gone, and a new nature exists; they do not coexist. In other words, by being born again, the conduct and focus of our lives have undergone a significant change. When we lived in the flesh, we set our minds on the things of the flesh; we were hostile to God and lived under the law of sin and death (Rom. 8:2-5). But now we live in the Spirit (Rom. 8:9). Although our bodies are still [spiritually] dead due to sin, they will be raised and given life by the Spirit of Christ in us (Rom. 8:10-11; Phil. 3:21). Romans 8:10 informs us that our physical bodies remain corrupt, not yet having been changed, that is, reconciled to God. Until our physical bodies are redeemed and reconciled, they will continue to afflict us with corrupt passions and desires (Gal. 5:17). But our souls, having been regenerated, are no longer enslaved by these passions and desires, having received the ability and willingness to resist, even to mortify them through atrophy and redirect our lives toward God. Thus, the old nature is gone, and Paul can exhort us not to gratify the passions and desires of the flesh (Rom 13:14), which only serves to strengthen them.

Since being born again, the Holy Spirit imparts increasing holiness, righteousness, and godliness to our new nature. The process is known as ***progressive sanctification***. During sanctification, the passions and desires that once enslaved us gradually lose their influence, though they will always remain present to some degree. The apostle calls us to actively engage in their mortification, an ability of the new nature that every saint possesses.

Jesus had to deal with the same infirmities of the flesh that we face today. In every substantive way, Jesus was tempted as we are tempted, yet he never sinned (Heb. 4:15). Paul refers to Jesus being "*in the likeness of sinful flesh*" (Rom. 8:3; Phil. 2:7). Paul goes on to say that the body is [spiritually] dead because of sin (Rom. 8:10). The point here is the capacity of the flesh to defile a person in nature and soul. It is this capacity for which the flesh is called sinful. In another place, Paul tells us to "*cleanse ourselves from all the defilements of the flesh and spirit*" (2 Cor. 7:1). It is essentially the same as "*put to death what is earthly in you.*" The problem is that what is earthly in us, including our flesh since it is derived from Adam, the man of dust (1 Cor. 15:47-49), can defile us. Romans 8:3 is about Jesus' life. The law could not free us from sin because it could not defeat the power of the flesh to defile us. Therefore, the law could not remove our corruption. However, the flesh tried in diverse ways but did not defile Jesus. Because Jesus was sent in the flesh and was not defiled by the flesh, he defeated the power of the flesh to rule. Thus, Jesus condemned sin in the flesh, in his own flesh, and fulfilled the law of righteousness for all who now walk in the Spirit and not in the flesh (Rom. 8:3-4).

The phrase "*what is earthly in you*" refers to all things that are not of God, stemming from our darkness and corruption by which we were previously enslaved. As the phrase points out, their influence is still with us as they are "*in*" us and continue to defile us if permitted (Gal. 5:17). Since we are told to put them to death, we should not deceive ourselves with such false claims as, "this is the way God made me," or "there is nothing I can do." The Father has delivered us from the corruption in the world (2 Pet. 1:4) and given us the ability to overcome the defiling influences that remain (1 John 5:4-5). Our deliverance from corruption and its eternal penalty was otherwise impossible, but we were not delivered to ourselves; we were delivered to the everlasting kingdom of our Lord Jesus Christ (Col. 1:13), not partway, not in increments, but entirely all at once. Peter issued a notable warning to everyone who believes they have been delivered from the domain of darkness and liberated from the world's corrupting influences, yet continues to embrace and live in them. He tells us that if this is your case, your final end will be worse than before (2 Pet. 2:20) because you were never in Christ and made a mockery of his atonement. As we move to the next verse, we will see Paul issuing his own warning.

In 2 Peter 3:14, to highlight the importance of putting off the old nature and mortifying the influences of the flesh, we are told to be diligent about our faith and manner of life as we wait for the coming of the Lord so that on that day, the Father will find us to be like Jesus Christ, without "s*pot or blemish and at peace*" (ESV). If we are found otherwise, I suggest we would be like the man who showed up at the wedding feast of the king's son without wedding apparel (Matt. 22:11-14), as referenced in the parable that parallels the Marriage Feast of the Lamb (Rev. 19:6-9).

sexual immorality

Should we fail to grasp the meaning of earthly, Paul presents a list of categories of sins that represent what is earthly. Paul's effort is to bring us to the realization that being delivered from the domain of darkness only prevents the darkness from re-enslaving us. However, the only way to know that is true for us is to acknowledge that darkness still influences us and that we must actively make an effort to put to death and cleanse ourselves of its defilements. Paul is not offering us a choice of which influences to mortify and which to embrace. Paul's exhortation is straightforward: put what is earthly in you to death.

Paul has been addressing the Colossian believers collectively about their calling and manner of life. He is endeavoring to elevate their understanding of what it means to be a faithful Christian and will proceed with instructions concerning the Christian life. In Paul's letter to the Ephesians, he covers the same issues of sin as mentioned here, but adds another dimension. We present a poor witness of the gospel and grace of Jesus Christ to nonbelievers if we continue to live in the defilements of the world (Eph. 5:3) while claiming to be Christians. His remedy is to live as imitators of God (Eph. 5:1).

Colossians 3:6
the wrath of God

We should not infer from Paul's statement that true believers in Christ will receive the wrath of God under any circumstances. When Paul wrote to the Ephesians, he told them they were once children of wrath, which implies they are now saints and no longer children of wrath (Eph. 2:3). Paul is telling us that God's wrath is coming upon those who live in the passions of the flesh, those categories of sin listed in the previous verse. The desires of the flesh are the source of disobedience and misery, and no man is free from them during this life. Because of them, humankind is divided between those who walk in them and those who, by grace, do not. Yet, there is a warning to saints in this verse. Saints need to be circumspect about the way they live and honor Christ. Faithful saints will endeavor to mortify the passions of the flesh, all that is earthly in them. Although they will never fully succeed, their reasonable efforts testify and bear witness that they are in Christ.

Scripture approaches this in other ways as well. Addressing who will receive God's wrath. John cut through the noise to state,

> " *whoever does not obey the Son shall not see life, but the wrath of God remains on him*" (John 3:36 ESV).

In the same verse, John says, "*Whoever believes in the Son has eternal life.*" The verse appears to suggest that simply believing in the Son results in eternal life. That is true, provided we understand what John means by the term *"believing."* This belief produces obedience, and thus, we are led to Paul's statement in Colossians about putting to death the things that are earthly in us or suffering the wrath of God, as he and John inform us. It is not obedience that leads to eternal life in some meritorious way. It is a genuine belief that is received as a free, gracious gift of God's mercy that produces within us a new nature, driven to honor God with our lives through obedience.

Those who believe in the Son have eternal life. They now have it as an inheritance. It is legally and substantially theirs. Such belief is reckoned in this life by seeing that it leads to living in a manner worthy of Christ, putting off the old man and putting on the new man. True belief is manifested in good works that are the products of grace having transformed the heart of the person (Jas. 2:17). Without such belief, the wrath of God remains on that person, and that person shall not only not even see or experience eternal life, but will never see or experience even the lesser spiritual life enjoyed by those born again. Remember that wrath *remains* on those who do not believe in Christ, indicating that it is not removed or removable. Saying that wrath *remains* on them indicates that it was upon all persons, even believers in Christ, until it was removed by grace (Eph. 2:3).

Both Paul and John testify to the wonderous grace of God that draws the elect to Christ (John 6:44) and instills in them belief and faith in Jesus Christ (Eph. 2:8). The elect, who have been born again, who have died and risen with Christ face no condemnation (John 3:18; Rom. 8:1). However, all those who live in darkness, who abide in the things within themselves that are earthly stand under judgment because their deeds are evil (John 3:19). We should see that the coming wrath of God that Paul has written about is a reference to a future judgment. The wrath of God and the judgment it leads to are no longer upon true believers. But nonbelievers are already living with the wrath of God upon them in a state of condemnation, which is a state of confirmed guilt requiring the punishment of death awaiting only its inevitable execution (John 3:18). This is the dividing line between eternal life and eternal death - the nature of the individual. Those who by nature love darkness rather than light (John

3:19), who live in the works of the flesh (Rom. 8:4; Eph. 2:3; Gal. 5:19), who reject Christ (Heb. 12:25; 1 Pet. 2:4, 7), remain under the judgment (John 3:36), which is to say they are condemned.

Paul writes in Colossians 3:6 that the wrath of God is coming. We should understand that the fullness of God's wrath is coming because his wrath is already upon the wicked. It is revealed from heaven, even now, against all unrighteousness and ungodliness (Rom. 1:18). Even now they receive in their flesh a foretaste of the fullness of God's wrath (Rom. 1:27). The sentence of death, which they have lived under, will be executed on the last day when Christ appears in glory and from that time on they will experience only the fullness of God's wrath. The Romans Chapter goes on to explain how evil people plunge themselves deeper and deeper into the depravity of sin as God gradually withdraws his restraining influences.

God's wrath is not coming to those in Christ. God's mercy and grace have spared them. Christ took the full weight of divine judgment upon himself for those being saved. He was crushed for their iniquity and healed his people by his wounds. There is no cheap grace. God's wrath is still coming on the unbelieving world, on the sons of disobedience, those who by nature are children of wrath (Eph. 2:2-3). Paul makes this point unmistakably clear: God's wrath is coming, and no power on earth or in heaven can prevent it.

Perhaps some nonbeliever, while contemplating the coming judgment and wrath of God, is moved to a deep concern for their eternal soul. Then, perhaps they will pass it off as mere foolishness, thinking that will be the end of it. And so the concern passes. On the other hand, if they are among the elect, that concern may be the voice of the Holy Spirit drawing them to Christ. Many people have been saved by reading warnings about the coming wrath of God upon all who do not obey the gospel of Jesus Christ.

Colossians 3:7
a reminder

Paul is clear and to the point. You also walked in the very things for which God's wrath is coming upon the world, just like those upon whom the wrath remains (Eph. 4:22). Once is not a moment in time but an expanse of time during which you walked in them because you lived in them according to your nature at that time. But even verse

7 implies a change has taken place. Paul anchors the Colossians' minds on what manner of life they lived before coming to Christ and the horrible end that awaits all who continue to live without Christ. We were all people of God's wrath, but we are now people of God's grace.

the church and the works of the flesh, a broader understanding

The letter to the Colossians prompts us to reflect on our past and how we formerly practiced the works of the flesh. What is earthly in us (Col. 3:5) is also referred to as the passions of the flesh (Eph. 2:3; 1 Pet. 2:11), the works of the flesh (Gal. 5:19), the works of darkness (Rom. 13:12; Eph. 5:11), and corruption (Gal. 6:8; 2 Pet. 1:4). Colossians was written to a young church in need of correction and guidance. Some issues are lightly addressed, giving readers a partial view of what is more extensively presented elsewhere in Scripture. Because people continue to practice earthly things, Colossians states that the wrath of God is coming. Colossians 3:5-6 can be viewed as a summary of the broader discussion of God's wrath coming upon people who abide in earthly things, the works of the flesh.

Chapter 3 of Colossians is aimed at preparing new believers who are struggling with their faith. They need to develop the proper focus of their lives, the manner in which they walk, and participation among God's people, the church. To that end, Paul has them recall their former sinful lives and the divine wrath they have escaped by having been called to Christ. However, there is much more in Scripture about this that we need to explore to grasp the gravity of what Paul is only summarizing for the Colossians. Colossians makes it clear how individuals are to deal with earthly things and what is personally at risk, but the broader issue also bears upon the church, which we need to understand.

The concept of God's wrath has two parts. There is wrath that is presently being manifested (Rom. 1:18) and a wrath yet to come (Rom. 2:5). What is coming is the fullness of God's wrath on the day of judgment. It is the fullness of wrath referred to in Colossians 3:6. Anyone who scoffs at this should read Chapter 3 of Peter's second epistle. The concepts of God's wrath and a coming judgment are not relics of an archaic culture. Judgment is real, pending, and as ready today as ever (1 Pet. 4:5). So, we, the church, should be aware of what Scripture informs us about these matters of earthly things and the coming wrath.

God does not deal lightly with unforgiven sin. The list of sins in verse 5 closely parallels the sins listed in Romans 1:18-32. There, Paul describes what God does with people who dishonor God as God. He gives them over to the inclinations of their own nature, allowing them to progressively dive deeper into their own depravity until there is nothing left for them except the fullness of divine wrath. In the Romans passage, approving those who practice the works of the flesh is just as unrighteous as practicing them. Both have a divine sentence of death hanging over them. We should realize it would be more egregious before God when this approval is in the name of the Lord. One of the points of Romans 1:32 is that all people are aware of God's righteous decree in this matter, and thus we, that is the church, should realize the righteousness of God's judgment against them.

The works of the flesh are also listed in Galatians 5:19-21 along with an expression of God's righteous judgment against them. These works are evident to all people for what they are (Gal. 5:19). They are surely evident to men who lead and minister to God's people. The Galatians passage, v. 21, specifies that those who practice such things are barred from the kingdom of God. The alternative is perdition, eternal death, hell. Anyone who ministers to God's people should read Chapter 2 of Peter's second epistle, which was written to warn the church about people who promote the works of the flesh, especially among God's people. Anyone who abides in these works of the flesh or gives approval to them heaps judgment upon themselves without excuse, for they have knowingly engaged in them for what they are. Should they also claim to have fellowship with God, they are liars and there is no truth in them (1 John 1:6).

Unbelievers still walk in the passions of the flesh just as believers did before being saved. Thus, what is said about those who walk in the passions of the flesh, who practice the works of the flesh, applies to unbelievers, people who have no fellowship with God (1 John 1:6). 2 Corinthians 6:14-18 addresses this issue head-on. The church is not to be mixed with unbelievers. The passage makes its point by contrasting righteousness with lawlessness, light with darkness, Christ with Belial, believers with unbelievers, and the temple of God with idols. Thus, until a person has been delivered from darkness (Col. 1:13) and has escaped the corruption that is in the world (2 Pet. 1:4), they have no place among God's people. The coming wrath of God against all unrighteousness (Rom. 1:18) continues to be Paul's warning to the world. It is not an outdated relic of the past.

COLOSSIANS 3:8-11
THE OLD SELF AND THE NEW SELF – PART 2

Paul has presented a then-and-now scenario of how our lives have been transformed by grace. Then, you lived in a manner worthy of God's wrath. Then, you were without Christ in your life. Now you are in Christ, and Christ is your life. Paul likens this to an old man and a new man. The old has been put away, and the new has been put on, but since we remain in the flesh, there are lingering effects of the old man to be put off and new abilities of the new man we need to exercise. This is Paul's way of exhorting us to be proactive in our sanctification, something we cannot initiate but can only engage in by God's power graciously working in us through a living faith.

Colossian 3:8-9
exhortation

But now, you no longer walk in the ways of the flesh, driven by sensual desires and passions. So, you must put them off, mortify them. Paul's mood is imperative. The list of things to put off is partial, but it makes its point. We are not given the option to choose one, two, or several sins to mortify while living in the others.

- Anger: hostility towards another person that is not conducive to their best interests, impairs fellowship and kindness, and is sustained and cultivated.
- Wrath: a form of human anger that is forceful and vindictive.
- Malice: an attitude that seeks another's injury or spite.
- Slander: an unwarranted statement that harms another's reputation. It does not have to be false to be malicious. It is just harmful and unnecessary.

- Obscene language: We are aware of its nature and the increasing prevalence in today's society. It does not emerge from godliness. It emerges from the inclinations left behind by our old nature. We cannot progress in godliness if we hold on to former inclinations. It is also disruptive to the fellowship of believers.
- Do not lie to one another: Do not attempt to gain an advantage of any sort over another by any means of deception. It also includes shaving the truth when it is to one's advantage.

Notice that there is a development in Paul's list of things to put off. He began in verse 5 with sins that are so egregious and flow from an inherent corruption of one's nature that they cannot be hidden. The sins now listed in verse 8 are interpersonal sins that continue to harass true believers who have put off the more egregious sins of verse 5, yet must be mortified. Paul will address these sins in further detail.

Colossians 3:9-10
the old man and the new man

The old man was spiritually dead and uncircumcised in the flesh (Col. 2:13), which is unholy and sinful. Let's outline the characteristics of the old man, also the natural man, as they are described in Scripture. The old man, or the natural man:

- is dead in trespasses and sin (Eph. 2:1),
- follows the prince of this world (Eph. 2:2),
- is a son of disobedience (Eph. 2:2),
- is a child of wrath (Eph. 2:3),
- can't come to Jesus (John 6:44, 6:65),
- suppresses the truth (Rom. 1:18),
- has a futile mind and dark heart (Rom. 1:21),
- doesn't seek after God (Rom. 3:11),
- is enslaved to sin (Rom. 6:6, 11),
- falls short of the glory of God (Rom. 3:23),
- is separated from Christ (Eph. 2:12),

- regards spiritual things as folly and has no spiritual discernment (1 Cor. 2:14), and
- does the works of the flesh (Gal. 5:19-21).

From Colossians Chapter 2, we see that initially the saints, as their former selves, were dead in their trespasses, sin, and state of uncircumcision (v. 13). However, by the power of God (vs. 12, 13) the saints have received Jesus Christ (v. 8), have been filled in him (v. 10), have been circumcised with the circumcision of Christ (v. 11), buried and raised with him (v. 12), and made alive with him (v. 13). The phrases "*you (plural) have put off the old self,*" and "*have put on the new self*" are not describing anything that the saints have done by or to themselves. The change from the old to the new man was accomplished and done to them by the power of God for his purpose, according to his sovereign will. It is another way of expressing that they have died and risen with Christ, while specifying that a transformation has occurred, requiring the work of a creator for what emerges. It occurred when the Father transferred them from the domain of darkness to the eternal kingdom of his Son (Col. 1:13), when, by his divine power, they escaped the corruption that is in the world (2 Pet. 1:4). The new man, does not coexist with the old man and is so radically different that he is called a new creation (2 Cor. 5:17; Gal. 6:15).

Believers have one nature, a new nature with new abilities, as established by verses 9 and 10. A believer is also a spiritual man as opposed to the natural man of his former life (1 Cor. 2:14-15). Verse 9 declares that the old nature has been put away, while verse 10 declares that the new nature has taken its place. These events have occurred and are done.

In context, "nature" or "self" refers to how we live in accordance with our spiritual abilities and inclinations. Therefore, we are discussing the soul and not the physical body. The spiritual aspects of nature lie in the soul and are manifested by the soul's abilities. The old nature is subject to the sensual desires of the flesh, which do not change during this life. They dominate the soul as a slave of sin that cannot extricate itself from its bondage and so is spiritually dead, alienated from God (Eph. 4:18). The exhortation Paul is giving cannot be complied with by the old nature and spiritually dead soul. The old nature is incapable of complying, so the soul is incompatible with compliance. By nature, the temptations and desires of the flesh enslaved the soul to sin. However, the new nature that is spiritually alive, while still capable of yielding to the temptations of the body and yielding to former inclinations, is not enslaved to them and is now capable of resisting.

Only the person possessing a new nature in Christ can respond to Paul's exhortation. But he does not do so all at once. When a person is raised with Christ with a new nature, that nature must be renewed in holiness and righteousness (Rom. 12:2; 2 Cor. 4:16; Eph. 4:23; Col. 3:10). The new nature requires teaching, learning, and sanctification. The knowledge that the soul must gain will conform its nature to the likeness of Christ, who created it in His image (1 Cor. 15:49). It is essential to understand that our new nature is not being restored to the prelapsarian nature of Adam, for Adam's state of holiness was mutable. In contrast, the final condition of the believer will be immutable (1 Cor. 15:49). Even now, being dead to sin and alive to God in Christ, the saints have already entered the eternal life of the soul, one of God's irrevocable gifts (Rom. 11:29).

Because you possess this new nature, you can put off all the earthly things in you, and as you work to do so, they will atrophy. Your success will always be achieved by the gracious work of the Holy Spirit, but faith that works for that purpose is a necessary factor.

Colossians 3:11

no ethnic benefits, only impartiality

Paul's purpose in verse 11 is twofold. First, it establishes that the exhortation to exercise godly living by putting to death the inclinations of our former self, which he has just presented, is not just another ordinance of men of no spiritual benefit. The outward acts of compliance with vain ordinances and the traditions that separate one background from another are among the earthly things to be put away so that we may live outwardly and inwardly to God through Jesus Christ. Our backgrounds afford us no advantage in Christ, nor do they necessarily hinder us.

When we come to Christ in faith, regardless of our background, we have all come to the same faith, the same Lord, and are filled with the same Spirit, and are engrafted into one body, the church (Eph. 4:4-6).

The second purpose found in verse 11 is that by the grace and power of the indwelling Christ, believers can mortify the things within them that are earthly, put them away, seek the things that are above, and set their minds on heavenly things (Rom. 8:10). But any raw outward acts of compliance with Paul's exhortation to mortify what is earthly in us are of no spiritual value in and of themselves. To be of spiritual benefit, they must arise from an inward desire for a transformed nature by the Spirit, by having Christ in us, and the new nature of our hearts (Rom. 2:28-29).

Take note of the phrase, *"but Christ is all."* On one level, Christ is all things conducive to building his church and more.

- Christ is the firstborn over all creation. (1:15)
- Christ created all things. (1:16)
- Christ holds all things together. (1:17)
- Christ is preeminent over all things. (1:18)
- Christ is the Head of the church. (1:18)
- Christ is the firstborn from the dead. (1:18)
- Christ is the reconciler of all things. (1:20)
- Christ is the head of all rule and authority. (2:10)
- Christ is the redeemer of the elect. (2:14)
- Christ is seated at the right hand of God. (3:1)
- Christ is our life; our life is hidden in Christ. (3:3,4)

However, Paul has something more profound in mind. In his Ephesians letter, addressed to Gentiles, he explains that Christ has brought Jews and Gentiles together as:

> "*he might create in himself one new man in place of the two, so making peace, and might reconcile us both to God in one body through the cross*" (Eph. 2:15-16 ESV).

In his letter to Colossians, Paul applies the concept of bringing two groups together by expanding it to encompass bringing many groups together. All the saints in the population groups named in Colossians

3:11 have been brought together as "*one new man.*" Paul is saying that Christ is in all of these without partiality and has brought them together in himself. We could express Paul's meaning of "*Christ is all, and in all*" by paraphrasing Ephesians 2:15-16 to read,

> he [Christ] might create in himself one new man in place of the many, so making peace, and might reconcile us all to God in one body through the cross. Christ has put away all that made us distinct identity groups, and now we possess a common identity in Christ, having come to one faith and one body by one Lord and reconciler of all things unto God. (an adaptation of Eph. 2:15-16)

Paul closes this section with the affirmation that Christ is *"in all."* Let's specify what this does not mean. It does not mean that Christ is in or ontologically all of creation. That's pantheism. It does not mean that Christ indwells all people. That's universalism. It does mean that the Spirit of Christ indwells all the regenerate elect believers (Rom. 8:9), whomever they may be, as exemplified by the foregoing list.

COLOSSIANS 3:12-13
THE OLD SELF AND THE NEW SELF – PART 3

Paul addresses us with the special status of being God's chosen people. Christians, whoever they are and wherever they may be, are God's chosen people. True Christians are holy and beloved. So, if you regard yourself as a Christian, live like you are holy and beloved of God; live as though that has meaning to you and is precious to you. We are reminded that Christians are not islands of faith unto themselves; each is part of a larger body, the church, and expected to be active participants. This exemplifies what is meant by putting on the new man. The old man, that lived in the desires and passions of the flesh, was corrupt in all aspects of his being, unable to please God or incline himself toward God, is gone. The saints no longer live in the old nature; the new nature has come, but it must be trained, exercised, and sanctified as the lingering temptations of the flesh are mortified. We are also reminded that all of God's judgments are impartial.

Colossians 3:12
as you are, so live

Your nature will dictate what you can do and how you live. You will live in the world if you have not been buried and raised with Christ. But if you have been buried and raised with Christ, you are among God's chosen ones who are holy and beloved (Eph. 1:4) and have been made able to live as such. Having Christ in you and having put to death that which is earthly in you, you now live to God.

The call that Paul says applies to the saints is often misunderstood and misrepresented as a universal invitation for all people to come to Christ. Indeed, such a universal call is consistent with God's ***preceptive*** or ***permissive will***. Sin prevents unbelievers from responding favorably to this call. There is no saving grace in it, and the devil blinds the minds of men to it (2 Cor. 4:4). Paul is referring to God's effectual call that goes out to the elect according to his ***decretive*** or ***absolute will*** (Rom. 1:7, 8:30; 1 Cor. 1:2). The saving grace in this call (Gal. 1:6) is irresistible because it is empowered by the power of Almighty God (2 Pet. 1:3). The call itself is holy and heavenly (2 Tim. 1:9; Heb. 3:1) and leads the saints to Christ (Rom. 1:6; 1 Pet: 5:10). Something we should dispense with is the notion that the gospel and salvation are ever offered to people or issued as an invitation. The gospel is preached, proclaimed, and taught, but is never offered in Scripture as a choice.

By calling the saints God's chosen ones, Paul draws our attention to election, the Father's free and sovereign choice made in love for them pretemporally, before creation, of who he would save through Jesus Christ. Election was thoroughly reviewed in the exposition of Colossians 2:2, which was founded on a detailed exposition of Ephesians 1:3-10. Paul is here emphasizing that our having died and been raised with Christ is all of God's sovereign will and plan for us through Jesus Christ, of which we contributed nothing to merit God's choice, and that we owe our lives and obedience to him for his great and free gift of pure grace that originated in election.

Those who have died and been raised with Christ have been chosen by God because he loved them before creation (Eph. 1:4). They were chosen to be holy and blameless and predestined through Jesus Christ for adoption as sons of the Father (Eph. 1:4-5). It is, therefore, altogether proper for Paul to call the saints holy and beloved because they were sovereignly called to be so (1 Thess. 4:7). Paul strategically places that here to emphasize the difference between what the saints were and what they have become and to be a motivating impetus (Heb. 12:14). Now, consequentially to what they have become, Paul can instruct them to live accordingly. We should be careful not to construe things in a backward manner. No one will ever become holy because of how they live or what they do. The saints are holy by decree, forensically confirmed, and manifested by their lives.

put on

Paul is not instructing the Colossians to put on new spiritual abilities. God's chosen ones, now holy and beloved with a new nature in Christ, already have these abilities and can exercise them. He instructs them to utilize these new abilities, to live in harmony with their new nature, and to live as the people they have become. Since they are holy, they can and should live as holy people. Since God loves them, they can and should live in a way that demonstrates their cherishing of his love. Of course, there are implications for us if we share the same faith and are called by God. Then, like the believing Colossians, we can and should live as people who cherish his love.

From verse 12 to verse 17, Paul describes the characteristics of persons living holy lives unto God. In actuality, he is instructing all of us to live as people who have put on the Lord Jesus Christ (Rom. 13:14; Gal. 3:27) and have been created after the likeness of God (Eph. 4:24). Paul also describes these things to put on as walking "*in a manner worthy of the calling to which you have been called*" (Eph. 4:1 ESV).

Our Lord and Savior, Jesus Christ, is the example of the way all saints should live. It is in his likeness we are being made, and thus, it is incumbent upon us to exercise the abilities we have been granted to walk in a manner that is honoring to him and worthy of our calling. James 5:1 tells us that our Lord is compassionate and merciful. The kindness of God is evident in our Savior (Titus 3:4). It will be demonstrated towards us evermore through Jesus Christ (Eph. 2:7). Paul referred to the meekness and gentleness of Christ in 2 Corinthians 10:1. In Philippians 2:8, we're told that Christ humbled himself. In 1 Timothy 1:16, we are told that Christ's patience is perfect. So, as we practice these same qualities and grow into them, we develop them as inherent to our nature. In that manner, we are putting on Christ.

Paul begins with the heart, the seat of our emotions, and tells us to be compassionate from the heart by nature. The world has a sense of what compassion is, and we should not settle for being of such compassion. Instead, we should look to Jesus, discern his compassion, and strive to exercise the compassion of Christ by nature. We may say this is a radical compassion. Kindness is a fruit of the Spirit. It is a characteristic of true love and includes being tenderhearted and forgiving (Gal. 5:22; 1 Cor. 13:4; Eph. 4:32). God favors humble people and declares that humility comes before honor (Ps. 15:33, 18:12; 22:4), indicating that there is no real honor without humility. He gives grace to the humble (1 Pet. 5:5) and salvation (Ps. 18:27, 149:4). He lifts up and exalts the humble (Ps. 147;6; Matt. 23:12, Luke 14:11; Jas. 4:10). True humility is marked by counting others more worthy than yourself (Phil. 2:3) and God opposes the proud (1 Pet. 5:5; Jas. 4:6). Meekness is a quality of the soul by which we are able to receive God's word internally (Jas. 2:1). It is a characteristic of wisdom (Jas. 3:13). And those who are blessed by God are marked by their meekness and are promised a great inheritance (Matt. 5:5). Patience is a fruit of the Spirit (Gal, 5:22). It is a quality of the soul that stems from an honest and good heart that bears fruit (Luke 8:15). Patience is part of the instrumentality of faith as we wait and seek for glory while doing good works, wait for unseen things, and inherit the promises (Rom. 2:7, 8:25; Heb. 6:12). Like the works of the flesh that we are told to put off, these qualities of our new nature are to be put on without exception.

In Colossians 1:21, Paul reminded us of the way we formerly walked. Recalling how we were is an interesting exercise from which only the saints can benefit. Only those who have been drawn into the light of Christ (2 Cor. 4:4, 6; Col. 1:12; Eph. 5:8; 1 Pet. 2:9) can perceive the works of darkness as they are (Eph. 5:13). Only the saints understand why God's wrath was righteously upon them (Eph. 2:3) and why it remains on everyone who walks according to the desires of the flesh (John 3:36; Rom. 8:4).

The following side-by-side lists outline the differences between walking in the flesh and in the Spirit, stemming from our inherent nature. Now that we are in the light of Christ, we should be repelled by our former nature that we can only now see and comprehend.

The saints' former nature The old man The natural man	**The saints' new nature The new man The spiritual man**
alienated and hostile in mind	holy and blameless
doing evil deeds	above reproach
dead in trespasses	beloved
sexual immorality and impurity	compassionate hearts
passion and evil desire	kindness
covetousness, which is idolatry	humility and meekness
anger and wrath	patience
malice and slander	bearing with one another
obscene talk	forgiving
lying	love

the natural man and free will: the case for grace alone

We've been discussing the old man and the new man as they apply to the saints. True believers in Christ have put on the new man and put off the old man. That cannot be said of nonbelievers. They are stuck in the old man, and the terminology of old and new man is not suited to them. When a nonbeliever is contrasted with a believer, we can say that the nonbeliever is a natural man and the believer is a spiritual man (1 Cor. 2:14-15).

The natural man is still under Adam's federal headship. He is still bound in darkness, sin, and corruption. All the characteristics previously discussed in verse 1:13 in the section "***dominion of darkness***" and repeated in the introduction to 3:9-1 describe the spiritual condition of the natural man. The nonbeliever, according to Scripture, is the natural man, and there is no other type or form of a nonbeliever.

The totality of the natural man's corruption is called ***total depravity***. Total depravity does not mean that the natural man is as depraved as possible, as one devoid of all human kindness and feeling. It means that the totality of what he is, in all his parts and being, is corrupted by sin.

Because the natural man is totally depraved as described, if he is going to be saved, God must save him despite himself. Being totally depraved, the natural man cannot contribute anything to his salvation, not even incline himself or prepare himself for it. Recall from the list of his characteristics: he does not seek God (Rom. 3:11), his heart and mind is veiled to the gospel (2 Cor. 3:16), he is a slave to sin (Rom. 6:17, Gal. 4:18), and he is the corruption that is in the world (2 Pet. 1:4). So, if the natural man is to be saved, it must be by the grace of God working alone to deliver him from his own darkness, corruption, and depravity. That soteriology is according to Scripture.

Where does this leave free will? Is there such a thing? Yes, people have free will, whether they are saved or not. Everyone is free to choose within the physical limits and abilities of their physical body, as well as the spiritual abilities and limitations inherent to their nature. Everyone is free to love their family, friends, and pets. However, the spiritual man is free to love Christ and seek God. In contrast, the natural man is incapable and unwilling since he is spiritually dead in sin (Eph. 2:1) and at enmity (Jas. 4:4). The natural man loves all sorts of idols, gods to him, but cannot love or even incline himself toward the Lord Jesus Christ as he is revealed to the saints and according to Scripture. He is tethered to sin in all his being. He is as free to choose, and will, and act only and always according to sin's dominion over him that restrains him from responding favorably to God's universal call to repentance. The natural man's inability is what Jesus meant in John 6:44 when saying, "*No one can come to me*." Jesus meant no natural man can come to him of their own will. They have to be drawn to Jesus by God's decretive will, effectual grace, as he goes on to say in the same verse.

Colossians 3:13

prepared saints

Paul is transitioning from instructing the saints as individuals to applying those instructions to the community of believers, the church. He has worked to "clean up" the saints by instructing them to put off the remnants of their old nature. Those who do not heed Paul's exhortation will continue to submit to the desires of the flesh that endeavor to defile them. So, after putting off the works of the flesh, the saints must look to Christ to see how they should live, as told in verse 12. From verses 5 through 12, Paul has cleaned up the saints and dressed them in Christ, so to speak, so that as God's chosen people they show themselves to be worthy of their calling (Eph. 4:1; Phil 1:27; Col 1:10; 1 Thess. 2:12; 2 Thess. 1:5, 11; Rev. 3:4). Now they are prepared to participate as part of the body, that is the church, and need to be instructed how members of the household of God should behave.

bearing with one another

Beginning in verse 13, the list of things to put on expands to what is necessary to maintain peace and unity among believers. This theme will proceed through the next several verses. Paul has begun presenting the proper conduct of everyone within the church. Our ability to heed Paul's instruction stems from our condition in Christ. Thus, we are without excuse if we fail to adhere to this excellent conduct, as clearly outlined, and we jeopardize the peace and unity of the church.

Bearing with someone does not mean merely tolerating or putting up with them; it involves actively supporting them, carrying their burden, regardless of any impulse to the contrary. In any engagement or exchange between believers, both parties are instructed to behave in the same manner. Paul explains by way of example. A complaint arises between two believers. Paul doesn't mention whether the complaint is valid or false. In either case, both parties are to forgive the other. This forgiveness is not a one-and-done deal. It is ongoing. Accordingly, you (plural) must do this just as the Lord has forgiven you (plural). Pause to consider the degree to which the Lord's righteous precepts were violated by us and the dishonor our sins brought him. If we are to forgive others as the Lord forgave us, is there anything we should never forgive?

COLOSSIANS 3:14-17
MEMBERS OF THE HOUSEHOLD OF GOD

Verses 14, 15, and 16 contain a triad of virtues paralleling our calling from the Father. The parallel consists of love, the peace of Christ, and the word of Christ. The parallel begins with the Father electing and predestinating the saints in love (Eph. 1:4-5). Scripture is clear: God loves us (believers) first (1 John 4:19), and without his love, we would be unable to love as Paul instructs us. Precipitating from the Father's love is his decree that those chosen are to be holy and blameless before him, which is peace with the Father, peace secured by the blood of Christ. We can have peace because God is the God of peace (Rom. 15:13, 16:20; 1 Cor. 14:33; 2 Cor. 13:11; Phil. 4:9; Heb. 13:20), who gives us peace (Phil 4:7; e.g., Col. 1:2). The saints then being predestined for adoption as his sons through Jesus Christ are to receive the word of Christ, the gospel, the mystery of Christ revealed and implanted in their hearts. Each part of this triad has a condition and a promise. Love is to be above all, and promises perfect harmony among the saints. Peace is to rule in your hearts, promising unity of the body, which is the church (1 Cor. 14:33). The word of Christ is to dwell richly in your hearts, leading to building one another up, corporate worship, and thanksgiving.

Colossians 3:14
put on love

In verse 14, love is placed at the pinnacle of our striving. So, we should explore why love is so important and how it binds everything in perfect harmony. The love referred to is *agapé* love, which is selfless, unconditional, and sacrificial in nature. Agape love is the love that God has for his people, the love by which the elect were chosen, and the love that Jesus said we are to have for God as the greatest of all commandments. He added that the second greatest commandment is expressing this same love to our neighbors (Matt. 22:37-39).

In Chapter 2, the term *"knit together"* was used to describe the saints. In verse 2:2, this knitting together was done "*in love.*" Two meanings were assigned to this. The first was that the knitting or bringing the saints together was done lovingly by the Father. Second, the result is a union of believers with love toward one another. Through this unity of deep affection, the saints can grow toward unity of faith, mature manhood, and reach the fullness of Christ (Eph. 4:13). Paul reiterates that unconditional and sacrificial love enables believers to strive together in perfect unity toward fulfillment in Christ.

In Chapter 13 of 1 Corinthians, the reason why love is above all the other qualities of our nature is explained in verses 1-3. Without love, we are nothing. No matter what we do with all excellency in speech, prophecy, understanding, faith, or sacrifice, if accomplished without love, they avail us nothing (1 Cor. 13:1-3).

The latter part of verse 14 states that love is the perfect bond of unity. Godly love is the highest of virtues. Since a pinnacle must rest on a foundation, affection without "*compassionate hearts, kindness, humility, meekness, and patience*" (Col. 3:12 ESV) is not love and cannot lead to harmony. The love that saints are required to strive for rests on putting off the works of the flesh, particularly those listed in verse 8, and certainly any lingering effects of those sins listed in verse 5. Paul's presentation builds the foundation for love perfectly by telling us what to remove from our lives and what to replace it with, so that love may abide and flourish among the saints, leading to the perfect bond of unity and harmony within the household of God.

The Father has brought us together in love, but we must practice it from within our hearts. Sometimes, the command to put things on is likened to putting on a garment or performing an external action. However, this is more akin to activating something internal, something implanted by God that needs to develop and mature through use and practice. The love the saints are growing into is frequently cited in marriage ceremonies to express the love between husbands and wives. Love is patient, kind, and rejoices with the truth. Love bears, believes, hopes, and endures all things. Love does not insist on its own way, is not irritable or rude, and does not rejoice at wrongdoing (1 Cor. 13:4-8). However, our concept of this love should not be so limited or pigeonholed. It must exist between all believers. John made this very clear by stipulating that someone who hates his brother is not of God, cannot love God, and lies if he claims to love God (1 John 3:10, 4:20). Jesus commands us to love our enemies and do good to them (Matt. 5:44; Luke 6:35). According to reason, since we are to love those who would harm us, we are most certainly to love our brothers and sisters in the Lord. The love we are to express to those who seek our harm is the same love we are to share among believers, a love that "*transcends human emotions and is rooted in the will and character of God*" (biblehub.com). This is a sound description of the love to which we are called.

The love that the saints are called to possess and express does not blind us to unrighteousness. The psalmist clearly states that Christ loves righteousness and hates wickedness (Ps. 45:7). Hate from a holy and loving God, the Lord Jesus Christ! Yes, hate is born out of holiness and the love of righteousness. Some people and churches approve of things under the pretense of God's love. The phrase "*God is love*" is found in 1 John 4:8 and 4:16. Using "*God is love*" to the exclusion of all else God is can potentially lead to approving things that are expressly condemned and forbidden in Scripture. But when they are embraced under the pretense of love, it is alleged that God approves such abominations (e.g., Lev. 18:22; Deut. 12:31). Here are several "God is" statements to consider in juxtaposition to "God is love."

- God is not mocked (Gal. 6:7) – Rationalizing unrighteousness under the pretense of his love mocks God.
- God is holy (Ps. 99:9) – Mocking God is an affront to his holiness.
- God is a righteous judge and a God who feels indignation every day (Ps. 7:11) – God is aware of those who mock him and will not acquit them.
- God is a consuming fire, a jealous God (Deut. 4:24; Heb 12:29) – A heavy penalty will fall upon those who mock him.
- God is light (1 John 1:5) – There is no unrighteousness in or condoned by him.

In addition, God is a God of wrath (John 3:36) and hatred (Prov. 6:16-19). Some things that are an abomination to him cannot be overturned or dismissed by the claim that God is love (e.g., Lev. 18:22; Deut. 12:31). The concept is well stated by King Solomon. That which God has made crooked, no man can straighten (Eccl. 1:15, 7:13).

Colossians 3:15
the peace of Christ

Variations in English translations of this verse arise from differences between the Greek manuscripts. Some Bibles have "*peace of [or from] Christ,*" translated from εἰρήνη τοῦ Χριστοῦ. Others have "*peace of God,*" translated from εἰρήνη τοῦ θεοῦ (biblehub.com). The King James bible here refers to God, but the next verse returns to Christ. In either translation, the peace referred to is that which ultimately is with the Father and from whom all peace emerges. It is through Christ that we obtain the peace referred to in verse 15.

This peace is no ordinary peace since it is the very peace that Jesus himself possesses (John 14:27). Although we can gain great assurance of this peace, with much understanding, it will always be beyond our ability to comprehend fully (Phil. 4:7). Thus, the peace we have is truly precious to us and glorious, even beyond knowing. This peace is so profound that its source, purpose, meaning, significance, attributes, and all else lie beyond our comprehension.

Before coming to Christ in a saving relation, we were children of wrath (Eph. 2:3). We had amassed a record of debt (Col. 2:14) for which a judgment of eternal death lay before us (Rom. 6:23). There are two crucial aspects of being called children of wrath. First, Ephesians 2:3 states that this condition was due to our nature, which was derived from our parents and spread throughout all mankind. It is a condition passed from one generation to the next, from parents to children. Paul elsewhere states, "*all have sinned and fall short of the glory of God*" (Rom. 3:23 ESV). Falling short of reaching the glory of God means not being justified and redeemed, leaving one to perish as a child of wrath. Second, the word *"wrath"* strikes our modern ears as discordant and archaic, as do other words such as *"blasphemy"*, *"perdition"*, *"sacrilege"*, and *"profanity"*.

Nevertheless, the reality of divine wrath persists and should be taken seriously, as indicated by the fact that God is a consuming fire (Deut.4:24; Heb. 12:29) and what it might be like to fall into his hands (Heb. 10:31). Divine wrath is not irrational, unwarranted, unjustified, or uncontrolled anger. Romans 1:18 informs us that God's wrath is due to man's ungodliness and unrighteousness and is presently being manifested, seen, and witnessed. As we read further in Romans Chapter 1, it becomes clear that the manifestation of divine wrath is evidenced by the gracious restraints against sin being withheld from the ungodly, allowing them naturally to dive deeper into unrighteousness.

Divine wrath is closely associated with God's rest and peace. Those under wrath are barred from entering God's eternal rest (Heb. 3:11, 4:3). They have fallen short of the glory of God to enter and are not at peace with God. But what is the remedy, if there is one, since all men are under God's wrath? The remedy is the gospel of peace (Eph. 6:5). God, who is the God of peace (Rom. 15:33, 16:20; Phil. 4:9; 1 Thess. 5:23; Heb. 13:20), has given us his Son in the person of Jesus Christ to be our peace (Eph. 2:14) by shedding his blood for us according to the eternal covenant (Heb. 13:20; Eph. 1:3-9). Thus, through Jesus Christ, we have been justified before God by faith and have peace with God. Propitiation is the setting aside of God's wrath to be replaced by peace. The Father sent his Son in the Person of Jesus Christ to shed his blood and to make propitiation (Rom. 3:25; 1 John 4:10) for our sins (Heb. 2:17; 1 John 2:2) that we may be at peace with the Father through faith and delivered from his wrath (Rom 5:9; 1 Thess. 1:10, 5:9).

The second line in the most beautiful hymn, "Hark! The Herald Angels Sing," reads, "Peace on earth and mercy mild. God and sinners reconciled!" This hymn is sung so often during Christmas every year that many have thought that the whole world should now be at peace, nation with nation, and neighbor with neighbor. Two points are to be made. (1) The peace we sing about in this hymn is the peace the saints have with the Father due to Christ's propitiation of sin. (2) The words of the angels, as recorded in Luke 2:14, specify that this peace is only with those with whom God is well pleased.

So far, we have discussed peace between God and his chosen people. We may say this is the vertical dimension of peace. Apart from no longer being children of wrath, the Father is now at peace with us and, through this peace, showers us with manifold blessings. From this peace we have a sense of salvation (Isa. 52:7). In all times, Christ, the Lord of peace, will in all ways give us peace (2 Thess. 3:16) as it is a fruit of the Spirit (Gal. 5:22). There is a sustaining power that flows from the God of peace that guards our hearts and minds in Jesus Christ (Phil. 4:7). Thus, as the herald angels proclaimed, we too proclaim, "*Glory to God in the highest*" (Luke 2:14 RSV).

There is also a horizontal dimension of peace that springs from our peace with God, and it is achieved by and through Jesus Christ when we pursue it. It breaks down the walls of separation between people (Eph. 2:14), enables us to live in peace and comfort one another (2 Cor. 13:11), and fosters mutual building up of one another (Rom. 14:19). Verse 15 encompasses these two dimensions of the peace we have in Christ.

What Paul means by writing "*let peace rule*" in verse 15 is to let peace be the rule and principle by which we live. By indicating this is to be from the heart, he demonstrates that this is the nature of the new man. To emphasize its importance, Paul points out that we were called to one body, which we understand is the church, and which we should regard with all thankfulness that peace is to rule within the church. That is, we are called to be at peace with each other within the church. That is only possible if that peace is of Christ. Those who disturb the church's peace, especially for personal gain, place themselves in great jeopardy before the Lord.

Paul adds a caveat to be thankful. As we read it, we understand that it is a thankfulness to God for the peace we have, which has been graciously given to us by the blood of his Son and which has set aside the wrath we had stored up against ourselves. Paul exhorts us to be thankful because it is necessary, and since we have short memories, we need reminders to do important things. It is an exhortation not to take our peace lightly, as it comes from the living God who previously regarded us as children of wrath. There are a great many things to be thankful to God for by all who were once children of wrath but are now adopted children of God (Eph, 1:5; 1 John 3:1). Consider Romans 1:21 in which a person knows certain things about God but does not honor him as God and does not thank him for what he has received from him. Paul's exhortation to be thankful to God is an exhortation to honor him as God. Failure to do the former is a failure to do the latter.

Usually, prospective new members are asked to pledge to uphold the church's peace, unity, and purity. Peter, Jude, and Paul warn us that false teachers will be among God's people, even today, to lead the saints astray. If you ever find yourself or witness someone confronting false teachers, you can be assured that they will likely accuse you or that person of disrupting the church's peace. Remember your oath and be steadfast in faith. Do not let one person carry the weight of confronting false teachers alone, for we are called to build one another up, and that must certainly include not allowing one person to be torn asunder for doing what we are all called to do together. Passive reconciliation or acquiescence to false teachers only sustains a false peace and leads the church into false teachings (***heterodoxy***) and practices (***heteropraxy***). As Peter establishes in his second epistle, this results in manifold blasphemies and a false witness of the gospel as perceived by the world.

Colossians 3:16
the word of Christ

The phrase "*word of Christ*" in verse 16 directly refers to the gospel. But it is not just the gospel; it is the gospel unveiled. The gospel is not an external artifact of religion for those desiring to live godly lives. The gospel and all it encompasses are meant to abide within us with abundance. Having the word of Christ in us is not simply referring to the initial acceptance of the gospel, as when we were first drawn to Christ, as if to say we have accepted the gospel and can move on. Not at all. Paul is exhorting us to embrace the gospel with persistence.

Additionally, although indirectly, Paul means all that Christ taught and commanded. All that Jesus spoke of concerning the Father, eternal life, faith, and the kingdom was given to him by the Father and was under the Father's authority (John 12:49). What the Father gave Jesus to say was not a suggestion or an outline; it was by ordinance, indicating its veracity and specificity. In the very next verse, John 12:50, Jesus reveals this commandment is eternal life, indicating the power to save abides in his words as given by the Father (Rom. 1:16, 1 Thess. 1:5). John was led to tell us that anyone who does not abide in Christ's teachings, the words of Jesus, does not have God (2 John 1:9). Therefore, to have the Father and the Son, one must abide in the words of Christ. Put another way, they must dwell in you richly. Jesus clarified that anyone who does not keep his commandments does not love him and is not a friend (John 14:15, 21, 15:10, 12, 14).

One of the more memorable statements made by Jesus is,

> "*I am the way, and the truth, and the life. No one comes to the Father except through me*" (John 14:6).

During Jesus' high priestly prayer, he proclaimed that he had given the disciples the words given to him by the Father, that they received them, and knew them to be true. Jesus asked that they be sanctified in the truth, for which and by their words, others would believe and know that Jesus was sent by the Father (John 17:8, 17, 20, 21). We conclude that even the words of the Apostles, given to them by Jesus and spoken in truth, are the words of Christ we are called to pursue, take hold of, and abide in.

Once the word of Christ dwells in our hearts, we can teach and admonish in all wisdom. Christ's words in our hearts are the wisdom that is from above, as opposed to that wisdom that is earthly and demonic. James tells us that the wisdom from above is pure, peaceful, gentle, reasonable, merciful, fruitful, impartial, and sincere (Jas. 3:17). These attributes of wisdom align with the new nature that has been born within us. What is taught is the pure, undefiled truth of the gospel, the Father, and the eternal kingdom by those sanctified in the truth according to Christ's high priestly prayer. What sanctifies them in the truth is the abiding word of Christ. To draw from a related verse, this is God's word, and should we ever be tempted to depart from it, that word will bring to our minds the staggering danger of our intentions in a manner sharper than "*any two-edged sword*" (Heb. 4:12). In addition to teaching and admonishing, worship with a heartful thankfulness to God naturally wells up within us drawing us to worship with songs and hymns.

Colossians 3:17
do everything in the name of the Lord

Paul ties all the essentials of the new nature together with one final summation. Whatever we say and do should be done in the name of the Lord. Christ is our redeemer, and we are now his possession. Whatever we do is under the authority of Christ, by which we must be governed. In all things, we are reminded to be thankful to God through Christ because it is only through Christ that we receive blessings from the Father.

Paul wrote to the Corinthians that they are epistles written in flesh to be read by all men (2 Cor. 3:3). Paul was using this expression as a validation of his teaching. Still, the greater reality is that all Christians, whether truly so or only in name, are "*read*" by other men as a representation of Christ's teaching and the doctrines of the Christian faith.

COLOSSIANS 3:18-25
EXERCISE HOLINESS IN ALL RELATIONSHIPS

Verses 18 through 22 contain instructions regarding personal relationships, outlined in the form of duties and responsibilities. These instructions are relatively brief compared to Paul's detailed instructions in his Ephesian letter, where he addressed each person's behavior in their respective role, dutifully to engage (Eph. 5). Peter gave us substantial details about these relationships in his first letter (1 Pet. 3). Throughout these instructions by Peter and Paul, the duties each person is least likely to perform because of the inclinations of sin are singled out and offset by explicit instruction in the Lord as to what is required and expected.

Colossians 3:18
wives

Wives are instructed to be submissive to their husbands. This duty is not to be taken as an unrestrained submission since Paul limits this duty to that which is appropriate in the Lord. Nevertheless, this duty is in the Lord, and wives who refuse this duty refuse the Lord. The verse establishes that husbands are the heads of their families and households, but likewise, "*as is fitting in the Lord.*" In the garden, when God addressed Adam and Eve after they had sinned, he told Eve that her desire would be for her husband, and he would rule over her (Gen. 3:16). This is precisely what Paul counseled concerning the family; the husband is the head of the household. However, due to sin, wives often tend to desire their husbands' authority. Verse 18 cuts directly to what wives need to remain aware of, regardless of the social norms of the day.

A verse in Proverbs speaks to the effect that a quarrelsome wife may have when she fails in her duty to her husband. The home becomes a battlefield, and to seek solitude, the roof or even the desert would be a preferable place to live (Prov. 21:9, 19).

Colossians 3:19
husbands

The duty of husbands to their wives is to love them, to which no limits are assigned. This obligation is an active, agape love in which believing wives are not only due as fellow heirs with Christ, but it is emphasized here because they are wives. Husbands who fail in this duty are doubly sinful. In addition, while loving their wives, husbands are not to be harsh with them, which is a warning that they must not abuse their authority. It seems like an unnecessary directive since husbands who properly love their wives would naturally not be harsh. But then there is sin, and as women all too frequently learn, men tend to disregard this directive.

In 1 Peter, there is a remarkable statement about the beauty of a wife. There is an inner person of the heart that possesses a gentile and quiet spirit that is most beautiful. It is a blessing to husbands who find this beauty in their wives, as it is an imperishable beauty that does not fade but grows more precious as the years pass (1 Pet 3:4).

Colossians 3:20
children

Children are to obey their parents in everything. Everything indicates that it is not up to them to decide when to obey or on what terms. Encouragement is added by informing children that their obedience pleases the Lord. Of course, children are naturally disobedient at times and must be reminded that the Lord oversees their conduct. By itself, the verse presumes parents love their children and will not abuse them or knowingly put them in danger by whatever they instruct. But just in case there is a wayward Father, the next verse appears.

Colossians 3:21
fathers

Fathers are to safeguard their conduct towards their children so as not to drive them from instruction or into rebellion. Curbing harshness follows on the heels of the previous verse out of necessity. Fathers who are harsh toward their children create an atmosphere in which obedience becomes more difficult. Children are to obey even if a Father is unduly harsh, provided it is not contrary to Christ. But an unduly harsh Father acts outside his calling/role as a parent and will answer before the Lord for his conduct.

Colossians 3:22-25
bondservants

These four verses are tied together and are addressed to bondservants. They closely parallel Paul's instructions to bondservants in Ephesians Chapter 6.

Slaves are the subject of these verses. Slaves serve two masters: one who is in the flesh, earthly, and one who is in heaven. Their service to earthly masters must be obedient in all matters, from the heart, and not only when seen but also when not seen. Since this is their duty, Paul adds that this is to be done in the fear of the Lord. We should consider this fear as having a proper reverence for the Lord. Who knows what the Lord's intended outcome is from the service of a slave? It would be better to serve the Lord in obedience than in disobedience.

Ultimately, slaves work for the Lord, not for men, and this should be the proper orientation of their thinking. We would do well to adopt it as our guiding principle for thinking about work and employment. Since slaves are inclined to be slothful and lax, Paul tells them to work heartily. The word translated as "*heartily*" comes from ψυχῆς (psychēs), which means "s*oul,*" "*life,*" "s*elf,*" and "*inner being*" (biblehub.com). We may understand that Paul tells slaves to put themselves into their work. Again, we would do well to adopt this ourselves in all our labors.

Emphasis and encouragement are added. As you serve your master here on earth, you know an inheritance is being kept for you that you may regard as a reward. If you imagine reading this as a hard-working, suffering slave, this brings to mind that the current conditions of your life have a terminal end when you will receive a great inheritance as a reward. It is a reward postponed for labors done now. Paul encourages all the saints to look beyond the trials of this life to the blessed hope and glory of the coming Lord and his eternal kingdom (Rom. 8:18).

The wrongdoer addressed in verse 25 is the disobedient slave and the harsh master. There is no partiality in divine judgment. Each will reap what they have sown. A slave who is being badly treated by his master can be comforted to know that retribution is not in his hands and that it would be wrong of him to retaliate against his master by violence or poor work. The Lord knows the wrongdoer and will pay him his due wages at the proper time. It does not challenge us to realize this application in an employee-employer relationship.

CHAPTER 3
SUMMARY

the old man and the new man

The Chapter is rich in Christian doctrine and its practical application. God is noted for his impartiality in all his judgments. Those whom he has called to Christ had no special benefit from whatever background they came from, nor do they among God's chosen people. Each was called from a life of corruption, unable to please God or even to be inclined toward him.

We had to iron out what was meant by the old man and the new man. When told to examine our former lives, we were being told to examine the old man, the way we lived before we were called to Christ. For a nonbeliever, living as it were in the old man is living as a natural man. The believer has died with Christ and has therefore put off the old man. When the believer rises with Christ, he rises as a new man with a new nature. But he is not yet complete and has to mortify the lingering effects of his former life.

by grace alone

As we explored the natural man, we took the opportunity to explore the possibilities of how such a person might be saved. We began by comparing the natural man's spiritual attributes to the attributes of the spiritual man, a believer. We saw that the Bible presents no other type, form, or degree of man other than the natural and the spiritual. The term total depravity was introduced and explained as an overall description of the spiritual condition of the natural man. Since the whole of the natural man's being is corrupt and in a state of spiritual death, he is incapable of doing anything to contribute to being saved. The conclusion is that God must act to save him, if he is to be saved, and that would be an act entirely of grace. Along the way, we encountered the concept of free will, which we defined as the freedom to act according to one's physical and spiritual abilities and limitations.

hidden with Christ

We are called to mortify those lingering temptations to sin, knowing what is at stake. Though we have left our former state of corruption, our future state is hidden with Christ in heaven. We have glimpses in Scripture of that glory and are exhorted to set our minds on such things as we endeavor to leave behind all that is in us that is earthly and perishing. God's pending judgment and wrath stand as an ever-present warning. For the saints, such a warning is an effectual remedy against the earthly that remains in them. It is also an example of God's guardianship of the saints through faith (1 Pet. 1:5).

Christian living

Although we have been called to Christ as individuals, no individual is an island of faith unto themselves. The saints come to Christ as members of the household of God, the church, the body of Christ. We are expected to be engaged and conduct ourselves properly, as we have been instructed to do. Agape love between the brothers and sisters is to be the virtue of virtues. The peace of Christ is the guiding principle governing the body. And by the word of Christ dwelling in our hearts, we are to build one another up into spiritual maturity.

The duties of wives, husbands, children, fathers, and slaves are outlined, encompassing submission to authority, mutual love, and service under the Lord's ruling oversight. Husbands are set before us as heads of their homes and are forbidden to be harsh. Wives and children are to be submissive and obedient as much as it is in the Lord to do so. We are encouraged to perform these duties from the heart to the Lord to receive an inheritance as a reward, and are reminded that the Lord will judge wrongdoers with impartiality.

The Chapter is a compelling rule for the Christian life. Many verses could be selected for special recognition, but these seem to encapsulate the theme of the Chapter and Letter.

> *Put on then, as God's chosen ones, holy and beloved, compassionate hearts, kindness, humility, meekness, and patience, bearing with one another and, if one has a complaint against another, forgiving each other; as the Lord has forgiven you, so you also must forgive.* (Col. 3:12-13 ESV)

CHAPTER 4
RENOWN MEN OF FAITH

INTRODUCTION

The Chapter opens with instructions regarding the proper Christian duties in relationships that began in Chapter 3. The odd way chapter designations have been assigned is exemplified by the first verse of this Chapter, which has been segregated from the previous Chapter where it belongs, as dictated by the context of the subjects addressed.

In a few verses, final instructions on Christian conduct conclude the application part of the letter. These instructions are directed to improving the Christian witness of the gospel. Paul gently draws them into his own ministry by asking for prayer and takes another opportunity to encourage the Colossians to speak graciously in all things.

The remainder of the chapter lists people Paul commends for their loyalty, faith, and service. Some personal instructions are included. All these recommendations are vitally important to the church during Paul's time and have served the church as historic examples of great works of faith and service used and empowered by God.

COLOSSIANS 4:1
CHRISTIAN DUTIES IN RELATIONSHIPS, CONCLUSION

The church subsequently made chapter divisions in the Biblical text. People have had to work with them since. Verse 1 seems to belong in Chapter 3, as a closing content of that Chapter.

Masters of slaves are reminded of their duty before God with a reason appended that is more akin to a warning. It is their duty to treat their slaves justly and fairly. By "*justly,*" Paul means that their treatment of slaves must be consistent with judicial precepts. Just treatment includes their reasonable care, not overburdening them, correction and punishment that is neither undue nor disproportionately harsh or cruel, and recognition and reward for good service. By "*fairly*," Paul means even-handedly, so that no one is treated differently without a valid reason. The reason cited for masters to do this has two meanings. First, Paul reminds earthly masters that they have a heavenly master to whom they will have to give an account of how they treated their slaves. Second, Paul urges masters to be Christ-like to their slaves, for the principles of justice and fairness that Paul exhorts them to follow are none other than those regarded by Christ, by which they will be judged. Slaves and masters should at all times recognize each other as image bearers of God and possibly heirs of the kingdom (Pro. 14:31; Col. 3:10; Eph. 3:16; 1 Pet. 3:7; Jas. 2:5).

These instructions have implications that bear upon the employer-employee relationship. When an employee requires instruction, correction, or reproof, it should be proportionate to the deficiency and delivered with equity.

The Bible neither condones nor condemns slavery as an institution. The Lord addresses slavery by graciously instructing how it should be conducted from both the slave's and the master's perspectives, offering encouragement and warning. The masters of Black slaves in America did not heed the warnings of these instructions and have reaped the due penalty of their actions.

COLOSSIANS 4:2-6
FINAL EXHORTATIONS

Paul reminds the Colossians to be vigilant in prayer, reminds them that he is in prison for the sake of the gospel, and requests that they pray for him and his ministry, including several specific requests. Always the evangelist, Paul instructs the Colossians and us how we should conduct ourselves as witnesses of Jesus Christ to this fallen world.

Colossians 4:2
vigilant in prayer

The Greek words employed for "s*teadfastly*" and "*watchful*" convey similar but not identical meanings to "*vigilant*" (biblehub.com). It appears that Paul is employing a tautology to emphasize the importance of prayer, especially since a person who does not pray may have a mind that wanders from the faith. Vigilance in prayer appears to be Paul's point for two additional reasons. (1) Prayer is to be at all occasions (Eph. 6:18). (2) The Colossians are reminded to pray with thanksgiving.

There are three key considerations regarding prayer. First, it must be earnest, deliberate, and frequent. When prayer occurs only out of a sense of duty or reluctantly, it is at least disrespectful towards God. Worse, prayer that is meant to be heard by others to draw attention to oneself is hypocritical (Matt 6:5). Second, when praying, be of sound mind knowing that prayer is to God the Father through Jesus Christ (Matt. 6:7). If that does not make us pause to consider our attitude in prayer and what we say and ask for, then we are approaching God improperly. Third, be thankful in all prayer, knowing that thanklessness is a characteristic of the reprobate and is included among those things for which they are condemned. If even the reprobate are expected to be thankful to God, how much more should those for whom Christ shed his blood be thankful unto God (Rev. 1:21)?

Colossians 4:3
requested prayer

Paul adds a request for the Colossians to include whenever they pray. Part of his request was that God might provide opportunities for him and those ministering with him to speak to people about the mystery of Christ. Paul's incentive and motivation are for the word of Christ to go forward, and he wrote to the Colossians with that perspective, as we should when we speak, write, teach, or preach about Christ and the things of God. At this time, Paul was under house arrest in Rome (Acts 28:17-31). While in Rome, "*From morning till evening he expounded to them, testifying to the kingdom of God*" (Acts 28:23). It's interesting that this opportunity was by the Romans' request. We see in Acts that Paul tried to convince the people of the gospel, but only some were convinced. Why some and not all? We'll see why in just a moment.

The mystery is that Jesus Christ is the promised savior of both Jews and Gentiles. The mystery part of Christ lies in belief. No one can believe Christ is their Lord, Redeemer, and Savior unless it is graciously revealed to their hearts to be true. Paul wants to be able to declare or speak boldly and authoritatively about Christ. It is essential to understand that Paul is not asking anyone to offer the gospel as a choice. All the English translations have words such as "*declare*," "*proclaim*," "*preach*," and "s*peak*," but none have "*offer*." This verse is an example of many that the gospel is never offered to people as a choice. Paul is asking only to speak about the mystery of Christ, knowing that it would be presumptuous to think he could reveal to spiritually dead hearers the secret things of God. The mystery of Christ can only be presented to people as a means for God to open their hearts and minds for them to receive it by grace, by grace alone, and thus be drawn to Christ according to the Father's will (Col. 1:13, John 6:44). Those who hear the mystery of Christ, the gospel, preached will only hear folly proclaimed if God does not graciously reveal it internally and calls them with a holy calling to Christ (1 Cor. 1:18, 23, 2:14; 2 Tim. 1:9). As we see in Acts Chapter 28, as much as Paul desired to be convincing, he still only expounded and testified about Christ without presenting the gospel as an offer. The results were according to the will and grace of the Father. Those convinced believed because they were appointed to eternal life (Acts 13:48).

As the Colossians pray for Paul's preaching ministry, they participate in it. In the same way, when we pray for our church leaders to serve faithfully, grow in wisdom and understanding, be respected as appointed shepherds of God's people, and protected from trials and suffering, we participate in their ministries, as we should.

in prison

Paul adds a reminder that he is currently in prison, and we will revisit this reminder in verse 5. There are two ways of looking at his bondage. Paul is in prison in Rome because he had been preaching about Christ. Or, Paul is in prison to preach about Christ to the Romans (Matt. 10:18). It is likely both reasons, and we see that Paul is asking the Colossians to pray for him to be able to continue to do the very thing for which he is now in prison and to do so even from prison. It isn't known whether Paul was released from prison or what he may have done if he had been. Theories abound. However, it seems from the nature of his prayer that he had some expectation of being released.

Colossians 4:4

making it clear

In addition to opportunities to preach, he asked that he preach clearly to those who hear him. Specifically, he is praying for his efforts to properly preach. This prayerful request affirms that Paul recognizes his preaching is accomplished through the power, ability, and outcome granted by God, yet it is achieved through his own efforts. The Greek word that is translated as clear means to make known, reveal, and make manifest (biblehub.com). Paul is striving for that level of clarity that is convicting and which only comes from the Holy Spirit.

There are many people who only cognitively understand the gospel account of Jesus Christ in detail, from the promises of his coming to his incarnation, crucifixion, resurrection, and ascension. Perhaps they understand even more than some Christians, yet they are not saved because they know but disbelief. They disbelieve because they stumble over the word of Christ that they understand. Even so, they were destined to disbelieve (1 Pet. 2:8). This is precisely what occurred in Rome when Paul spent an entire day lecturing clearly on the Scripture concerning Christ and his kingdom. It was with clarity to the degree prayed for, but only some who heard him were convinced (Acts 28:24).

Colossians 4:5
walk in wisdom

In verses 2 through 4, Paul, while in prison, asked the Colossians for their prayerful assistance in his preaching. Now, he guides them on how to conduct themselves with people outside the church, who are sometimes referred to as strangers or outsiders. His request for prayer and his guidance are interconnected. His outreach ministry, proclaiming the good news of Jesus Christ to outsiders as an apostle and evangelist, exemplifies their calling to witness to outsiders through their words and actions, but to a higher degree.

Paul's instruction aims to promote the gospel's witness to the unchurched, using the term "*outsiders*" to be unoffensive and foster peace among all parties. In other places Paul had no reluctance to refer to some outsiders derogatively as Gentiles (Eph. 2:11, 4:17; 1 Thess. 4:5). That was not done to shame outsiders or to encourage distain for them, but to recall the manner of life that has been left behind by the saints who once lived that way and must not return to it.

How we conduct ourselves in thought and action is our "*walk*." There are two ways a person can walk. They can walk according to the flesh that leads to death or according to the Spirit that leads to life and peace (Rom. 8:4-6). In Colossians 4:5, Paul highlights an important aspect of walking in the Spirit, for one who walks in the Spirit will necessarily walk in wisdom toward outsiders. One cannot be separated from the other. In this, we encounter an aspect of the Christian life that exceeds merely consenting to a creed.

Some aspects of wisdom must be explained to understand what is meant by "*walk in wisdom toward outsiders*." The saints cannot walk in wisdom with outsiders because outsiders do not share the wisdom that Paul draws our attention to. Paul is referring to wisdom that is from above, spiritual (Jas. 3:17). It is Christ (1 Cor. 1:23:24). Whatever wisdom an outsider has is earthy, unspiritual, even demonic (Jas 3:15) and is derived from and confined to human teaching (1 Cor. 2:13). The saints are believers in Christ who is for them the power and wisdom of God. In contrast to the unbelieving outsiders, he is a stumbling block and folly (1 Cor. 1:23-24). This difference must be kept in mind when interacting with unbelievers.

Since outsiders are not of Christ, our discourse with them must be conducted with the perspective taught by Jesus to those he was sending out to evangelize. They would be as sheep among wolves (Matt. 10:16; Luke 10:3). Jesus' statement is a metaphor that tangibly describes the danger he was sending them into. Those sent were to be gentle, peaceful, kind, and not return evil for evil (1 Pet. 3:9-12). They would encounter judgment, slander, malice, abuse, and rejection (Col. 2:16; 1 Pet. 4:4). They were to be as wise as serpents but as innocent as doves (Matt. 10:16). Genesis 3:1 helps to shed light on what this means. It states that the serpent that tempted Adam and Eve was more crafty than any other beast. The Greek word, which is translated as "*crafty,*" also means "s*hrewd,*" "*cunning,*" and "*prudent*" (biblehub.com). What applies in Matthew 10:16 is more akin to being more shrewd and prudent than those being visited, yet as innocent as a dove. In which innocent means to be without sin, and dove frequently symbolized the Holy Spirit (Matt. 3:16; Mark 1:10; Luke 3:22; John 1:32).

In Chapter 5 of Ephesians, Paul describes people who have no inheritance in the kingdom of Christ. They are sexually immoral, idolaters, and whose speech is profane (Eph. 5:5,6), an apt description of wolves used in Matthew Chapter 5. Following that description, he exhorts the Ephesians to walk as wise, not unwise (Eph. 5:15) and discern what is pleasing to the Lord (Eph. 5:10). In another place Paul told the saints that he wanted them to be wise in what is good and innocent in what is evil (Rom. 16:19). But they must be mature and with practice able to distinguish good from evil (Heb. 5:14). The whole of the matter of Matthew 10:16 is that those sent out to evangelize are to be shrewd and prudent being wise in what is good and able to distinguish good from evil, so as not to be drawn into sin, remaining innocent in what is evil, since sin is precisely what the people they encounter will encourage, bait, or deceive them into, just as sheep are led astray by ravenous wolves masquerading as sheep (Matt. 7:17; Acts 20:29). We must incorporate this in our exposition of Colossians 4:5 to fully appreciate what Paul means by walk in wisdom toward outsiders. We conclude the following:

1. Outsiders do not possess the spiritual wisdom of the saints. The saints are children of light, but the outsiders are still children of darkness and wrath.
2. Walk in the Spirit, in a manner worthy of your holy calling in Christ.
3. Be as gentle as a lamb, but remain shrewd and prudent, knowing that wolves among the outsiders will seek to shipwreck your faith and draw you into sin. Resist them.

Paul took being shrewd and prudent, yet without sin, to a high level, as he explained in 1 Corinthians Chapter 9. He said that he became all things to all men so that he might win some to Christ by any means (1 Cor. 9:19-22). What an amazing example of walking in wisdom toward outsiders to advance the gospel. He exhorts us to do the same, though to a far lesser degree. By honoring Christ in ways that convey we have a special hope, some people may then ask us to explain what it is. Then being ready to present a good reply (1 Pet. 3:15) is one way we can walk in wisdom with outsiders.

Walking in wisdom is not as easily accomplished as it sounds, since so much goes into it. Paul had informed the Colossians that he always prays for them to be filled with spiritual wisdom and understanding, so they can walk worthy in the Lord (Col. 1:9-10). Here, Paul encourages them to exercise what God has given them, what he has been praying for, to walk in wisdom among the saints and toward outsiders as witnesses of Jesus Christ and the gospel.

the best use of the time

There are translation differences in the English versions of this phrase. A literal translation of the Greek text from biblehub.com is, "*the time redeeming*." The Greek word for "*redeeming*" is ἐξαγοραζόμενοι (exagorazomenoi), which may be translated as "*redeem*", "*buy back*", or "*make the most of*" (biblehub.com). Thus, we find in different English translations the following:

- redeeming the time
- make the most of each opportunity
- making the most of the time
- make good use of the time

- use your time in the best way you can
- make the most of your chances
- and other variations

As we proceed, we'll find that redeeming the time is the appropriate translation and versions that do not refer to time or buying it back fail to reach the theological depth of Paul's meaning.

It isn't time itself that is evil, but what is done during the time. We find the same construction of this phrase in Ephesians 5:16. Moreover, the same exhortation in verses 15 and 16 as in Colossians 4:5. However, in verse 16, Paul explains why the time must be redeemed – the days are evil. When we juxtapose the Ephesians and Colossian verses, we see that the outsiders are doing things that render the time or days evil. In his first epistle, Peter addressed the concept of time being or containing evil. Regarding the saints, he wrote that their past was sufficient for doing what the Gentiles want to do, sin (1 Pet. 4:3). Peter means that the days of walking in the passions of the flesh are over for each saint. For the sake of understanding Colossians 4:5, we must recognize that the days preceding a person's conversion to Christ were the most evil periods of their lives. With that understanding, the days are still evil for outsiders who continue to walk in the passions of the flesh.

However, when the faithful walk in wisdom towards outsiders, some outsiders may receive Christ, and thus their days will no longer be evil or filled with evil. Whatever the saints did in word, deed, suffered, or sacrificed as a means to that outcome shortened the time when evil was being done by "*buying it back*," literally redeeming the outsiders' time.

As just explained, the concept of redeeming the time is not unlike what was previously discussed in Colossians 1:24, where Paul wrote, "*I am filling up what is lacking in Christ's afflictions.*" The afflictions of the saints on behalf of the body of Christ, that is the church, (1) do not add to Christ's own afflictions or efficacy since nothing is lacking in them, and (2) are made effectual by the power and grace that Christ secured by his afflictions (see section: *suffering for the sake of the elect*). Redeeming the time does not add to Christ's redemption or make it effectual. The afflictions of the saints and the witness of their walking in the Spirit or wisdom, as observed by outsiders, are means of God's saving grace to them.

Colossians 4:6
gracious speech

Continuing with his guidance on discourse with outsiders, Paul instructs us to always be gracious in our speech. The word grace has special significance to all who have been saved, especially to those who do not mingle God's saving grace with their own alleged merit. The Greek word χάριτι (chariti) may also be translated as "*favor*", "*kindness*", or "*blessing*" (biblehub.com). These possible translations align with the context of the verse and chapter, offering a broader perspective on the nature of our speech to outsiders. Gracious speech means to speak favorably and kindly to outsiders without them having to earn or merit it, even when we feel that they have given us an excuse to address them otherwise. We have ceased to be gracious once we put the tiniest condition on outsiders to deserve our kindness.

The phrase "s*easoned with salt*" refers to the previous exhortation to actively guard our speech so that it remains gracious and never becomes a reason for offense. Peter tells us we should be prepared to make a wise, gentle, and respectful defense of our faith and hope whenever asked (1 Pet. 3:15). Notice the similarity between Peter's text and Paul's "*gracious speech*." Peter's counsel is essentially the same as Paul's. When we are circumspect of the people we come in contact with, by treating them with kindness at all times, we honor Christ and create opportunities to witness our hope in Christ in greater detail. Even when shamed and abused, we should remain gracious, which honors Christ.

Witnessing to the mystery of Christ to outsiders is of paramount importance and deserves our prayer and active participation. It is an activity fraught with danger and personal sacrifice for which we need the wisdom of Christ. Without heeding Paul's guidance, one might fail to be a witness of the gospel, bring contempt upon it, or bring persecution upon themselves. Paul informs the Colossians of the possible consequences by reminding them that he is in prison because he has brought the gospel to outsiders, but at the same time presents himself as an example of making the best use of the time by requesting God to provide opportunities for him to continue preaching from prison. As he does so, he redeems the time for those who are converted through his ministry.

COLOSSIANS 4:7-9
TYCHICUS AND ONESIMUS

From verses 7 to 17, Paul commends several servants of the Lord for their faithful service to the church and to him. They are men who should be well-received among all the churches. Do not pass this list of commendations by as something superfluous. It serves multiple purposes. (1) In the early church, false teachers were a problem. Such lists of faithful men helped protect the saints from wolves entering the fold under false pretenses. If an apostle of Christ did not recommend someone, they should be received with caution and scrutiny. (2) There is much for the modern church to learn from the accounts of these men who suffered as they served, whose lives were dedicated to the preservation of the truth and the advance of the faith. They speak to us today and teach great lessons of faith, service, loyalty, and dedication. Many of them suffered great hardships because the truth was precious to them.

Colossians 4:7-8
Tychicus

Paul sent Tychicus to Colossae to report to them concerning himself and encourage them, and likely to deliver this letter. As we will see, Tychicus' mission was much larger. Tychicus had been engaged in the activities mentioned that would be the subject of his report. He is introduced as "*the beloved brother and faithful servant and fellow bondservant in the Lord,*" as rendered in the Greek text (biblkehub.com). This introduction informs us that Paul highly regarded Tychicus as a man of faith who ministered faithfully and with deliberate persistence. Additionally, his service was in the Lord, indicating that his efforts were entirely devoted to benefiting God's people. His introduction is elevated by the use of a definite article, which helps establish that this is not just Paul's opinion of Tychicus. Tychicus and his report should have been well received with such an introduction.

Tychicus is frequently mentioned in Scripture, and we have much to learn about this servant of God. After Paul had been in Ephesus for about three years, he began planning further travels (Acts. 19:21). Among the men who traveled with him to Macedonia and Greece were Timothy, Aristarchus, Tychicus, and others (Acts 20:4). During the three months of winter that they spent in Nicopolis (Titus 3:2; Acts 20:3), Paul arranged for Titus to join him from Crete where he was overseeing a church and planned to send either Artemas or Tychicus as his replacement (Titus 3:12). Artemas was likely sent because Tychicus continued to travel with Paul (Acts 20:3-5). It is noteworthy that Paul considered Tychicus worthy of overseeing the church in Crete, although the appointment did not occur.

Also, while in Greece Paul asked Timothy to oversee the church at Ephesus to guard it against false teachers (1 Tim. 1:3). After leaving Greece (Acts. 20:4-6), Paul and Tychicus, along with others, went to Jerusalem but Timothy went to Ephesus to oversee the church (Acts 20:16). Later when Paul was in prison in Rome, and Tychicus was with him, he arranged for Tychicus to travel to Ephesus and Colossae to report on Paul and the church in Rome (Eph. 6:21). It is believed that Tychicus delivered Paul's epistles to Ephesus and Colossae. Tychicus' mission to Ephesus also freed Timothy to travel to Rome to see Paul (2 Tim. 4:12-13). Timothy already knew Tychicus, as they had traveled with Paul from Ephesus to Macedonia, Greece, and Troas.

Colossians 4:9

Onesimus

Paul's letter, that we know of as Philemon, is a personal letter to Philemon (Phlm. 1). Philemon hosted the Colossian church in his home (Phlm 2), and knew Paul and Epaphras personally, not just by reputation (Col. 1:7, 4:12; Phlm. 23). In that letter, verses 8 through 21 are devoted to Onesimus. In Colossians, we encounter Onesimus, who was sent by Paul from Rome to Philemon as a traveling companion of Tychicus and a servant of Christ. As we explore the facts we have about Onesimus, an epic story of slavery, flight, concealment, conversion, faithful service, and acceptance unfolds, testifying to the mercy, grace, and sovereignty of God, by which an extraordinary service to the church is performed.

The story of Onesimus begins in the home of Philemon, where Onesimus is a slave. The conditions of his slavery are not disclosed in the Bible; however, several things are known about Onesimus, and other things can be surmised. (1) Since the Colossian believers met in Philemon's home, Onesimus likely overheard their meetings and thus the account of the gospel. (2) Possibly, Onesimus heard of Paul being in Rome and his reputation by overhearing conversations about him during these meetings. (3) During this time, Onesimus is not a believer. (4) At some point, Onesimus fled Philemon and left Colossae (Phlm. 10-12). (5) When he fled, he may have taken something of value that belonged to Philemon, but this is not certain (Phlm. 18-19).

Roman law required the return of a runaway slave. But Rome, as large as it was, was a good place to hide or be lost. A runaway slave in a small town would be noticed, however. It was not an easy journey to Rome. Did Onesimus go there to blend in and conceal himself, or was his purpose to seek Paul? We don't know his motive, but he met Paul, and they spent a considerable amount of time together. We may glean only a few details about this time from the letter to Philemon. Onesimus became a believer, a servant of Christ, and an aid to Paul while Paul was in prison, which would have been Paul's first Roman imprisonment, according to tradition. The relationship was very much that of father and son. Although Paul had requested that Onesimus be allowed, with Philemon's consent, to remain in Rome with Paul, Onesimus was sent back to Colossae. He traveled with Tychicus, first to Ephesus, where they spent some time before going to Colossae. Long before his return to Colossae, Onesimus became a man of God and a fellow believer in Jesus Christ. We may assign two meanings to Paul's writing, "*who is one of you.*" First, he is a resident of Colossae, and second, he is a brother in the Lord. The latter is the central purpose Paul has in mind, that Onesimus should be received as a fellow believer.

Additionally, both Tychicus and Onesimus will report on Paul's activities and the state of the church in Rome. Onesimus should be recognized for at least helping deliver the Colossian, Philemon, and Ephesian letters. Imagine receiving a report on Paul and the church in Rome from a man who was formerly a runaway slave but is now entrusted with helping deliver three of the New Testament's original books. Paul offers an uplifting insight to the circumstances of Onesimus' flee from slavery, conversion, and return to his master as God's sovereign will and adds the perspective that Philemon may now spend eternity with Onesimus as fellow saints in glory (Phlm. 1:15). Indeed, all things work for good for those who are in Christ (Rom. 8:28).

COLOSSIANS 4:10-13
ARISTARCHUS AND OTHERS

Colossians 4:10
Aristarchus

Aristarchus was a Macedonian from Thessalonica (Acts 27:2) who traveled with Paul during his third missionary journey from Ephesus but may have begun traveling with Paul earlier (Acts 19:29). He is mentioned as a fellow prisoner. Although we could construe alternative meanings to what Paul might mean by "*fellow prisoner*," I think it is best to take him literally, which would apply to Paul's first Roman imprisonment. Although Aristarchus is from Thessalonica, he is identified as being among the circumcision, indicating he is a Jew (Col. 4:11).

When King Agrippa sent Paul to Rome for trial, other prisoners were sent with him. Although Aristarchus sailed with Paul, it is not indicated that Aristarchus was one of the prisoners at that time (Acts 27:1-2). However, this does not detract from the interpretation that Aristarchus and Paul were imprisoned in Rome.

In Paul's final greeting to Philemon, he mentions greetings from Aristarchus and refers to him as a fellow worker. From this, we may conclude that Philemon is acquainted with Aristarchus. We may notice that Aristarchus is not referred to in the Philemon letter as a fellow prisoner as he is in Colossians 4:10. Epaphras, on the other hand, is referred to as "*my fellow prisoner in Christ Jesus*" (Phlm. 1:23-24). Again, we may construe a variety of possible meanings. Still, I think it is best to regard Aristarchus and Epaphras as prisoners in Rome with Paul. Their imprisonment may explain why Tychicus was sent to Ephesus and Colossae instead of Epaphras, who had planted the Colossian church and lived there (Col. 1:7).

Mark

Here is a name that is most familiar among the men listed. Mark the Evangelist is credited with writing the gospel account that bears his name, though it was written anonymously. Mark is his Roman name, and John is his Jewish name (Acts 12:12, 25). His mother was Mary (Acts 12:12), and Barnabas was his cousin. Mark is known for traveling with Paul and Barnabas to Antioch to evaluate and teach the church there, and then went with them to distribute famine relief from Antioch to the elders across Judea (Acts 11:22-30, 12:25). He also accompanied Paul and Barnabas on Paul's first missionary journey (Acts 13:5). When they came to Perga in Pamphylia, Mark returned to Jerusalem (Acts 13:13). This caused a rift between Paul and Barnabas so that instead of Barnabas accompanying Paul on his second journey, Barnabas took Mark to Cyprus where they had previously visited (Acts 15:39).

There are only a few details in Scripture about when Mark and Peter were together. Nevertheless, a deep bond formed between them (1 Pet. 5:13).

Barnabas

Paul only mentions Barnabas as Mark's cousin. The rift between them is not mentioned again in Scripture, and it does not appear they ever traveled together again. Yet, Barnabas pursued missionary work, having been sent to evangelize and minister to the Gentiles as was Paul (Gal. 2:9). Paul acknowledges Barnabas' ministry in his first letter to the church at Corinth (1 Cor. 9:6). It also indicates that Barnabas was known as an evangelist among the churches. Mark was with Paul during his first Roman imprisonment (Phlm. 1:23-24). During Paul's second Roman imprisonment, he requests that Timothy bring Mark with him to Rome (2 Tim. 4:11). This suggests that Paul was aware of Mark's whereabouts and activities. These positive references to Barnabas and Mark indicate that the falling out that occurred years earlier had been resolved. The instructions mentioned in Colossians 4:10 apply to Barnabas, whom Paul exhorts the Colossians to welcome if he comes to them. We may conclude that Paul is aware that Barnabas continues to minister and travel, but is unaware of his specific itinerary. It seems that simply telling people to welcome someone lacks the enthusiasm Paul typically has when asking a church to receive someone who is serving the Lord. The undisclosed instructions remain a curiosity.

Colossians 4:11
Justus

There are several men named Justus mentioned in the Bible. The one named here is the only Biblical reference to this individual. Unfortunately, nothing more can be said of him beyond what Paul wrote in verse 11. But like all those mentioned by Paul, Justus is commended as trustworthy and should be received as a trusted believer. Such recommendations are critical in a world of false teachers and scoundrels.

Colossians 4:12-13
Epaphras

Of all those named, Epaphras is the most written of, and rightly so. He was a resident of Colossae and the likely founder of the churches at Colossae, Laodicea, and Hierapolis. His visit and report to Paul are likely the reason Paul wrote the letters to the churches at Colossae and Laodicea. Paul is not praising Epaphras for Epaphras' sake. He commends him as an example and an encouragement to the believers in these cities, us, and all who minister as church planters or overseers.

COLOSSIANS 4:14-18
LUKE AND OTHERS

Colossians 4:14
Luke

We are familiar with Luke as the presumed writer of Acts and the gospel according to Luke. There is very little biographical information about Luke in the Bible. Much of what we think we know about him today is by tradition. Verse 11 informs us that Luke is a physician. Luke's noteworthy loyalty to Paul is expressed by the fact that, for a time, Luke was the only one with Paul during his second Roman imprisonment (2 Tim. 4:11).

Demos

During the first time Paul was in prison in Rome, he was under house arrest, having been sent to Rome by King Agrippa (Acts 26:32). Many friends and coworkers were with him (Phlm. 1:23-24), including Demas. The second time in prison, under Nero, was more severe as Paul was imprisoned as an evildoer and in chains (2 Tim. 1:16). Demas had a favorable relationship with Paul during Paul's first imprisonment as can be seem in the Colossian and Philemon letters (Col. 4:11; Phlm. 1:24). By the time Paul is in prison the second time, Demas' attitude had changed, or his true colors emerged, and Paul reported it (2 Tim. 4:9-10). While several people left Paul (2 Tim. 1:15, 4:10), Demas is singled out for being in love with the world and deserting him. Such a statement should be received as a warning to readers to be cautious of Demas.

Colossians 4:15-16

Laodicea, letters

Laodicea was a neighboring city to Colossae. The church there was likely planted by Epaphras, as was the church at Hierapolis (Col. 4:13). Philemon hosted the church in Colossae (Phlm. 1:1), while Nympha hosted the church in Laodicea.

Paul previously mentioned the saints in Laodicea and how he has also struggled for them (Col. 2:1). Here, we're told that Laodicea has also been sent a letter. Although the verse does not disclose its author, it seems safe to say that Paul wrote it since he is asking the Colossians to read it along with their own. That means the Laodicean letter has Paul's approval as a document of sound and edifying substance, something he would not know unless he knew its contents. Recall that the Colossian believers struggled to mature in the faith because of outside influences they had not put off. So, Paul would not have them read the Laodicean letter in the same manner as their letter unless he knew and approved its contents. The same applied to the Laodiceans reading the Colossian letter. In my opinion, the letters to Colossae and Laodicea were so similar that preserving both was unnecessary.

Colossians 4:17
Archippus

Although the letter to Philemon is personal, it is not entirely private. Philemon 2 indicates that Paul is writing to Philemon, Apphia, and Archippus, who may reside in Philemon's house. It also seems to be addressed to the church that meets in Philemon's house. Since Archippus is identified as a fellow soldier, we may construe that Archippus shares some type of solidarity with Paul, Timothy, and Philemon, which aligns with the information in Colossians that Archippus has been given a ministry from the Lord. Paul is likely intending to draw Archippus' attention to it.

What is Archippus' ministry from the Lord? There are two possibilities to consider. (1) At this time, Epaphras, who founded the church in Colossae, is in Rome with Paul. Who's overseeing the church there in Epaphras' absence? Perhaps it is Archippus who needs assurance from the believers. (2) Alternatively, Paul's instruction to the church to tell Archippus to fulfill his ministry seems to imply that the church oversees Archippus, as when a church sends someone out from them on a mission. Since Archippus hasn't yet left Philemon's home, Paul's instruction to the church seems fitting. Whatever Archippus was to do, it seems he, in particular, was assigned to do it.

Colossians 4:18
greeting

Paul concludes the epistle with a note that he has written this greeting, emphasizing that it was done by his own hand. Not all of his letters were written in Paul's handwriting. Romans was written by the scribe Tertius, who identifies himself in the letter and whom we may conclude was also a believer (Rom. 16:22). The use of a scribe does not diminish the authority of the letter, since the scribe is recording what is being dictated to him and overseen by the author. Paul's letter to the Galatians seems to have been written entirely in Paul's handwriting as does the letter to Philemon (Gal. 6:11; Phlm. 1:19). Most letters only mention that the closing greeting was written directly by Paul (1 Cor. 16:21; Col. 4:18; 2 Thess. 3:17). Paul made it a point to mention it was he who wrote the closing greetings to authenticate his letters (2 Thess. 3:17). Here, in Colossians 4:18, we may take this greeting to be such an authentication of the authorship and authority of the letter.

chains

"*Remember my Chains*" seems out of place when we consider that Paul is held under house arrest in Rome. Most English translations have *chains* or *bonds*, including ESV, KJV, NKJV, and NIV. However, NASB has "*remember my imprisonment*." The Greek word in question is δεσμῶν (desmōn), which can be translated as "*bond*," "*chain*," "*fetter*," or "*imprisonment*" (biblehub.com). While "*chains*" and "*bonds*" may not be incorrect translations, they fail to capture the broader context of the circumstances involved. In Philemon, verses 1:10 and 1:13, the same or a similar Greek word is translated as "*imprisonment*." The Greek word in Colossians indicates possession, whereas it indicates being acted on in Philemon. So, what do we get from all of this? (1) Paul is under house arrest in Rome for the sake of the gospel of Jesus Christ. (2) Paul bids us to remember his circumstances, what they are, and why. (3) Paul especially acknowledges ownership of his imprisonment. In the Philomen verses, the case of the Greek word indicates Paul's imprisonment was done to him, but in Colossians, it is his imprisonment. (4) While there are no literal chains involved, his imprisonment is real, and his request to remember it is a plea for prayer. Our prayers would be for Paul's relief in suffering and release from arrest, but also when faced with being imprisoned ourselves for Christ, we would be steadfast in our faith.

"*Grace be with you*" is a benediction that expresses God's continued work in the church, growing every believer to the full maturity of the faith and completing the work he has already begun in them (Phil. 1:6).

CHAPTER 4 SUMMARY

relationships

The opening exhortation completes the relationship instructions presented in Chapter 3 by addressing masters of slaves regarding their duties before the Lord. Paul's address to slaves lies in Chapter 3. Here, he reminds masters that though on earth they are masters among slaves, they also serve a Master in heaven, and thus should be just and fair themselves. Briefly stepping back to the last verse of Chapter 3, Paul points out that wrongdoers will be paid back with impartiality; we may infer that this warning applies to wives, husbands, and masters, though it seems attached to the instructions for slaves. These instructions, in principle, can be applied to the present-day work environment, as they should.

prayer

Paul exhorts the Colossians to be watchful and steadfast in their prayers with thanksgiving. Watchful and steadfast was interpreted as being vigilant in prayer, praying on all occasions with thankfulness. This instruction was to be followed whenever they prayed, as it is an exhortation to the church today as we pray.

In particular, Paul requested prayer for his group to have opportunities to preach. The emphasis of his request was for the mystery of Christ to be proclaimed with further opportunities. Paul reminded the Colossians that he was in prison for his preaching ministry. That may be construed, considering his times, as a warning of what to expect if you proclaim the mystery of Christ. Today's saints can still answer Paul's request for prayer, that the mystery of Christ be proclaimed, by praying for their local church leaders and other evangelists who faithfully proclaim the Word of Christ.

walking in wisdom

Instructions and warnings follow regarding how believers are to interact with people who are not part of the church, referred to as outsiders. Church members will always be measured by outsiders, for better or worse, as representatives of their faith and Jesus Christ. Godly wisdom is to be used, and as was determined, by being shrewd and prudent, because outsiders are likened to wolves operating with earthly and demonic wisdom. In all situations, the saints are to be gracious to outsiders, avoid sinning, and be prepared to answer each outsider appropriately to honor Christ. The saints are unavoidably evangelists, and by adhering to these instructions, they may shorten the time some outsiders spend as outsiders, as it is said, "*redeeming the time*" (Eph. 5:16 KJV).

men of faith recognized

The church in Colossae was established by Epaphras, who loved the gospel and shared it with the surrounding towns. He was the church planter and leader in Colossae, and when false teachings infiltrated the church, he sought help from Paul. Epaphras traveled to Rome, where Paul was in prison, to report on the status of the Colossian church. The report prompted Paul to pen the letter to the Colossians. Another faithful man, Tychicus, who was traveling with Paul, was tasked with delivering the letter to the Colossians. Epaphras' and Tychicus' service is often overlooked because our gaze is fixed on Paul. However, they were men of great faith whom God used mightily in the service of his church and without whom this great work of the Apostle may not have been penned or handed down to us. It is a lesson that even the smallest thing we may be tasked to do for the Lord may have history-changing implications.

We must not overlook Onesimus because his story is a great testimony to the love, grace, and sovereignty of God for those the world thinks of as least among us. It is also a testament to a man's spiritual conversion that led a runaway slave to help deliver several original books of the Bible while returning to serve in his master's house. When fleeing Colossae, Onesimus did not know he was bound for glory.

Key verses, worth remembering when outsiders get to us, are 5 and 6.

> *"Walk in wisdom toward outsiders, making the best use of the time. Let your speech always be gracious, seasoned with salt, so that you may know how you ought to answer each person"* (Col. 4:5-6 ESV).

COLOSSIANS SUMMARY

Colossians is a wonderful epistle written to a small, struggling church. The letter is filled with the love and glory of Christ.

Paul presents the Lord in his preeminent glory, the one who alone reconciles all things to himself, who ransomed and redeemed the church by his own blood, in whom are all the unfading treasures a man could desire, and in whom all fullness dwells. In Christ, the fullness of deity was pleased to dwell in human flesh. Those in Christ were buried with him and raised with him. Thus, the old man has been put to death with its body of sin, and the new man has risen with Christ to live unto God.

Various false teachings are exposed stemming from legalisms, human teaching, traditions, and empty philosophies. The Colossians are challenged to consider who they are and how they live their lives. If you have been buried with Christ and raised with Christ, changes will be manifest in your life that testify to these things. Important instructions for Christian living follow, aiming for unity and peace among God's people and a faithful witness to the fallen world of the gospel of Christ and the hope of glory we have.

We encountered the concept of our former life being that of the old man who was by nature enslaved to sin, which separated us from God and placed us under his pending wrath. Having been called to Christ, we died to the old nature, were buried with Christ, and rose with Christ as a new man freed from the bondage of sin and created in righteousness and holiness (Eph. 4:24). With new abilities, we can put to death the lingering presence of our former inclinations toward sin. We concluded that a new creation has replaced the old man. It is not the old man we are to mortify; it is the lingering effects of the corruption he bore.

Further instructions are presented to guide the saints as members of Christ's body, the church. Love among the saints is lifted as the pinnacle of virtue, with peace from the heart being the guiding principle. The word of Christ should dwell richly in every heart to build one another up into full maturity in Christ.

Paul concludes the text with a list of saints serving the church faithfully. He commends them as brothers who may be trusted and received as faithful stewards of what the Lord has entrusted to them. The letter begins with an invocation for grace and ends with a benediction of grace.

The theme of Colossians is Christ, the head of the universal church (1:18).

> *"And He is the head of the body, the church, who is the beginning, the firstborn from the dead, that in all things He may have the preeminence"* (Col. 1:18 ESV).

Many verses could be chosen as key verses from this letter. If Christians could wrap their minds around one thought and embrace it for the reality it is, for an enduring benefit, I suggest that such a thought is as follows.

> *"For you have died, and your life is hidden with Christ in God"* (Col. 3:3 ESV).

What wonderful assurance we have when we believe from the depth of our hearts that we have a life with Christ in God, even now and abundantly more yet to be revealed.

www.ingramcontent.com/pod-product-compliance
Lightning Source LLC
Chambersburg PA
CBHW051822040426
42447CB00006B/332

* 9 7 9 8 2 1 8 7 6 5 1 2 5 *